Ideogram History of a Poetic Method

Ideogram
History of a Poetic Method

by Laszlo Géfin

University of Texas Press, Austin

Publication of this work has been made possible in part by a grant from the Andrew W. Mellon Foundation.

First edition, 1982

Library of Congress Cataloging in Publication Data

Géfin, Laszlo K.
  Ideogram, history of a poetic method.

  Bibliography: p.
  Includes index.
  1. American poetry—20th century—History and criticism. 2. Picture-writing in literature. 3. Pound, Ezra, 1885–1972—Influence. I. Title.
PS323.5.G37   811'.5'09   82-1920
ISBN 0-292-73828-5   AACR2

To Lajos Németh *and* Pál Lengyel,
teachers of my youth in Hungary,
to whom I owe the awakening of my abiding interest
in literature and history,
this book is gratefully dedicated.

Contents

Contents

Preface

This study is the result of my interest in poetic continuity; more specifically, it reflects a concern about the continuity of the paratactic mode of composition developed by Ezra Pound. It may be an exaggeration to say that our present literary consciousness is going through a reactionary, antimodernist phase comparable to the period between the two world wars. Yet it may not be untimely to affirm—reaffirm, actually—Pound's poetic method as the main contribution to modern aesthetics, and to show that the method—the method of the ideogram—is still alive by tracing it from its source in Pound's work to its subsequent use in the theories and practices of other American poets. This, then, is the subject of this book: the definition of an ideogrammic tradition within modern American poetry, the identifying of the nature and variousness of this tradition, and the assessment of its larger conceptual significance.

In the course of the study I touch upon several literary movements —imagism, vorticism, objectivism, and so on—but it is beyond the scope of this project to deal with them exhaustively; for the most part, their histories have already been written. Similarly, although I intend to establish relations between theory and practice in the case of the ten poets I discuss in this work, I offer no comprehensive analyses of their creative achievements, taking only a limited number of examples mainly from their longer poems.

This study is the first historical survey of the ideogrammic line, and as such, it stands as a modest relation of such pivotal works as Roy Harvey Pearce's *The Continuity of American Poetry* and the more recent *The American Quest for a Supreme Fiction* by James E. Miller, Jr. Although my study intersects these works at several points, I feel that it is sufficiently different from them in concept, approach, and execution.

Ideogram is a revised version of my doctoral dissertation (McGill University, Montreal, 1979). I am grateful to my advisor, Professor William C. Wees, for his help and encouragement. Animated discussions with Professor Louis Dudek have clarified several issues. Research was conducted mostly at Yale University and at the Humanities Research Center at the University of

Texas. In Austin I received friendly and expert assistance from Ellen Dunlap, research librarian, and her colleagues, for which I am thankful. Professors Hugh Kenner of Johns Hopkins University and Joseph Slate of the University of Texas have read the manuscript, and it has greatly benefited from the incorporation of their numerous suggestions. I thank them both.

Although intended primarily for a scholarly audience, my work is not a detached exercise in criticism. My motto has been Goethe's advice: "Where one cannot love, one should pass by." I only hope my love did not prove too inadequate for my subject.

Introduction

"The future of poetry is immense," wrote Matthew Arnold one hundred years ago. Meditating on the state and future of poetry, I wonder how many responsible people engaged in literature today would be willing to make such an assertion. Not many, I would venture. The reasons for our inability to share Arnold's confidence and self-assuredness are various, one of them being the obvious fact that we can now hardly speak of *poetry* as a concept with a distinct and solid reality behind it. Poetry today is no longer what it was for Arnold, a kind of mighty stream uniting in its flow all good verse written from Homer to his own day; it is now at best a myriad of rivulets trickling away in all directions. Not that poetry was ever as homogeneous as the notion of a great river seems to imply, but it is still our own, not only Arnold's, paradisaical image of a condition that existed "before the fall."

The "fall," of course, came about as a result of the modernist movement in English and American poetry. This event is our beginning, the origin of a new "history." Consequently our own questions about the continuity of poetry and our hypotheses in response to them must radiate from this source. The questions which prompted my inquiry must also be specifically formulated, for a set of general queries (such as "What is the future of our poetry?") cannot be answered without having to resort to mere speculation and conjecture.

The questions which I find meaningful are the following: Can we pinpoint the most important methodological achievement of modernist poetics? Has it been found valuable by subsequent poets? If so, has there been, among the many "rivulets" of twentieth-century poetry and poetics, a single "stream" which has preserved, enriched, and carried forward this poetic to our day? And is it still flexible enough so that the continuity of the modernist trend is, if not assured, at least made possible?

My answer to these questions is a more than tentative "yes," one which I hope to substantiate in this study. It is obvious from the way I phrased these questions that I consider the "fall" resulting from modernism a *felix culpa*, a necessary and fruitful revolt. The questions also express my assumption that the real and concrete contribution of modernism can be measured with some accuracy only if we concentrate on the methods it introduced—more concretely, if we isolate that method which brought about the most radical changes in poetic composition and in poetic *thinking*. The model of this method must be constructed in such a way that its appearance and reappearance in subsequent poetics and actual works—in whatever metamorphoses and variations—will serve as a guide in our effort to do more than speculate about the present and the future of modernist, or postmodernist, poetry.

The central method and the main form of modernism I call the *juxtapositional* or, to use the name given to it by its "inventor" Ezra Pound, the *ideogrammic* method. To juxtapose, of course, means to situate side by side two or more things. The method may also be called *paratactic*, based on the Greek verb παρατάσσω, to place beside one another. Parataxis is the opposite of hypotaxis, from ὑποτάσσω, to arrange under, which signifies a dependent construction or relation of parts with connectives. On the simplest rhetorical level such a mode is an asyndetic composition (from the Greek ἀσύνδετος, unconnected), where connectives have been omitted. The Chinese ideogrammic method, in Ernest Fenollosa's view (from which Pound built a poetic theory), relies in its juxtapositions on a close observation of natural processes. In his view the basis of the method is metaphorical: the juxtaposed "material" images imply "immaterial" relationships. From a deliberate juxtaposition of pictures of things, without any connectives, the Chinese written language can draw not only more pictures of things (that, too), but more important, it can point to concepts and universals. For example, the juxtaposition of the pictograms of "man" and "fire" produces a new meaning, the color "red." For Pound, the setting side by side, without copulas, of verbal pictures will perforce establish relationships between the units juxtaposed. Such juxtapositions he called *images*. The image is the basic form of ideogrammic composition; it is not simply a visual impression but a union of particulars transposed onto the conceptual plane.

Even from this outline the antecedents of Pound's method in his earlier poetics are obvious, and it is quite reasonable to assume that had he not been an imagist and a vorticist, Fenollosa's essay would not have aroused his interest the way it did. It is in this light that I see the significance of Fenollosa for Pound, and I share the belief that "the advent of the Fenollosa materials was the single most important event in the development of Pound's poetics."[1] The method as Pound came to use it in various forms, and as the ideogrammic poets employed it after him, is not simply a form of poetry in the same sense that the sestina or villanelle are forms; it is much more than the scheme of juxtaposition suggests. The method constitutes the tip of a whole congeries of concerns related to the problem of representation in art. It opened up for Pound and others the possibility of organizing the poetic

utterance in such a way that it would present an accurate model of the processes of modern reality.

Indeed, the modernists' revolt, like all artistic revolts, began as a reaction
against what they believed was an intolerable state of affairs in the arts, particularly in poetry. For Pound, "the common verse of Britain from 1890 to
1910" was "a horrible agglomerate compost, . . . a doughy mess of third-
hand Keats, Wordsworth, heaven knows what, fourth-hand Elizabethan
sonority blunted, half-melted, lumpy."[2] Pound's view, especially for a new-
comer (he came to London in 1908), was characteristically harsh. Yet it was
shared not only by the younger writers who gathered in London at that time
(several Americans among them), but also by a few critics who saw new possibilities in Pound's earlier books, several years before imagism. Edward
Thomas wrote, in a review of *Personae*, that Pound "has hardly any of the
superficial qualities of modern versifiers; . . . he has not the current melan-
choly or resignation or unwillingness to live; nor the kind of feeling for
nature that runs to minute descriptions and decorative metaphor."[3] The last
observation is particularly astute, not only because Pound eschewed all
forms of ornamental metaphor, but because the motive underneath his
modernist poetics, culminating in the ideogrammic method, was a desire to
move beyond metaphoric construction. Such a statement may seem to go
against the grain of Fenollosa's assertions about the links between metaphor
and ideogram, but I hope to show in this study that a significant aspect of the
Poundian method stems from his antimetaphoric stance. With some
simplification, Pound's theory of poetry may even be summarized as a critique of and an alternative to metaphor. His own formulation of his poetics-
in-a-nutshell confirms this: "From dead thesis, metaphor is distinct. Any
thesis is dead in itself. Life comes in metaphor and metaphor starts
TOWARD ideogram."[4] This is the crucial fact which the poets in the ideogrammic stream came to recognize, and this is one of the reasons why they
adopted and incorporated the method in their own poetics.

There are, of course, other aspects of Pound's contribution to modernism
that received due recognition; the entire modernist period has even been
called "the Pound era." This is Hugh Kenner's designation, and in his
monumental book by the same name he presents a total image of Pound
within modernism. We see him not only as poet and theorist but also as
editor, agent, correspondent, tireless propagandist for the arts and certain
artists, literary impresario—in Kenner's words, "as ground-bass and part-
time conductor."[5] The value of Kenner's book, both as scholarly treatise
and work of art, cannot be denied. Yet I cannot quell my unease that such an
encyclopaedic overview paradoxically tends to enclose Pound in his "era,"
making him a *figure* (albeit a towering one) *in literary history*. Now it seems to
me that the peculiar quality of the "Pound event" inheres in its ability to extend beyond its "era," so that subsequent writers could turn to his most

important poetic contribution to modern poetics without becoming epigones. Of the great moderns both Yeats and Eliot have had their following. Yet more often than not their example encouraged traditional poetic modes, conservatism, and reactionary tendencies. On the other hand, all postmodernist poetic renewals and upheavals in America—William Carlos Williams's achievement, Louis Zukofsky's objectivist group, Charles Olson's projectivism, the Beat movement, the San Francisco poetry renaissance—have invariably stressed the seminal importance of Pound. His importance was seen to lie not in the fact that he was an organizer of *poets* but that he was an organizer of *poetic form*; and for those poets who continued to explore and experiment with new modes, he was, if not a "conductor," then certainly an ever-present "ground-bass."

The poets and movements mentioned above constitute what I call the ideogrammic stream, in which the main form of modernism has been successively perpetuated and revitalized, and its basic philosophy—*make it new*—kept active and alive. The idea of a line of "ideogrammic poets" beginning with Pound inevitably means a confrontation with the problem of influence. First, there is the problem of influence on Pound himself, primarily that of Ernest Fenollosa, which was instrumental in his formulation of the ideogrammic method. But more important, there is the task of demonstrating Pound's influence on the later poets. Although no critic has failed to refer to Pound as one of the most influential poets of this century, only one book has been published on this topic: K. L. Goodwin's *The Influence of Ezra Pound*. Goodwin, however, has not attempted to treat Poundian influence as a case of direct and indirect genealogy; he is mainly interested in turning up "signs" and "traces" (actual words, images, formal devices) in the widest variety of poetic works. He considers influence purely on biographical grounds and comes to the absurd conclusion that Pound's effect was strongest on poets who were his personal friends and acquaintances, weaker on those who only corresponded with him, and most minimal on those who "merely" read his works.

In contrast to Goodwin's approach, I hold with Harold Bloom that "the profundities of poetic influence cannot be reduced to source-study, to the history of ideas, to the patterning of images."[6] But, I hasten to add, neither can they be reduced to Bloom's own ingenious categories (his "revisionary ratios"), nor is influence an "anxiety." Wielding Freud as previous theorists wielded Plato, Bloom constructs his poetics on a theory essentially inimical to art; his is a reductionist model of an already reductionist original.[7] My intention is to treat the problem of influence as a dynamic and *conscious* process—an influence, in the words of Louis Zukofsky, "acting in common upon individual temperaments." Zukofsky distinguishes three types of influence: first, "its presence in the air"; second, the coincidence of temperaments; and third, "conscious choice or rejection of a literary tradition."[8]

It is evident that the starting point for my study cannot be other than Zukofsky's third point, as I am concerned neither with "signs" and "traces," nor with subliminal infighting. My investigation is based on certain poets' deliberate choice of aligning themselves with a poetic tradition and with a method they considered vital and beneficial for their own poetic practice and for the continuity of modernist principles. The succession of poets which I see extending from Pound (or Fenollosa and Pound) through Williams, Zukofsky, and the objectivists to Olson, and from them to Duncan, Creeley, Ginsberg, and Snyder constitutes a tradition in which the poets are not arbitrarily included but *include themselves*. Their presence is not based on random selection but is *given*. In many respects the theory and practice of these poets is quite different, and that is as it should be; their importance lies in the fact that they have produced discrete poetics that in themselves are coherent wholes in which the juxtapositional-ideogrammic method has become fully integrated, "made new," and is used to embody urgent, vitally interesting "ideas in action." In reality, the ideogrammic line is not a line at all but a complex web of interrelationships, a live network of intellectual and emotional currents.

Turning again to Zukofsky's definition, I do not think the second type of influence—coincidence, or affinity—is really germane to the present discussion since there, as Zukofsky himself writes, influence is merely apparent and not really affecting. But the point about "presence in the air," if one transposes the notion from the merely biographical to a wider conceptual plane, directs attention to the fundamental question of the nature, the ontology, of the ideogrammic method itself. The appearance of the method in the 1910s was not an accident, nor can Pound's continued insistence on its importance be ascribed to the idiosyncratic quirkiness of one poet. The form itself was "in the air" in seemingly unrelated fields of modern thought. The emergence of the method in a variety of endeavors testifies to a common human effort in the early part of our century to make the world whole again, to heal the rupture (caused, as some believe, by Plato) which has characterized Western thought over two millennia. Powerful mental energies operating in different areas have organized and channeled themselves in similar patterns in order to arrive at an up-to-date, objective image of reality and of our place in that reality. The modernist revolution in the arts is closely related to the new vision of the universe provided by Einstein, Planck, and the "new atomists" (Rutherford, Bohr, Schrödinger, Heisenberg) as well as to the findings of archeologists and anthropologists.

Simultaneously with this aim to arrive at a new *imago mundi* there was the desire to recover our lost heritage, to reach back to pre-Socratic, pre-logical strata of human time and space in order to find our true roots. "The archaic is one of the great inventions of the twentieth century," Guy Davenport has written; "as the first European renaissance looked back to Hellenistic Rome for a range of models and symbols, the twentieth century has looked back to a deeper past in which it has imagined it sees the very beginnings of civilization."[9] Behind the holistic direction of the modern will lies the fundamental insight that the universe in all its manifestations is isomorphic. The sayings of Heraclitus, for example, long held to be "illogical" and "mystical" —such as "The nature of things is in the habit of concealing itself" or "Latent structure is master of obvious structure"—became fully modern and meaningful in the light of the Bohr model of the atom as a miniature galaxy. Fenollosa's reaching back to the Chinese ideograph finds its philosophic counterpart in Wittgenstein's reference to the Egyptian hieroglyph; Fenollosa observed that "relations are more real and more important than the things which they relate" because true relations do not point to analogy but to "identity of structure." His statement shows concerns similar to Wittgenstein's as they are formulated in the latter's picture theory, for "there must be something identical in a picture and what it depicts," and this is an identity of the Heraclitean "latent structure." Incidentally, the importance of relations has been stressed by Gestalt psychology. The stroboscopic movement in perception, as demonstrated by Wertheimer (in 1912!) and further argued by Köhler and others, has given rise to the principle of psychophysical isomorphism, the identical structure of objects perceived and the underlying neural processes.

This brings us back to the problem of representation, that is, to the form that would adequately depict the isomorphic nature of reality. Behind the modernists' dissatisfaction with traditional (logical, anthropomorphic, transitional) modes, we can now perceive the underlying motives: these modes are useless because by their very forms they have helped perpetuate a false image of reality, of human beings, and of their relation. "What any picture," wrote Wittgenstein, "of whatever form must have in common with reality, in order to be able to depict it . . . is logical form, i.e. the form of reality."[10] But it is essential to note that the true logic of depiction is not platonic but a unified logic combining archaic vision with empirical observation. The perceptible universe consists in discrete particulars, and they "lie" in seemingly unrelated juxtaposition; but we can discover their hidden unity. Artists in representing reality must preserve the true relation of the objects of reality; they must strive to show the isomorphism of nature's processes and human cognitive processes in an objective way.

The method of the ideogram asserts that a true representation of reality (one that is in accord with nature's own movements) is possible in poetry (and in art in general) by an asyndetic juxtaposition of linguistic (or pictorial, spatial, tonal) particulars which the mind of the reader (onlooker, listener) will organize into a coherent whole just as he or she does with particulars in the real world. Not only are connectives relics of an outmoded transitional practice, but they are redundant, in fact, because they are not present in nature. To use Wittgenstein's example, in the descriptive sentence "The book is on the table" we can point to objective referents in the world of "book" and "table," but we cannot point to the copula "is on." The ideogrammic method obviates such artificial "meddling" with and intrusion upon nature. Herein lies perhaps the source for Pound's (and the ideogrammic poets') mistrust of metaphor; hence their move "TOWARD ideogram" as an accurate mode of depicting reality.

Depiction is not synonymous with a copying of nature; ideogrammic writing is mimetic only in the sense that it attempts to enact natural processes. An illustration of the poetic ideogram may be helpful here. Kenner writes that "Joyce's catalogue of Bloom's books in *Ulysses* is the simplest possible application of the ideogrammic method; so is Pound's transcription of the contents of Sigismondo's post-bag."[11] With the Pound example, Kenner is referring to Canto IX where Pound presents the reader, without connectives and comments of his own, letters and parts of letters written to the Renaissance condottiere Sigismondo Malatesta. This juxtaposition of the letters, all the while preserving the particularity of the documents, presents us with an ideogram of Malatesta in his family and social relationships. "Renaissance man" is a general term, perhaps a concept; "Sigismondo Malatesta" is a particular individual. But Malatesta's "factive" personality emerging from its dispersed state, from "ready-mades," as it were, gives us an additional, closer image, neither all-general nor all-particular. Furthermore, the method itself is its own meaning: the ideogram of the man thus arrived at follows the logic of natural processes. Structurally, it is identical with them.

Such composition is a poetic application of the main form "in the air," of the new *forma mentis*, to use Pound's words. The principle is the backbone of cubism and also of collage composition which had appeared in the 1910s, first in the work of Braque and Picasso and in its full flowering in the constructions of Max Ernst and Kurt Schwitters. The montage technique of the cinema is the purest visual realization of the ideogrammic form. It is interesting that Eisenstein, like Fenollosa and Pound, received confirmation of it as a creative process directly from the Chinese ideogram. In other fields, in the music of Stravinsky, Schönberg, Bartók, and later in the work of Webern, Berg, and Cage, linear and traditionally predetermined harmonic sequences and repetitions give way to musical equivalents of collage and montage. In Bartók's case, for example, jazz rhythms, folk melodies, and atonal phrases are abruptly juxtaposed.

This, then, is the brief outline of the form with which the poets in the ideogrammic stream chose to align themselves. While no doubt aware of the "presence in the air," for these poets it was Pound's method that provided the primary instigation. As Wai-lim Yip has written, "Pound's language, in particular his paratactical structures and line divisions, . . . has been followed and modified by other American poets, notably Williams, Olson, Creeley, and Snyder."[12] My addition of Zukofsky, Reznikoff, Oppen, Duncan, and Ginsberg does not signify completeness; they, and not others, are included because their total *oeuvres* to date appear to be the most weighty and vital. On this basis the exclusion of some poets is perhaps justifiable; some readers may still object to the absence in this study of a centrally important poet—T. S. Eliot. But Eliot, apart from *The Waste Land*, is not ideogrammic; and even *The Waste Land*, similar to Pound's *Mauberley* and *Homage to Sextus Propertius*, is *analytical* in approach and form, whereas *The Cantos* and the major work of the later poets (*"A"*, *Testimony*, *Paterson*, *Maximus Poems*, *Passages*, *Pieces*, *The Fall of America*, *Myths and Texts*) are *synthetical*. It is also important to remember that many of the more violent disjunctions and montages in *The Waste Land* owe their existence to Pound's editing. Furthermore, Eliot fostered a following which sought to negate ideogrammic composition or any version of open form; these poets (along with Eliot) were openly opposed and renounced by the poets in the Pound tradition.

Some readers and critics may object to the use of the term "ideogrammic" in describing the Poundian method of composition. But whether we substitute "paratactic" or "juxtapositional," or talk about a vorticist combination of "pattern units," or employ phrases like "qualitative progression," "nontransitional sequence," "fugal construction," "montage," or "collage," or, specifically, "Poundian juxtaposition," we are really speaking about the same thing: the literary or poetic version of the *forma mentis*. Similarly, the poets in the ideogrammic tradition have given new names to the method to fit their own individual poetics. For Olson, for instance, it is "composition by field"; for Zukofsky it is the fugue; for Duncan it is "collage," while Snyder describes his method as "riprapping" and Ginsberg calls attention to his "elliptical" mode of composition. But in spite of the shades of meaning, the same organizing principle is behind their diverse methods.

Throughout the book I have tried to establish the contemporary relevance of ideogrammic composition, which I see as an aesthetic form extending from a postlogical and even posthumanist consciousness, according to which the human being is not the apex but a creature of the universe. Should this process of revaluating our relation to the cosmic environment be carried on by poets in the future, the achievement of the ideogrammic poets will, I believe, continue to remain an ever-widening "live tradition" from which new compositional techniques and methodologies may be derived.

Part One
Toward a New Logic of Depiction

Felicem cui datum est dispersiones cordis in unum colligere.

—Richard of St. Victor,
Benjamin Major

Part One

1. From Metaphor to Vortex

The poets in the ideogrammic tradition have all been, to a greater or lesser degree, "archeologists." Williams's digging into archives to gather material for *In the American Grain* and *Paterson*, Olson's literal digging up and laborious deciphering of Mayan hieroglyphs in Yucatan, Snyder's "field work" in translating ancient Chinese poems from the original and his collecting of Hopi legends—all these have in common the desire to unearth the natural foundation of human thought upon which a new poetics and poetry may be constructed. Their aim has been to retrieve and put to use those valuable elements in our cultural heritage which had become well-nigh obliterated by the tyrannical superstructure of postplatonic reason and logic. The entire modernist movement in all the arts is inseparably tied to such "digging," and in fact cannot be understood without it. Brancusi's "Ancient Figure," Picasso's "Les Demoiselles d'Avignon," Wyndham Lewis's "Creation," even Stravinsky's "Sacre du Printemps"—to cite a few examples—are in reality "transparent" works: behind the shocking contours of modernist forms there loom archaic shapes created by Babylonians thousands of years ago or by contemporary "primitives" in Africa and Oceania.

In modernist poetry, Pound was the first "digger" to resurrect certain specific areas of the past in order to build upon them, as he said, "the airy fabric of my heresies." Pound's first book that drew serious critical attention and made his name known in literary circles was *Personae*, published in London in 1909. In *Personae*, the formal "heresies" were combined with a highly idiosyncratic subject matter and treated with great originality: transliterations, adaptations, derivations from Provençal troubadours and medieval Italian poets, translations from Heine, poems with suggestive titles such as "De AEgypto" and "Paracelsus in Excelsis." Even his most sympathetic reviewer, Edward Thomas, had to admit that "it is easier to enjoy than to praise Mr. Pound, easier to find fault with him, easiest to ridicule."[1] Strange as it may seem, William Carlos Williams was among those who took the "easiest" course. His response to the idea of an international poets' meeting in France is a thinly veiled attack on Pound: when the poets meet, he wrote,

"Paris will be more than slightly abashed to find parodies of the middle ages, Dante and Langue d'Oc foisted upon it as the best in United States poetry."[2] He wrote these words just a few years before he was to begin his own "excavating."

Eliot, on the other hand, was fully aware of Pound's intentions and their significance. He saw these methods as a modernist gesture of doing away with romantic notions of "originality" in poetry. In its proper meaning, originality was seen by Eliot to lie in grasping certain things which are "permanent in human nature." Accordingly, in Eliot's view, "Pound is often most 'original' in the right sense, when he is most 'archaeological' "; and "One of Pound's most indubitable claims to genuine originality is . . . his revivification of the Provençal and the early Italian poetry."[3] Eliot's introduction of the term "archeological," though enclosed in inverted commas, is noteworthy in that the ideogrammic poets were to appropriate and use it with almost the same connotation in describing their own "digging."[4] Pound's Provençal and Italian research is important for a number of reasons, not the least of which is the poetic-pragmatic aspect. As Pound characterized his "pawing over the ancients and semi-ancients," his aim had been "to find out what has been done, once for all, better than it can ever be done again, and to find out what remains for us to do."[5] But it is more important, I believe, that his early "field work" already contains much of the material from which the mature poetics were to be constructed. Simply stated, Pound was already moving away from metaphor and groping toward ideogram when he investigated Dante and Arnaut Daniel. The very basis of the ideogrammic method, Pound's "intuitive affinity for description by particulars,"[6] is present in *The Spirit of Romance* (1910) and in "I Gather the Limbs of Osiris" (1911-1912). These works, together with his "Cavalcanti" essay, contain the fruits of his research in the romance tradition. The vehicle is ostensibly a kind of unorthodox philology, but the substance is an incompletely articulated theory of poetry.

The first clearly and unequivocally formulated poetics of the modernist movement is Pound's imagist manifesto and its three often-quoted principles:

1. Direct treatment of the "thing" whether subjective or objective.
2. To use absolutely no word that does not contribute to the presentation.
3. As regarding rhythm: to compose in the sequence of the musical phrase, not in the sequence of a metronome.[7]

These points and the definition of the "Image"—"that which presents an intellectual and emotional complex in an instant of time," a complex which results in a sense of "sudden liberation," a sense of "sudden growth"—have not come about because Aldington, H. D., and Pound "decided," as he claims, upon these principles. Their antecedents can be found in the earlier works of romance, just as imagism was a preliminary stage of the ideogrammic method. In fact, as Hugh Witemeyer correctly diagnosed, the ideogrammic mode "'... flows from his [Pound's] earlier aesthetic programs and 'isms.' The essence of the method is that general concepts are most meaningful (perhaps only meaningful) when expressed through a cluster of particular cases."[8] This "intuitive affinity" for presentation via particulars is rooted in Pound's firm grasp on the "new *forma mentis*," which suggests a creative process isomorphic with natural processes.

The new *forma mentis* demands natural expression; but Pound in the earlier works seems to be vacillating between what we may call the "normative" and the "organic" methods of writing poetry. "I think," Pound writes, "that some poems may have form as a tree has form, some as water poured into a vase."[9] The ambivalence may be due to several factors, one being the paradoxical side effect of Pound's work in romance: his great admiration for Dante and Dante's poetics as set forth in *De Vulgari Eloquentia* with its rigid norms of *ars, ingenium,* and *scientia*.[10] The other, equally important factor may have had to do with an almost congenital dislike of any notion even remotely romantic and transcendentalist, the most obvious manifestation of which he saw in the work of Whitman. It would seem that in the early transitional stage of Pound's poetic theorizing the espousal of an "organic" concept would have been tantamount to a rejection of Dante, of *form* itself, and an alliance with Whitman, and through Whitman with Emerson, Wordsworth, Coleridge, and the German romantics. For it was Whitman who said that "the rhyme and uniformity of perfect poems show the free growth of metrical laws and bud from them as unerringly and loosely as lilacs or roses on a bush and take shapes as compact as the shapes of chestnuts and oranges and melons and pears."[11] And it was Emerson who had written before Whitman that "it is not metres, but a metre-making argument that makes a poem,—a thought so passionate and alive that like the spirit of a plant or an animal it has an architecture of its own."[12]

Yet the philosophy of modernism in all the arts is nothing if not "organic," which is simply another term for "open composition" or composition from nature. If Whitman's (and Emerson's) statements seem "romantic," what would one say about the pronouncements of the archmoderns, like Hans Arp's statement that "Art is a fruit growing out of a man like the fruit out of a plant, like the child out of the mother"? It is obvious that this sense of "organic" composition precludes a sharp difference on this point between "romantic" and "modernist"; what we can talk about is a difference of emphasis and not of kind.

The difference is crucial nonetheless. Though it is true that it was Pound and not Wordsworth who wrote, "Emotion is an organizer of form"; and he, not Whitman, wrote that the emotions organized in the image "must be in harmony, they must form an organism, they must be an oak sprung from an acorn,'' his ''organicism'' is tempered by a Dantescan or Arnautian *precision*. According to Pound, it was the ''precision of observation and reference'' in Arnaut Daniel which made this Provençal poet ''accurate in his observation of Nature.''[13] Arnaut's chief virtue, as defined by Pound in 1911, is measured almost according to the second principle of imagism: Arnaut ''conceived of a manner of writing in which each word should bear some burden, should make some special contribution to the effect of the whole.''[14] The difference in emphasis lies in exactness; the poem, for Pound, is likewise an organism, but it is ''an organism in which each part functions.'' The poem, then, is a *functioning organism*, created, like nature, out of precise particulars whose juxtaposition will establish relations between them and will give the reader ''a sudden insight.'' This is the intended effect of the image or the ideogram. In the pre-imagist period Pound called it ''sudden insight'' or ''ecstasy'' (''Great art is made to call forth, or create, an ecstasy''); in the imagist period he defines it, as we have seen, as ''sudden liberation,'' and when he is directly describing the ideogrammic method, he speaks of it as ''revelation.'' The objective of the artistic process—resulting from an accurate observation of particulars, their juxtaposition, and a grasp of their relation to revelation—is to arrive at *true seeing*, the vision of nature's oneness. The final image-in-revelation may approach the state of a general idea, yet it will never become one, for Pound's merging ''of essentiality and definiteness of conceptual and perceptual images is in fact the determinative form of the particular containing the universal.''[15] The mind ''in ecstasy'' holding fast to the suddenly realized concept will not release the individual and real objects which embody the concept.

The method of the ideogram, then, is implicit in the early works on romance in the discussion of the ''luminous detail'' in the series of essays ''I Gather the Limbs of Osiris'' and in the theory of ''language beyond metaphor'' in *The Spirit of Romance*. The latter, Pound's first published prose work, is also important because it foreshadows several important points which Pound elaborated after reading the Fenollosa essay on the Chinese character and after his more exact formulations of the ''image'' and the ''vortex.''

It is also in *The Spirit of Romance* that Pound begins to use scientific terms to define his aesthetic ideas. It is Pound's ''normative'' predilection for verbal precision which determines the value he places on the Provençal poets, especially on Arnaut Daniel, and his definition of poetry is in line with that ideal precision: ''Poetry is a sort of inspired mathematics, which gives us equations, not for abstract figures, triangles, spheres, and the like, but equations for the human emotions.''[16] He writes later that ''the arts, literature, poesy, are a science, just as chemistry is a science.''[17] And in describing the ideogrammic method twenty years later, he writes, ''That, you see, is very much the kind of thing a biologist does (in a much more complicated way) when he gets together a few hundred or thousand slides, and picks out what is necessary for his general statement."[18] I shall discuss in some detail the problem of science and art in Pound's aesthetics in a later chapter. I make mention of it at this time merely to point to the correlation of the particular phraseology to the *forma mentis* as it was present "in the air" and to the particular virtues Pound saw operative in the best Provençal and early Italian poetry. Arnaut Daniel's method of composition is "scientific" in that the Provençal poet "is not content with conventional phrase, or with words which do not convey his exact meaning." And in a close analysis of Arnaut's canzone "L'aura amara" Pound praises the precision of the verbs much as Fenollosa does in connection with Chinese poetry: "In this song . . . one can still follow the shadowy suggestion of medieval ceremonies, due to Daniel's choice of verbs."[19]

It is in connection with another canzone of Arnaut's, "Sim fos amor," which Dante himself had singled out for praise, that Pound introduces the term "language beyond metaphor." He refers specifically to the second stanza: "three times in this stanza," he writes, "the Provençal makes his picture, neither by simile nor by metaphor, but in the language beyond metaphor, by the use of the picturesque verb with an exact meaning."[20] Later in the book Pound defines what he means by "language beyond metaphor." In discussing Shakespeare and Dante, he writes that while Shakespeare's language is "more beautifully suggestive," Dante's is "more beautifully definite," "more apt in 'comparison.' " Then, after quoting Aristotle on metaphor ("The apt use of metaphor, arising, as it does, from a swift perception of relations, is the hallmark of genius"), Pound explains:

> I use the term "comparison" to include metaphor, simile (which is a more leisurely expression of a kindred variety of thought), and the "language beyond metaphor," that is, the more compressed or elliptical expression of metaphorical perception, such as antithesis suggested or implied in verbs and adjectives.[21]

I feel quite certain that by "language beyond metaphor" Pound does *not* mean a kind of metaphysical conceit or catachresis. True, the conceit is a comparison, but in contrast to Aristotle's (and Pound's) emphasis on "aptness," it is "a comparison whose ingenuity is more striking than its justness," for "a comparison becomes a conceit when we are made to concede likeness while being strongly conscious of unlikeness."[22] Pound's intentions are exactly the opposite. He is aiming at a "natural picture," an elliptical or antithetical juxtaposition of words whose relations will reveal larger and fundamental relations existing in nature. Pound's term the "epithet of primary apparition" follows directly from the "language beyond metaphor." "Epithets of primary apparition," he writes, "give vividness to description and stimulate conviction in the *actual vision* of the poet."[23] The emphasis is mine, for here again it is clear that Pound is alluding to a process where the artist, by precise perceptions, attains a vision of the relationships between the particulars observed and the workings of nature. From the exactness of these perceptions the artist recreates this vision in the literary work; and from this, acute and attentive readers may attain their own vision or revelation.

The idea of "luminous detail," which Pound develops in his other study of romance, the essays "I Gather the Limbs of Osiris," is a further step toward ideogrammic expression. All disciplines (history, science, the arts) work with "luminous details," says Pound, for they all deal with facts. Pound is concerned with "hyper-scientific precision" when he writes that "we must know accurately a great number of minute facts about any subject if we are really to know it."[24] But "luminous details" are not *any* facts; they are of a kind which "give one a sudden insight into circumjacent conditions, into their causes, their effects, into sequence, and law." Pound also calls it the method of "multitudinous" or "interpreting detail." In the hands of a great historian (he cites Burckhardt) such an array of significant particulars "can give us intelligence of a period"; they govern human knowledge "as the switchboard governs an electric circuit." The creative artist uses these details in a similar fashion: "The artist seeks out the luminous detail and presents it. He does not comment." Also, "he does not, as a rule, sling generalities; he gives the particular case. . . ."[25] Such luminous details are, then, the "language beyond metaphor" of Arnaut to which Pound drew attention; the concatenation of these foci can give us an approximation of the poet's vision and an insight to the "intelligence" of that period. The method is not static but dynamic; the rapid succession of luminous data reaches a point where the particulars will shine forth in their unique reality, yet stand transformed. The method of ideogram is implicit here. This is the fruit of Pound's research—his "digging" into the works of Arnaut, Vidal, Cardinal, Sordello, and Bertrans de Born. Their method was the creation of an idea-image through the relation of compressed metaphors. "Pound called it the ideogrammic method," observes one critic, "but he discovered it in Provence long before he came across the Fenollosa manuscripts."[26] While this is an exaggeration, it is safe to say on the basis of the evidence that Pound's mind was prepared by his Provençal studies so that the seeds of Fenollosa's essay fell on fertile ground.

Pound's "archeology," at the same time, prepared him for imagism, which in turn led to vorticism and the ideogram. The idea of luminous, interpretative details presented without subjective comments is very near to the "direct treatment" principle in the imagist manifesto. But in addition to studying the Provençals and Dante Pound had also assimilated, before turning to imagism, other ideas currently "in the air." Most important among these ideas were Ford Madox Hueffer's insistence on the Flaubertian *mot juste* and T. E. Hulme's theory of the image. The effect of Hueffer (later Ford) on Pound has been clearly demonstrated by critics, and Pound himself was never reluctant to pay tribute to Ford, whom he acknowledged as his first initiator into modernism in London. "The revolution of the word," Pound wrote, "began so far as it affected the men who were of my age in London in 1908, with the LONE whimper of Ford Madox Hueffer," for Hueffer was "one who really understood the question of clear expression."[27] Pound was no less ready to own a portion of the debt to Hulme for the latter's possible influence on the imagists, whom he called "the descendants of the forgotten school of 1909," i.e., the circle of poets who gathered around Hulme. There has been no consensus among critics, however, as to the nature of the Hulmian influence. While some have chosen to call him the "father" of imagism, others have called attention to the fundamental difference between the Hulmian and the Poundian concept of the poetic image. A difference certainly does exist, and it may even be quite crucial. But the *evidence* of Hulme's writings and their correlatives in Pound's thought incontestably point to a relationship, discernible in the Hulmian terminology which Pound adopted for the purpose of putting the results of his inquiries into poetic form in exact theoretical language. Hulme's ideas certainly constituted a part of the "new *forma mentis*" and, as such, represented a vital body of thought "in the air" to which all ideogrammic poets could turn for inspiration and clarification.

Yet, although Hulme *confirmed* the direction Pound set out to follow, his theory of the image stopped short of the more exalted role Pound intended for it. The image for Pound does not mean something almost purely visual, nor is it based on analogy in the Hulmian sense. It presents "an intellectual and emotional complex," a whole, where the juxtaposed particulars project for an instant, through their interrelatedness, a vision of both concrete and conceptual realities. An image has nothing to do with *size*, either. Pound's "In a Station of the Metro" or H. D.'s "Oread" present an image, and so does a canto. Pound had even gone so far as to say that "Dante's 'Paradiso' is the most wonderful *image*" (Pound's emphasis).

In the light of the foregoing, just how should one understand this statement? It is important to note that Pound gave his most complete theoretical account of the image when he was already a vorticist; the above statement on the "Paradiso" appeared in his 1914 essay "Vorticism." In his mind "image" and "vortex" became inextricably bound together, and in this essay he in fact defines the one in terms of the other: "The image is not an idea. It is a radiant node, or cluster; it is what I can, and must perforce, call a VORTEX, from which, and through which, and into which, ideas are constantly rushing."[28] This new definition of the image as vortex may sound as if it were lifted from a vorticist manifesto, but beyond the tone, it is significant for at least two reasons. First, it shows Pound's habit of appropriating and amalgamating older poetic practices under a new concept, as if his earlier experiments were suddenly flooded with the light of clear and distinct theoretical understanding. A similar "naming" and appropriation occurred in the early thirties when he began to propagandize the "ideogrammic method," as if he had just then found a name for the method of composition he had been practicing for a decade and a half. Second, the dynamic nature of the vorticist image does in fact date back at least three years, to the time of his Provençal and Italian studies. A year before the essay on vorticism he had already said that "the thing that matters in art is a sort of energy, something more or less like electricity or radioactivity, a force transfusing, welding, unifying."[29] And even in the "Osiris" essays a primitive version of the vortex and of the ideogrammic method proper appears in a revealing simile:

> Let us imagine that words are like great hollow cones of steel of different dullness and acuteness. . . . Let us imagine them charged with a force like electricity, or, rather, radiating a force from their apexes —some radiating, some sucking in. . . . Some of these kinds of force neutralise each other, some augment. . . . When this conjunction occurs . . . three or four words in exact juxtaposition are capable of radiating this energy at a very high potentiality. . . .[30]

The passage also foreshadows Fenollosa's energy-transfer theory and Olson's concept of the poem as energy construct and energy discharge.

In Pound's view, therefore, the image of the "Paradiso" is an image in much the same way as a canzone by Arnaut is an image. His attention focuses on the verbal metaphors whose juxtaposition initiates a growth, a mental climb toward insight or revelation. "The form of sphere above sphere, the varying reaches of light," he writes, "the minutiae of pearls upon foreheads, all these are parts of the Image"; the rest, "the discourses with the calendar of saints and the discussions about the nature of the moon, are philology."[31] In discussing the "Paradiso" Pound imagistically intuits a structure which he will use and develop for his own long poem. In a 1915 essay called "Affirmations—As for Imagisme", he prepares the theoretical groundwork from which longer imagistic or vorticist poems could be made to grow:

> Intense emotion causes pattern to arise in the mind, . . . perhaps I should say, not pattern, but pattern units, or units of design. . . . By pattern-unit or vorticist picture I mean the single jet. The difference between the pattern-unit and the picture is one of complexity. The pattern-unit is so simple that one can bear having it repeated several or many times. When it becomes so complex that repetition would be useless, then it is a picture, an "arrangement of forms."[32]

Another example may be quoted from a note appended to the 1914 article on vorticism which further amplifies the idea of the "Paradiso" as one complex image:

> I am often asked whether there can be a long imagiste or vorticist poem. The Japanese, who evolved the hokku, evolved also the Noh Plays. In the best "Noh" the whole play may consist of one image. I mean it is gathered about one image. Its unity consists in one image, enforced by movement and music. I see nothing against a long vorticist poem.[33]

The larger image, then, such as Dante's poem or a Noh play or a canto of Pound's, can be imagined as a force field where centripetal and centrifugal (mental) energies interact. The units of design are verbal "natural pictures," attracting and transforming ideas "constantly rushing" into their vortices. Such pattern units may be natural (objective) or emotional (subjective) images; they have the capacity to stand alone as "one-image poems," which Pound defined as "a form of super-position" where "one idea is set on top of the other." The definition is inexact, for "ideas" arise only from the collision of the juxtaposed images and from the arrangement of verbal forms. Also, "superposition" is physically impossible in writing; only juxtaposition is available to the poet. Superposition can come about in the mind of the reader, somewhat as in a Chinese ideogram the pictures are set side by side, from which the mind can grasp invisible "things"—ideas, concepts, universals.

Pound's entry into vorticism (he coined the term, though "the Great English Vortex" was primarily a painters' movement) was preceded by his acquisition of the Fenollosa papers, but there is no evidence that he read the essay on the Chinese written character until several months after delivering his lecture "Vorticism," where he speaks of the "one-image poem" and "superposition." The example he offers for such a poem is his "In a Station of the Metro." The poem, Pound tells us, is the result of a process of gradual condensation of his initial response to an experience during which he saw "a beautiful face, and then another and another, and then a beautiful child's face, and then another beautiful woman," after which he tried to find words to convey the emotions created by the experience. He finally arrived at the "hokku-like sentence" after an interval of some twenty months.

Pound explains that "in a poem of this sort one is trying to record the precise instant when a thing outward and objective transforms itself, or darts into a thing inward and subjective."[34] The terminology is vorticist, or at least it owes something to the expository style of the painters and sculptors whom Pound began to know and admire between 1912 and 1914. It is strongly reminiscent of Kandinsky's idea of "inner necessity," which is "the inevitable desire to express the objective," the effect of which is "a progressive expression of the eternally objective within the temporarily subjective.''[35] In that sense the "Metro" poem is a vortex—in Pound's words, a "cluster of fused ideas . . . endowed with energy"—as well as an image, an "intellectual and emotional complex." But it is also an image in the Provençal or Dantescan manner, the way Pound defined it in discussing Arnaut's canzones or Dante's "Paradiso." The poem's title (which is an intrinsic part of the poem) is "philology," the historical or biographical background. The first line is the image of the "thing outward," already approaching the subjective realm as seen in the connotative richness of the word *apparition*. And the second line is the "inward" "natural picture," coalescing for an instant with the superimposed external image, so that "faces in the crowd" and "petals on a wet black bough" are *one*. The poem is *not* a metaphor nor an implied simile; a paraphrase with the connectives supplied effectively destroys the poem. The poet's subjectivity is submerged; his emotions do not intrude, and he does not allow his intellect to arbitrarily order and predicate through the use of "is" or "is like." Only one thing is implied, and that is the Heraclitean "latent structure" that binds the two images together: the "latent" verb *grow*, which is implicit in all of nature.

Pound's aim is "letting realities manifest themselves, rather than settling for subjective affirmation or denial."[36] That is, he follows a nonmetaphorical, paratactic mode to reestablish through art, as he says, "our kinship to the vital universe." And the result of contemplating this poem is a kind of insight or revelation, or, in the Poundian sense, ecstasy. For ecstasy, according to Pound, is not something arcane or mystical; it is not "a whirl or a madness of the senses, but a glow arising from the exact nature of the perception."[37] It arises from the real and the actual. It in fact cannot come into being and cannot exist without it.

In another sense, the "Metro" poem is an image of Pound's poetic development. It is an image in which he combines his earliest "digging," his imagism, and his vorticist crystallizing of all previous efforts toward a realization of an accurate mode of recreating the world through art. This mode combines twentieth-century awareness with archaic, pre-logical drives to achieve a total, natural vision of reality. The words of Wyndham Lewis can be applied to Pound: "The artist of the modern movement is a savage . . . : this enormous, jangling, journalistic, fairy desert of modern life serves him as Nature did more technically primitive man."[38] In this "desert" Pound continued to lead a "double" life: while participating in one of the most radical and vociferous movements of modern art he began a new series of archeological explorations that were to give final form to his theory of poetic creation.

2. The Impact of Fenollosa

In the second (and last) issue of *Blast*, published in July of 1915, Wyndham Lewis wrote a brief description of Pound. Lewis was rarely given to flattering fellow artists, but the paragraph about Pound is quite complimentary as well as informative. Pound is described as a "demon pantechnikon driver, busy with removal of old world into new quarters. In his steel net of impeccable technique he has lately caught Li Po."[1]

The poems by Li Po—for this is what Lewis was referring to—were "caught" by Pound from the manuscripts of Ernest Fenollosa. A collection of the poems, including a few by other Chinese poets, was published in April of the same year under the title *Cathay*. Pound described the collection as "translations . . . from the notes of the late Ernest Fenollosa, and the decipherings of the Professors Mori and Ariga."[2] The book was a turning point in Pound's poetry, and it struck a new note in English literature.

Cathay has been justly praised and written about at length by several critics. Eliot's words that "Pound is the inventor of Chinese poetry for our time" are still valid today. Behind the "translations" there stands not only Pound's "net of impeccable technique," the results of all his earlier gropings and "diggings" in Provençal, in Dante and Cavalcanti, in the Anglo-Saxon from which he had "translated" "The Seafarer"—but there is also another of Fenollosa's works: his lecture notes for *The Chinese Written Character as a Medium for Poetry*. When Pound mentions Fenollosa in a general way in his correspondence or in his critical writings, he is usually referring to Fenollosa's essay on the Chinese written character. It came to occupy a central place in Pound's poetics, and as the subject of much controversy, it is a document of some importance in its own right. It is therefore well worth the trouble to establish as exactly as possible Fenollosa's intentions and meanings as developed in his essay, and then examine how Pound understood him and to what purpose he put Fenollosa's findings.

Pound received the manuscripts of Fenollosa (some sixteen notebooks) from his widow, Mary Fenollosa, sometime in November of 1913. It would appear that it was Pound's poetry that convinced her of the young

American's suitability to edit and publish the notes, translations, and essays lying untouched and undiscovered since her husband's death in 1908. Pound's first significant reference to Fenollosa's essay on the Chinese written character occurs in an article entitled "Imagisme and England," published on February 20, 1915, in *T. P.'s Weekly*. While not claiming absolute originality for "imagisme," Pound perceived that the kind of poetry the imagists were writing was strikingly similar in some ways to the Chinese poetry translated by Fenollosa. His earlier ideas about "luminous details," "language beyond metaphor," "intellectual and emotional complex," and "pattern units" appear to have fallen into place as soon as he read Fenollosa's essay. For Pound realized that his search for a new form, a natural poetic expression, had finally met with the exact model which could be the basis of a new poetics. He wrote in the article, "We have sought the force of Chinese ideographs *without knowing it.*" It was therefore hardly an accident that Mary Fenollosa had picked Pound as literary executor; in fact it was due to her uncommon insight of perceiving a relation between some of Pound's poetry and Chinese verse.

Pound's next mention of the essay comes in a letter to his ex-professor, Dr. Schelling, a few months later: "Fenollosa has left a most enlightening essay on the [Chinese] written character (a whole basis of aesthetic, in reality), but the adamantine stupidity of all magazine editors delays its appearance."[3] He gives examples of ideograms in the letter. For instance, the ideogram for the verb "to visit, or ramble" is a king and a dog sitting on the stern of a boat. It is, he writes, "an exquisite example of the way the Chinese mind works."

In June of 1916 Pound wrote the following to an aspiring poet, Iris Barry, who had asked him for advice:

> You should have a chance to see Fenollosa's big essay on verbs, mostly on verbs. . . . He inveighs against "IS," wants transitive verbs. "Become" is as weak as "is." . . . "All nouns come from verbs." To primitive man, a thing only IS what it *does*. That is Fenollosa, but I think the theory is a very good one for poets to go by.[4]

Again, to Iris Barry, a month later:

> The whole art of poetry is divided into:
> a. concision, or style, or saying what you mean in the fewest or clearest words.
> b. the actual necessity for creating or constructing something; of presenting an image, or enough images of concrete things arranged to stir the reader.[5]

Point *a* is an almost verbatim reiteration of the second principle of the imagist manifesto. But in point *b* Pound is formulating something new. Here, for the first time, we find him defining what he subsequently named the ideogrammic method of poetic composition. He was already at this time busy working on his "cryselephantine poem of immeasurable length," later to be called *The Cantos*, where the method was to become the poem's chief organizing principle. Pound continued to reiterate in letters and essays that Fenollosa's study of the Chinese written character "is one of the most important essays in our time," for "Fenollosa saw and anticipated a good deal of what has happened in art (painting and poetry) during the last ten years, and his essay is basic for all aesthetics. . . ."[6]

Other critics have also extolled the virtues of the essay. Hugh Kenner has called it "the *Ars Poetica* of our time," and Donald Davie has said that it is "fit to rank with Sidney's *Apologie*, and the Preface to *Lyrical Ballads*, and Shelley's *Defence*" and that although the essay did not fulfill Pound's expectations of receiving wide recognition, it nevertheless constituted an indispensable methodological tool for Pound himself in constructing his long poem.[7] Other writers have been less generous. According to Noel Stock, "The result of Fenollosa's essay was that in the end Pound almost gave up thought altogether, and instead concerned himself with arranging isolated gists, phrases and facts."[8] Before determining the extent of Fenollosa's influence on Pound, we must turn to the essay itself and uncover Fenollosa's own concerns and concepts.

It is important to note at the outset that *The Chinese Written Character as a Medium for Poetry* was published only in the shape Pound gave to it when he edited it. Furthermore, there are *two* manuscripts of the essay, both intended for public lectures. The earlier version of the lecture (dating about 1904) is less finished and more rambling than the later one, but it embodies Fenollosa's central insight in poetics: his continuous insistence on metaphoric construction as a *natural mode of composition* and on the isomorphic vision, which permeates not only the later version of the essay but is at the center of Fenollosa's thought—a part of the new *forma mentis*. According to Fenollosa, "a metaphor is only a strong way of forcing thought back upon the original unities of things. It deals not in fanciful analogies but identities *of structure*."[9] This idea is followed by a strong image of metaphor which Fenollosa then decided to cross out: "It is a Roentgen ray which pierces through bone and tissue, and lays bare the pulsing of nature's heart." He also includes a quite Aristotelian description of "the joy of a pure metaphor" which lies "in the sudden flash with which we perceive an identity of relationship between groups of facts ordinarily conceived as remote."

It was the later, finished version which Pound worked on and which was first published, with his changes, deletions, and additions, in the fall and winter of 1919 in four successive issues of *The Little Review*. Pound's editing is on the whole salutary and his stylistic changes certainly improve on the text, but there are certain deletions and transformations of Fenollosa's thought which are again revealing.

In the beginning Pound leaves out two long paragraphs in which Fenollosa sets forth his motives for propagating Chinese culture in the West. The motives are only in part aesthetical: a cross-fertilization of cultural forces between China and the United States and Britain should promote not merely an understanding of a rich and varied tradition but also a political alliance with a strong and independent China as a means of maintaining Anglo-Saxon hegemony in world affairs. Pound was right in excising this passage from the essay as it is not wholly germane to the general theme, but its prophetic insight has diminished little in the ensuing seventy-five years.

Fenollosa begins by comparing Chinese and Western modes of poetic composition, taking the first line from Gray's "Elegy Written in a Country Churchyard" and a Chinese line "Moon rays like pure snow." He demonstrates that in spite of the apparent dissimilarity there is no essential difference between the two ways of writing. There is a cause-and-effect scheme discernible in both, for poetry is a *time art*, and the flow of thought follows a *natural* pattern instead of merely an arbitrary one. "Thought is successive," Fenollosa writes, "because the operations of nature are successive. The transferences of force from agent to object, which constitute natural phenomena, occupy time."[10]

Fenollosa then gives an example. We see the temporal process of a man observing a horse in its linguistic representation: "Man sees horse." In Chinese the process is identical, but it is denoted in symbols different from ours.

人　　　　見　　　　馬

Man　　　Sees　　　Horse

In the English representation the symbols on the paper signify sounds. Chinese notation, on the other hand, "is based upon a vivid shorthand picture of the operations of nature":

> . . . The Chinese method follows natural suggestion. First stands the man on his two legs. Second, his eye moves through space: a bold figure represented by running legs under the eye, a modified picture of an eye, a modified picture of running legs, but unforgettable once you have seen it. Third stands the horse on his four legs.[11]

This group of symbols is "alive," writes Fenollosa; it is something like "a continuous moving picture." Chinese picture writing combines spatial and temporal qualities in that we witness the phenomenon of things working out their own fate. (It is an interesting coincidence that just as Pound's expository prose is full of scientific, medical, and mathematical analogies and similes, Fenollosa also makes use of the latest technological innovations to illustrate his points.)

The next important statement Fenollosa makes is that the shorthand pictures of Chinese writing do not depict *things* but actions and processes. After the single pictograms of his man-sees-horse example, he turns to "compounds." "In this process of compounding," he observes, "two things added together do not produce a third thing but suggest some fundamental relation between them."[12] Here we have the first precise definition of the working of the ideogrammic method, the theoretical formulation of a mode of natural composition toward which Pound had been groping. The method does not exhaust itself in giving us "vivid shorthand pictures of actions and processes in nature," for, as Fenollosa writes, "the best poetry deals not only with natural images but with lofty thoughts, spiritual suggestions and obscure relations." The idea of "latent structure" behind the scheme of things is formulated thus: "The greater part of natural truth is hidden in processes too minute for vision and in harmonies too large, in vibrations, cohesions, and in affinities."[13] The sentence may be admirable for its concision, but it is Pound's contraction. For a fuller meaning (and as an example of the flavor of Fenollosa's style) it is worth quoting the original version:

> The larger and more important part of natural truth is hidden from the physical eye, yet it is no less real. It is hidden both in the processes too minute for vision, and in harmonies too large;—in vibrations, cohesions, affinities; in orders, analogies, proportions, affections and character. Virtue, religion, beauty, law, social amenities, family ties, political responsibilities, all these exhibit immaterial planes of true being, in which the chief poetic values of the world are realized.[14]

Poetry, according to Fenollosa, is able to deal with the unseen relations between things through the process of metaphor, through "the use of material images to suggest immaterial relations." Primitive metaphors upon which languages have been built, Fenollosa asserts, are not subjective but objective in that they follow the objectivity of natural relations as they exist in the world. "Relations are more real and more important than the things which *they relate.*"[15] Natural processes operate through forces cutting into and across resistances; the energies producing vegetal or human growth are present in the seed. "This is more than analogy, it is identity of structure," states Fenollosa, stressing the principle of isomorphism. Pound leaves out the illuminating example of Fenollosa's original manuscript: "Laws of structure are the same in the spiritual and the material world. Human character grows with the same stresses and knots as mountain pines."

Isomorphism in all of nature and its metaphoric representation in human language and in poetry is closely interwoven with Fenollosa's idea that things and actions form inseparable wholes, functioning unities. "All processes in nature are interrelated,"[16] he writes, for nature is in eternal flux and knows no completeness. This is somewhat reminiscent of Heisenberg's idea that we can only consider the properties or mass of an object while we disregard its motion, just as we must neglect its mass if we wish to measure its speed. But, as Fenollosa writes,

> A true noun, an isolated thing, does not exist in nature. Things are only the terminal points, or rather the meeting points, of actions, cross-sections cut through actions, snapshots. Neither can a pure verb, an abstract motion, be possible in nature. The eye sees noun and verb as one: things in motion, motion in things, and so the Chinese conception tends to represent them.[17]

It is relationship that is truly important, for only through the dynamic relationship of an object and its function, and its ties to other things and their motions, that we can grasp the reality of their being. Things-in-motion and motion-in-things are eternally involved in *metamorphosis*, in transference of energy. Forces are constantly being redistributed between the "meeting points" of actions, which Fenollosa, for the sake of convenience, designates with the triad

agent — act — object

which the Chinese language follows in its sentence structure, as does English. The syntax most isomorphic with nature's processes is the transitive sentence, for it appears to imitate a natural succession of force distribution. Fenollosa's illustration, "Farmer pounds rice," is a linguistic depiction of an actual process, for "in uninflected languages, like English and Chinese, there is nothing but the order of the words to distinguish their functions." Only the transitive form of the sentence and its motor, the transitive verb, express a natural sequence. Intransitive sentences, says Fenollosa, are "weak and incomplete," and the "ultimate weakness of language" he locates in the copula "is," for it robs any natural process of its essential grounding in action. To introduce the copula "is" into Fenollosa's example, we can say "A farmer is a rice-pounder." But by doing so the verbal action actually grinds to a halt. It becomes static, and its natural dynamism evaporates into thin air. Therefore, Fenollosa concludes, "There is in reality no such verb as a pure copula, no such original conception: our very word *exist* means 'to stand forth,' to show oneself by a definite act. 'Is' comes from the Aryan root *as*, to breathe. 'Be' is from *bhu*, to grow."[18]

Fenollosa contends that the most ancient strata of our languages demonstrate a verbal quality beneath their nominal, objective, and adjectival shells, in line with the things-in-motion and motion-in-things principle. Like a thing in nature, a part of speech "is only *what it does*." As I mentioned above, the terms "agent-act-object" (or noun-verb-object, their equivalents in language) are posited by Fenollosa merely to facilitate describing a process. He knows full well that a person is not a noun but "a bundle of functions." Consequently, even the "Farmer pounds rice" form of a process is only partially accurate. In such a primitive sentence, writes Fenollosa,

> the agent and the object are nouns only in so far as they limit a unit of action. "Farmer" and "rice" are mere hard terms which define the extremes of the pounding. But in themselves, apart from this sentence function, they are naturally verbs. The farmer is one who tills the ground, and the rice is a plant which grows in a special way.[19]

It may be interesting to carry Fenollosa's example one step farther and say that this particular relation of farmer and rice is a temporary one: it lasts as long as they are bound together by the action. They are combined in a momentary unit until the farmer's specifically directed energy is redistributed. It was the action that accented one of the many possible functions each of them possesses, and it brought out only one of the many potential relations that can exist between them. After this transference of force comes metamorphosis: the farmer goes and tends to his animals; the rice has become rice flour. Even though they may be *statically* described, the one a "cattle-feeder" and the other "flour," they have not ceased to be "bundles of functions" on a related but different plane. And only through a verbal expression can we intimate the new wholes into which they have recombined themselves: "Farmer feeds cattle" and "Flour awaits cooking." On a different but related level, after other metamorphoses, they meet again when we say "Farmer eats rice cake." During which phase of these contiguous "sub-wholes" is the farmer truly *farmer*, and the rice, *rice*? We cannot say. Or rather, only through the meaningful juxtaposition of particular actions, apparently different but united by their relations, can we approximate the total reality of each functional "bundle" as the two entities ceaselessly unite and separate and unite again in new wholes according to their functions. "Things in motion, motion in things" is the pattern of natural processes: potential action in things, juxtaposition of things, release of energy (transference of force), new relation between things, temporary unity, decombination, metamorphosis. All things in nature act and are acted upon according to this "latent structure"; they are constantly regrouping and redistributing power. "No unit of natural process can be less than this," writes Fenollosa. "All natural processes are, in their units, as much as this." All things are structurally identical in their adherence to this law.

Poetic composition, in Fenollosa's view, must follow similar lines in order to fulfill its function. It is the poet's role to create forms in language that approximate nature's processes and show that the universe is *alive*, "full of homologies, sympathies, identities." As we have seen, the method recommended by Fenollosa is metaphoric construction relying on vivid, strong, transitive verbs. At the same time he attacks the copula "is" as an unreal verb, something that is not present in nature. (We may remember Wittgenstein's illustration of this idea in his example "The book is on the table.")

This "quasi-verb," as Fenollosa called it, has been used not only to designate actual relations between things, but as a linguistic, metaphoric tool to affirm "immaterial relations." Concepts and metaphysical ideas have been established with its aid; it is an implement with which the human mind has "invaded" reality and attempted to "tame" it, remake it, and possess it. With this tool we have attempted to build a home for ourselves in the universe *in our own image*, setting ourselves up in a unique position in the cosmos. We have believed in a supranatural *telos*, and our intellect and passions have been constantly fuelled by this belief in a metaphysical destiny, producing "truths" like "God is our father," "Heaven is our home," or, on a less exalted plane, "My love is a red rose." In times of existential crisis poets have made extravagant use of this connective verb to avert spiritual disaster and to keep us on our self-made pedestal; the poetry of the early seventeenth century is a good illustration of such metaphoric abuse. It has ever been a manifestation (to reverse Keats' famous adage) of our "positive capability," our overriding passion to elevate ourselves above nature and seize the world with logic.

This aggressive assertiveness, and its concomitant metaphoric device, began to crumble with the romantics' first hesitant steps toward organic composition and with their turning away from this "irritable reaching after facts and reason." But it was the modernists, following in the steps of the emerging empirical sciences, who dispensed with it completely. It was a modernist who said, "A rose is a rose is a rose." It was another, Brancusi, who said, "It's man's thoughts that break the universe." Another (Schwitters) wrote, "In a piece of art it is only important that all parts are correlated to the whole." It was Pound who wrote, "From the thing to the grouped things, thence to a more real knowledge." He pointed the way from metaphor "TOWARD ideogram," a more natural form of representation.

We can safely include Fenollosa among the theoreticians of modernism. When he insisted so passionately on metaphor, he most definitely did *not* intend for modern poets to continue filling their poems with the false metaphors of an arrogant, anthropocentric world view. His background was in Emersonian organicism, and in Japan he found close resemblances between this theory and the method of Chinese ideographic writing and poetic techniques. So when he spoke of metaphor, he meant *true* metaphor as he had seen it operate in the "natural pictures" of the ideogram. The examples in Fenollosa's essay confirm this idea:

> The sun underlying the bursting forth of plant = spring.
> The sun sign tangled in the branches of the tree sign = east. . . .
> "Rice-field" plus "struggle" = male. . . .
> "Boat" plus "water" = boat-water, a ripple.[20]

The word Fenollosa uses is "metaphor," but he means "ideogram," and so Pound understood him. Fenollosa writes that all languages are built on such true metaphors, upon "vivid verbs." Since "poetry only does consciously what the primitive races did unconsciously," poets must "feel back along the ancient lines of advance." At this point Pound adds the following footnote:

> The poet, in dealing with his own time, must also see to it that language does not petrify on his hands. He must prepare for new advances along the lines of true metaphor, that is interpretative metaphor, or image, and diametrically opposed to untrue, or ornamental metaphor.[21]

The image interprets; it does not interpose or encroach. In the "Metro" poem, the apparition of the faces *is not* a black bough with petals. In the ideogrammic composition the mind *re-creates*, or rather *creates*, in accordance with nature's processes; it tries not to "break the universe." Such metaphoric juxtapositions evince a reticence on the part of the poet, an unwillingness to tamper with reality. The form extends from an attitude which does not seek to appropriate nature but to explore it, which sees the human being as a participant in natural processes rather than some kind of *corona naturae*. An important passage in Fenollosa's essay affirms this, though in a somewhat curious way: "Metaphor, the revealer of nature, is the very substance of poetry. The known interprets the obscure, the universe is alive with myth. The beauty and freedom of the observed world furnish a model, and life is pregnant with art."[22] The first sentence is clear. But the other two sentences are not "logical," transitional constructs. Each of them is made up of two halves, and the halves are juxtaposed paratactically. They read like mildly anglicized Chinese sentences, the "rough" version reading something like this:

		Known	Interpret	Obscure
		Universe	Alive (with)	Myth
Beauty	Freedom (of)	Observed World	Furnish	Model
		Life	Pregnant (with)	Art

Even though Fenollos was steeped in Oriental poetry, he did not *think* ideogrammically; the rest of his essay attests to that. The matter is cleared up when the printed version of Fenollosa's essay is compared to the original manuscript. Not suprisingly, the paratactic structuring is the result of Pound's "editing." The original reads:

> . . . Metaphor, which reveals nature, is the very substance of Poetry. The known of man interprets the obscure world, hence the universe grows alive with myth. In turn, the beauty and freedom of the observed world furnish model and law to perplexed man, hence life grows pregnant with art.

The Fenollosa version is superior to Pound's because Fenollosa uses strong metaphoric verbs ("grows") while Pound is content to rely on the "quasi-verb" *is*. Had Pound made all the changes he did while leaving Fenollosa's verbs in their place, his sentences would not only have been stronger but clearer as well, despite the asyndetic composition. For here Fenollosa is pointing out the crucial difference between myth and poetry, the former investing the world with human values, the latter taking its cues from nature itself by constructing metaphors in accordance with natural laws. The distinction is not as clear in Pound's version, due also to his omission of informative data. But in spite of these shortcomings, Pound's modification is revelatory: he shows an ideogrammic intention. He is in fact manipulating Fenollosa's text in a way similar to his use of the John Adams papers or de Mailla's *Histoire générale de la Chine* in *The Cantos*: he interprets or re-creates them by selecting and juxtaposing significant material. From a group of such particulars the reader will then (so Pound expects) feel out the relations established through their interaction.

Fenollosa did not openly call the method ideogrammic in his essay, but he alluded to it several times during the exposition of his theme. The method springs from the method of Chinese characters, which have a "power of combining several pictorial elements in a single character." The ideogram is by its very metaphorical composition poetic, and Fenollosa is almost anticipating the vorticist position (and here Pound did not make changes in the text):

> Poetic thought works by suggestion, crowding maximum meaning into the single phrase pregnant, charged, and luminous from within.
>
> In Chinese character each word accumulated this sort of energy in itself.[23]

Based on the unique potential of the Chinese compound, Fenollosa formulates his definition of the method: ". . . the poet selects for juxtaposition those words whose overtones blend into a delicate and lucid harmony." In a poem "a word is like a sun, with its corona and chromosphere; words crowd upon words, and enwrap each other in their luminous envelopes until sentences become clear, continuous light-bands."[24] True art in any medium must strive for the creation of harmony, writes Fenollosa, and "refined harmony lies in the delicate balance of overtones." "In music," he writes, "the whole possibility and theory of harmony are based on overtones." Pound allowed this reference to music to stay in the essay, but he cut out a section devoted to painting, and more significantly, he left out the passage in which Fenollosa summarizes his theory of poetry. The original reads:

> In painting, great color beauty springs not from the main color masses, but from the refined modifications or overtones which each throws on

the other, just as tints are etherialized [*sic*] in a flower by reflection from petal to petal. One false radiation, or suspicion of conflict between any two of these overtones, breaks up the magic impression, and deadens art to the commonplace.

In this sense Poetry seems a more difficult art than painting or music, because the overtones of its words, the halos of secondary meanings which cling to them, are struck among the infinite terms of things, vibrating with physical life and the warm wealth of human feeling. How is it possible that such heterogeneous material shall suffer no jar, how that its manifold suggestions shall blend into an etherial [*sic*] fabric clear as crystal? . . . One device is clear in all three arts, namely the dominance of a single permeating tone. In music we get this by the unity of key—painting achieves it by mixing a suspicion of one tone color through all tints. In poetry it requires that the metaphorical overtones of neighboring words shall belong in the same general sphere of nature or of feeling.[25]

Fenollosa chooses an example from Chinese writing in which "a single dominant overtone colors every plane of meaning":

Fenollosa comments:

The sun, the shining, on one side, on the other the sign of the east, which is the sun entangled in the branches of a tree. And in the middle sign, the verb "rise," we have further homology; the sun is above the horizon, but beyond that the single upright line is like the growing trunk-line of the tree sign.[26]

Pound's deletion of the passage on the harmony of metaphoric overtones is, of course, revealing, and will be further commented upon. Obviously the poet, who from his earliest research on had been attempting to move *beyond* metaphor, was not impressed by harmonies and overtones. What he did notice and find exciting were the implications and the possibilities inherent in the Chinese ideogram as explicated by Fenollosa: that there exists a *natural unity* in a group of ideograms because the written symbol in Chinese, as Fenollosa wrote, "bears its metaphors on its face." Its etymology is, so to speak, at all times on the surface. "Thus a word," added Fenollosa, "instead of growing gradually poorer and poorer as with us, becomes richer and still more rich from age to age, almost consciously luminous."[27] Pound was clearly impressed by Fenollosa's assumptions about ideograms, which were twofold: (1) the Chinese written character is composed of "natural pictures" and their metaphoric juxtaposition, and (2) Chinese writers—especially poets—are aware of the metaphoric significance of the characters when they combine them to attain "a delicate and lucid harmony," and so are readers when they read the text. The ideographs in their accumulated metaphoric richness "are like blood-stained battle-flags to an old campaigner."

These are the two points which have provided the handiest targets for critics wanting to discredit Fenollosa's aesthetics and Pound's subsequent ideogrammic method, or at least to show that the method is based on false assumptions and deficient scholarship. Several critics have taken the trouble to disprove Fenollosa's notions,[28] and of course they are right. First, simple characters (like 人, "man," or 門, "door") and ideograms (or logical compounds) comprise only about 10 percent of the total number of characters. The rest are phonetic compounds, i.e., one part of the word is the so-called radical, indicating the sense and the other part suggests the way to pronounce the word. This side of Chinese writing Fenollosa patently ignores. Though he alludes to "Chinese lexicographers" who say that certain compounds have only a phonetic value, he cannot be convinced that at one time in the distant past even such phonetic combinations were not of a concrete metaphoric nature, the metaphor having been eroded by time. He is right in that the most ancient Chinese characters *were* pictograms and metaphoric ideograms. But he does not recognize the fact that to carry the ideogrammic mode *ad infinitum* would have required an inordinate amount of ingenuity and at the same time would have increased the possibility of confusion. He refuses to acknowledge the fact that the introduction of the phonetic compounds was a necessary step in the evolution of Chinese writing (occurring during and after the Chou dynasty, 1027-256 B.C.[29] With this discovery the creation of new characters at will was made possible. The sinologue's second objection is also valid: Chinese writers and readers are ordinarily unaware of the metaphoric "overtones" undeniably present in pictograms and ideograms, and such a reading of phonetic compounds is quite impossible. Many of the errors in Fenollosa's and Pound's translations from the Chinese are the result of such "ideogrammic reading."[30]

But does the validity of some philological points invalidate the entire framework of Fenollosa's thought, and subsequently Pound's, about ideogrammic composition? Evidently not, especially if we recognize the kind of intention and mental drive that prompted the two men to seek confirmation of their theories in the direction of the earliest forms of written expression. The drive was toward the source, a short-cut through the detour of 2,000 years of Occidental logic to the natural ground from which a new poetics could take its sustenance. In Kenner's view, Fenollosa's "great, his unassailable originality stemmed from his conviction that the unit of thought was less like a noun than like a verb, and that Chinese signs therefore denoted processes"; and that Fenollosa's "rejection" of phonetic compounds not only did not harm his general theory but in fact had encouraged him "to universalize his intuition about verbs and processes."[31] As for "ideogrammic reading," Pound recounts in a footnote to the Fenollosa essay that Henri Gaudier-Brzeska was able to read certain ideograms at sight, and "he was amazed at the stupidity of lexicographers who could not, for all their learning discern the pictorial values which were to him perfectly obvious and apparent."

And surely this is the central issue. As Hugh Gordon Porteus writes in an important essay on the ideogrammic method, Pound (and Fenollosa and Gaudier)—despite their lack of scholarship, or perhaps because of it—see something or look for something in Chinese characters "that sinologues in general are blind to." Metaphoric overtones are lost, or may be lost, on the general reader, both in Chinese and in English writing. And it is quite true, as Porteus notes, that

> for those educated in the written language, writing rapidly becomes so far an automatic gesture that the written word is hardly analyzed. It is probable that few, however steeped in the classics, have even the faintest suggestion of astrology when they read or write such a word as "disaster."[32]

But Porteus significantly adds: "The answer here, and it should settle a crucial point, is that it is precisely those *few* who matter, at any rate in connection with poetry."[33] Pound was one of the "few." In connection with the "east" ideogram, he said, "I think in a well-brushed ideogram the sun is seen to be rising."

For Pound, as for Fenollosa, the character of the Chinese written sign, as well as the quality of Chinese poetry, inheres in this natural capacity to recreate processes. And it was not Pound or Fenollosa but a sinologue (and a Chinese sinologue at that) who observed that "much of the art of Chinese poetry lies in the way in which the poet captures the visual events as they emerge and act themselves out before us."[34] Such a method not only lies at the heart of Chinese poetic composition but applies as well to Pound's techniques and those of the poets in the ideogrammic stream, particularly of projective verse. The same Chinese scholar (Wai-lim Yip) underlines the "cinematic visuality" and the paratactic formation of lines in Chinese verse so that the natural actuality of "things in motion, motion in things" is not lost. In his words, "the successive shots do not constitute a linear development (such as *how this leads to that*). Rather, the objects coexist, as in a painting, and yet the mobile point of view has made it possible to temporalize the spatial units."[35] Immaterial relations are depicted by juxtaposing pertinent concrete data in a suggestive way.

This simultaneity of perceptual units and their actions in a functional whole is the essence of Chinese ideograms to which Fenollosa called attention, and to which Pound responded with such enthusiasm. What Pound took to be Fenollosa's central message came through to him loud and clear because he was ready for it at that particular stage of his poetic development. The message was that poets should abandon logic as the principle of poetic organization. Instead, their compositional process should attempt to follow nature's processes, juxtaposing "meeting points" of energy transference to attain a nonhierarchic series of functionally interrelated particulars. "The prehistoric poets who created language," wrote Fenollosa, "discovered the whole harmonious framework of nature, they sang out her processes in their hymns."[36] It was perhaps at this time that it became especially clear to Pound—modernist poet, archeologist, synthesizer of archaic vision with "hyperscientific precision"—that to sing out the *process* would become his lifelong poetic occupation.

3. The Poundian Ideogram

It is a remarkable outcome of the Fenollosa-Pound relationship that in spite of the many outstanding features of *The Chinese Written Character*—isomorphism, transference of power, science over logic, and the theory of metaphoric overtones—it was not these aspects of it that constituted the Fenollosian influence on Pound's poetics. For when Pound praised and commended the unique importance of Fenollosa's insights as "the basis of a new aesthetic," he meant something else—what he in the early thirties began to call the ideogrammic method. He even denied that Fenollosa had explicitly defined the method in his essay, and allowed only that the ideogrammic method was "seriously indicated in Ernest Fenollosa's *The Chinese Written Character*, there dealt with narratively rather than formulated as a method *to be used*" (Pound's emphasis).[1] It is obvious that Pound did not mean the theory of dominant metaphoric overtones, for, as we have seen, he deftly excised it from his published version of the Fenollosa essay as something redundant or irrelevant. What he stressed was this "something else," the "narratively" formulated method: "Fenollosa accented the Western need of ideogrammic thinking," he wrote. "Get your 'red' down to rose, rust, cherry if you want to know what you are talking about. We have too much talk about vibrations and infinities."[2]

Here is the ideogrammic method he gleaned from Fenollosa's essay: the juxtaposition of seemingly unrelated particulars capable of suggesting ideas and concepts through their relation. He expounded the theory in *ABC of Reading* and *Guide to Kulchur*; but before he clearly formulated it he had already been practicing it in *The Cantos* for over a decade. Just as the theory of the image had solidified in his mind when already a vorticist, so his systematic definition of the method he named ideogrammic came about when he renewed his Chinese (particularly Confucian) studies in the thirties. Although explicit propaganda for the method does not begin until this relatively late date, the practical evidence of its influence is visible on every page of *A Draft of XXX Cantos*, published in 1930. And the method Pound saw partially formulated was in Fenollosa's *The Chinese Written Character*.

Clearly, the genesis of the method is to be found in the Fenollosa material, and there appear to be two possibilities as to how Pound extracted the method. In either case we are confronted with a certain benign misunderstanding by Pound of Fenollosa's examples given in the lecture notes, wherein he saw "something" only he could see: the basis of a new poetics.

In the case of the first possibility we must look for clues in the Fenollosa essay, which Pound had been preparing for its first separate edition while he was engaged in writing *ABC of Reading* in 1933 and 1934. On page 12 of the essay in its printed version Fenollosa puts forth the notable assertion that the sentence is not a man-made artifact: its form "was forced upon primitive man by nature itself," and it is "a reflection of the temporal order in causation." But before he develops his theme of agent-act-object power transference in nature as well as in the transitive sentence, he takes issue with the grammarians' definitions of the sentence and proceeds to demolish them. One definition, that a sentence expresses a complete thought, he finds untenable since "in nature there is *no* completeness," because all acts and happenings are successive. Consequently, "no full sentence really completes a thought." Subject, verb, and object are meeting points of action in an endless process of "things in motion, motion in things." The other definition, according to which a sentence is a uniting of subject and predicate, he dismisses because of its arrogant subjectivity which postulates that the form of the sentence is an adjunct of ego function.

Fenollosa attributes these artificial concepts to the logic of the Middle Ages, which disregarded the values and qualities inherent in concrete things, believing that thought arrives at them through the "sifting process" of abstract reasoning. Fenollosa contrasts this kind of logic with scientific thinking and attacks it later in the essay in the form of an analogy or parable. According to this logic, he writes,

> thought is a kind of brickyard. It is baked into little hard units or concepts. These are piled in rows according to size and then labeled with words for future use. This use consists in picking out a few bricks, each by its convenient label, and sticking them together into a sort of wall called a sentence by the use either of white mortar for the positive copula "is," or of black mortar for the negative copula "is not."[3]

By this method, says Fenollosa, we are capable of predications or negations which are wholly alien to nature, such as "A ring-tailed baboon is not a constitutional assembly." Then Fenollosa continues with another exemplum.

> Let us consider a row of cherry trees. From each of these in turn we proceed to take an "abstract," as the phrase is, a certain common lump of qualities which we may express together by the name cherry or cherry-ness. Next we place in a second table several such characteristic

concepts: cherry, rose, sunset, iron-rust, flamingo. From these we abstract some further common quality, dilutation or mediocrity, and label it "red" or "redness." It is evident that this process of abstraction may be carried on indefinitely and with all sorts of material. We may go on for ever building pyramids of attenuated concept until we reach the apex "being."[4]

Now, writes Fenollosa, predication will occur if we keep passing the things up and down the pyramid until we get at the correct classification, so that we can say, "Cherryness is contained under redness," or "The cherry is red."

According to my first hypothesis, it is from these two paragraphs—the one containing the brickyard example, the other the cherry tree and the color red—that Pound derived his ideogrammic method. In the preamble to his exposition of the method in *ABC of Reading*, Pound reiterates his view that Fenollosa "did not proclaim his method as a method," but only contrasted the validity of Chinese thinking with the erroneous ways and habits of Western thought. Pound proceeds to give his own example of the difference between the two:

> In Europe, if you ask a man to define anything, his definition always moves away from the simple things that he knows perfectly well, it recedes into an unknown region, that is a region of remoter and progressively remoter abstraction.
>
> If you ask him what red is, he says it is a "colour."
>
> If you ask him, what a colour is, he tells you it is a vibration or a refraction of light, or a division of the spectrum.
>
> And if you ask him what a vibration is, he tells you it is a mode of energy, or something of that sort, until you arrive at a modality of being, or non-being, or at any rate you get in beyond your depth, and beyond his depth.[5]

Following in Fenollosa's footsteps, Pound declares that this mode of defining things was the work of the medieval logicians who used abstract terms instead of looking at things. In the West science began to develop only after Bacon and Galilei suggested "the direct examination of phenomena." In China, by contrast, such direct dealing with things has never given way to abstract thinking; the ideographic writing there attests to it. And so Pound gives "his" example of how a Chinese would define the color red.

He puts (or his ancestor put) together the abbreviated pictures of

ROSE	CHERRY
IRON RUST	FLAMINGO

That, you see, is very much the kind of thing a biologist does (in a very much more complicated way) when he gets together a few hundred or thousand slides, and picks out what is necessary for his general statement.

The Chinese "word" or ideogram for red is based on something everyone KNOWS.[6]

The first critic to point out Pound's error (i.e., that "red" in Chinese is 赤, ch'ih[4], the juxtaposition of "man" and "fire") was Christine Brooke-Rose in her *A ZBC of Ezra Pound*; and while she also discussed the more serious aspect of the problem—that Pound also misinterprets Fenollosa's thought—she did not account for its occurrence in the first place.

The explanation, as I see it, is quite simple. If we look at the two contiguous paragraphs in *The Chinese Written Character*, it is quite clear that Fenollosa is treating *one* theme in both of them: the "brickyard" of medieval logic, of which the cherry tree example is a further illustration. But Pound did not see it that way. He assumed that Fenollosa was not continuing with one metaphor but rather contrasting the first with another, its opposite or its counterpart in the Chinese language. In other words, he believed that Fenollosa was writing ideogrammically; that he juxtaposed the two modes of thinking paratactically. Parataxis there is, but it is only apparent, not real. The second paragraph ("Let us consider a row of cherry trees") is actually hypotactically subordinated to the first one. Pound failed to notice the several warnings in the text—such as "we proceed to make an 'abstract,' as the phrase is," or the words "dilutation or mediocrity"—that neither Fenollosa's tone nor his intention signifies approval. Also, the original version of the final sentence of the first paragraph reads, "We may go on for ever building dizzy pyramids of attenuated concept until we reach the apex 'being.' " Pound chose to delete "dizzy," a rather tell-tale epithet.

The other possibility for the "birth" of the ideogrammic method is perhaps even simpler. Included with the first version of *The Chinese Written Character* were pages of diagrams, listing lantern slides to accompany Fenollosa's lecture. One version of the diagrams was reproduced by Hugh Kenner in *The Pound Era* (p. 158); the manuscript page seen by this writer differs slightly from the one Kenner gives, but substantially they project an identical notion; that rose, sunset, iron rust, flamingo, and cherry equal red or redness. The diagram serves to illustrate the point made in the lecture that "the true formula for thought is: The cherry tree is all that it does" as well as the process by which the tree, this "bundle of functions," becomes a bloodless idea when subjected to the "brickyard" method of logical classification. Fenollosa means that if we consider all its functional attributes, the cherry tree is no more *just red* than the farmer in his other example is a rice-pounder. In reality, the cherry tree is "all that it does," and only a language which re-creates the multiplicity of particular actions involved in the natural process can begin to do justice to it.

Whichever version we follow, it is clear that Pound saw things in the Fenollosa material that he *wanted* to see: the incomplete blueprint for a method to be developed and applied. It is a clear misunderstanding, but perhaps the most fruitful misunderstanding in English literature. Furthermore, Pound's derivation of the ideogrammic method from Fenollosa's rose–cherry–iron rust–flamingo example is, as Kenner later puts it, "right in principle but wrong in fact."[7] The principle is the juxtaposition of particular objects or their linguistic counterparts, and this juxtaposition establishes a mental energy field which generates a vision of unseen relations—of qualities, concepts, ideas. It underlines the conviction which Pound had begun to hold during his earlier archeological activity and which grew steadily stronger: that "art does not avoid universals, it strikes at them all the harder in that it strikes through particulars."[8] The artist must remain close to nature, to natural processes and actual manifestations, in order to create a true "natural picture" of the world. The method Pound drew from Fenollosa, in whatever manner, does not mean that Pound "gets stuck" in a mindless hoarding together of individual phenomena; he does not "give up thought." Rather, he is ever intent on presenting universals but, as James Wilhelm wrote, "without the blurring effect, the abolition of the particular."[9]

Pound made the "rose-cherry" mode of ideogrammic juxtaposition (for it is only one of several types of ideogrammic techniques Pound developed, as we shall see later) the basis of his entire artistic activity. It became a tool in literary criticism, in the composition of textbooks, in the arrangement of musical pieces for concerts. He believed that in opposition to the outmoded abstractions of medieval logic, this method was the expression of the new logic of the modern age: the logic of science. He continued to spread propaganda for Fenollosa well into the fifties because of his conviction that Fenollosa "emphasized a difference between the approach of logic and that of science." Specifically, he wrote in *ABC of Reading*, "The first definite assertion of the applicability of scientific method to literary criticism is found in Ernest Fenollosa's *Essay on the Chinese Written Character*." "The so-called 'logical method,' " he wrote elsewhere, "permitted the methodist to proceed from inadequate cognizance to a specious and useless conclusion. . . . This is *not* good enough for the age of Marconi."[10] He asserted that "the scientist to-day heaps together his facts and has to find organizations that fit them. He must consider his field of reference." Pound never tired of repeating with relish the story of Louis Agassiz and the fish as the most illuminating example of modern scientific approach.[11]

The gist of the anecdote is that a scientist must *look at* the object or objects under examination before drawing certain conclusions. Using the method of direct observation, the scientist formulates general laws via an inductive method, as does the biologist (another of Pound's examples), using the actual evidence present on slides. The axiom is the scientist's ideogram, based on relations between objectively juxtaposed functional particulars.

Pound insists on the existence of close ties between this aspect of the new science, i.e., axioms emerging from observation, and the new art because he sees science (natural science as well as the *sciences humaines* of psychology, anthropology, and archeology) as the foundation of the new *forma mentis*, validating—because it links them to the processes of nature—the emergence of nonlogical nontransitional modes in literature, painting, sculpture, cinema, and music. Poetry, Pound argues, must adopt as its working method the method of science in order to fulfill its role in the modern world. "Method of science" here of course means empirical science, the way Fenollosa had defined and defended it in his essay, the science which is "utterly opposed" to logic because it bases its premises on observation. Hence Pound's linking of the ideogrammic method with the "method of the biologist," who derives theory from a selection of slides.

Pound has been accused of having oversimplified the issue of theory versus observation; however, it must be admitted that even some of the greatest scientists of our century differed considerably as to the primacy of one over the other. In physics, for example, Heisenberg maintained that "a good theory must be based on directly observable magnitudes," whereas Einstein said that "it is quite wrong to try founding a theory on observable magnitudes alone" because "it is the theory which decides what we can observe."[12] Einstein argued that observation is a complicated process wherein observer and observed are dynamically involved:

> The phenomenon under observation produces certain events in our measuring apparatus. As a result, further processes take place in the apparatus, which eventually and by complicated paths produce sense impressions and help us to fix the effects in our consciousness. Along this whole path—from the phenomenon to its fixation in our consciousness—we must be able to tell how nature functions, must know the natural laws at least in practical terms, before we can claim to have observed anything at all. Only theory, that is, knowledge of natural laws, enables us to deduce the underlying phenomena from our sense impressions.[13]

But Einstein does not say how we arrive at the knowledge of natural laws upon which we must base our theory: by relying on other, previous theories or by our own observation of natural processes? This is the difference that for Fenollosa and Pound is so crucial. The "laws" deduced by abstract reasoning from logical constants produce a distorted view of the operations of nature, for these laws are not founded upon natural processes but upon human powers of thinking, the ability to rearrange the cosmos to suit ourselves. Einstein is of course opposed to such a method, and says that "in science we ought to be concerned solely with what nature does," and not what we think or know about it.

It would seem, therefore, that theory and observation must go hand in hand. While it is undeniable that the scientist begins with a set of theoretical concepts (partly original, and partly derived from established, traditional views on the subject), it is essential that these observations be allowed to influence the scientist's *a priori* notions, whatever their origin. Heisenberg says that one can think up experiments whose outcome may be predicted from theory. "And if the actual experiments should bear out the predictions," he goes on, "there is little doubt but that the theory reflects nature accurately. . . ."[14] But if preconceived theory and observed facts clash, then the theory must be modified in accordance with the results of the observation *and not vice versa*. Logical constructs cannot take precedence as far as validity is concerned over constructs based on observed data.

Pound did not in reality say anything very different. He did not disparage theory when he said that the scientist "must consider his field of reference" when he tries "to find organizations that fit" his facts. He simply meant that *whatever the theory*, the final conclusion must grow out of the observed material. It is safe to say that his view is a sound one, even if he did not insist on the necessity of theory as a starting point in any experiment. If a physicist states that certain atoms behave in a certain way in a given set of conditions, the statement is valid because it is based on actual observation of the particles in a cloud chamber. An ornithologist who states that the migratory habits of the *Hirundo rustica* are such and such must have directly observed the flight patterns and movements of the bird in question for this conclusion to be accepted as fact. Of course, a serious ornithologist will not say that, based upon the habits of the *Hirundo rustica* (the common swallow), we can *assume* that the entire family of swallows *must* migrate in a similar fashion. To make the statement "All swallows fly in such and such pattern," the ornithologist needs to have observed all the various types of the bird, or sufficiently representative samples of them, as functioning organisms, and must set these findings side by side to establish an "organization" that fits them all.

Pound proposes something similar when he applies the method (the "rose-cherry-rust-flamingo" type of the ideogram) to criticism and to poetic creation. Contrary to widespread misconception, Pound does not suggest the "heaping together" of any and all kinds of heterogeneous data. It is very important to bear in mind his insistence on a "field of reference" which determines the type of data the scientist (or poet) is going to take into consideration in making an observation. In Pound's view, then, the literary critic, instead of handing out vague generalities, must present an "ideograph of the good" by selecting and setting side by side the particular works the critic considers lasting and valid. Pound's own criticism is unabashedly didactic; he envisaged *ABC of Reading* as a textbook, and he repeatedly stressed that the functions of critic and teacher are in close alliance. While Pound's aim with the ideogrammic presentation in poetry is to induce an intellectual-emotional ecstasy or revelation, for the critical ideogram he intends an effect of more decidedly intellectual enlightenment. The teacher-critic should proceed via the "dispassionate examination of the ideogrammic method (the examination and juxtaposition of particular specimens—e.g. particular works, passages of literature) as an implement for acquisition and transmission of knowledge."[15] He recommends the use of the ideogrammic method because the critic's judgment will be sharpened and "will gain one more chance of soundness if he can be persuaded to consider Fenollosa's essay or some other . . . elucidation of the Chinese written character,"[16] by which Pound means the cherry-rose type of ideogrammic juxtaposition.

Pound's own critical activity was part of a larger attempt to bring about a "new renaissance." From Frobenius he adopted the term *paideuma*, or New Paideuma, the conscious delineation of cultural forces tending toward just such a renaissance and a revaluation of values. Pound wrote that he "approached" the ideogrammic method "in at least one case" in his 1913 essay "The Serious Artist." He is referring to a juxtaposition of lines by Dante, Cavalcanti, Villon, Yeats, and the Anglo-Saxon author of "The Wanderer." Such a type of juxtapositional criticism may in some respects be an offshoot of Arnold's "touchstone" theory, particularly as Pound writes in *ABC of Reading* that "certain verbal manifestations *can* be employed as measures, T squares, voltmeters, or can be used 'for comparison,' and familiarity with them can indubitably enable a man to estimate writing in general. . . ."[17] But the later critical ideograms do not merely aim at fixing in the reader's mind some few peerless lines from the classics (or from Pound's own highly personal literary pantheon). The intention is to effect formation of functional wholes of the juxtaposed poetic "blocks" in the perceptive reader, to point out relations that may or may not have been apparent before.

Pound implemented another use of the ideogrammic method in his organization of musical concerts in Rapallo. A typical concert consisted of music by Jannequin, Corelli, Bach, and Debussy. In another he included in the same program a string quartet by Boccherini and Bartók's Quartet no. 5. "The point of this experiment," commented Pound, "is that everyone present at the two concerts now knows a great deal more about relations, the relative weight" of the composers.[18] Again, the distinction must be made here, too: the music of Corelli and Debussy is not expected to form a whole in the way a poetic ideogram is a whole of particulars. The aim is a better knowledge of the musical values of the juxtaposed compositions. In fact, their salient qualities will truly emerge after they have been in close proximity to works of different weight and order.

Pound's fullest realization of the ideogrammic method of criticism is to be found in *Guide to Kulchur*, an unquestionably major work. It is also significant because Pound works out the method of the ideogram on the surface, as it were, supported by a number of explicit statements to the effect that while he is "heaping together" his facts in the manner of a scientist, the process of heaping is not without direction or interest.

The beginning of the book is hardly fortuitous: Pound starts by giving a "digest," an ideogram of the Confucian analects which he considers, along with the other three books by Confucius, the root of human wisdom and conduct. Pound's carefully juxtaposed excerpts accent Confucius' concern with particulars, the clarity of exact terminology, the value of real knowledge based on actual processes in nature as opposed to generalities. Kung's (Confucius') dicta serve to give the backbone and the intention of the work:

> Said Kung the Master: I have passed whole days without food, entire nights without sleep for the sake of my meditation, and in this there was no real use. It wd. have been better to have studied something in particular.

In the next cluster Pound sets out the method on which *Guide to Kulchur* is based, as inspired by Kung and Fenollosa:

> If so lately as the week before last one of the brighter scholars still professed ignorance of the meaning of "ideogramic" I must try once again to define that term, necessary to the said student if he still wishes to follow me or my meaning.
>
> Ernest Fenollosa attacked, quite rightly, a great weakness in western ratiocination. He pointed out that the material sciences, biology, chemistry, examined collections of fact, phenomena, specimens, and gathered general equations of real knowledge from them, even though the observed data had no syllogistic connection one with the other.

On the subsequent pages Pound proceeds to round out the definition by particular examples. He mentions his "real knowledge" of paintings, which is different from the knowledge gleaned from textbooks. He brings up Confucius' commendation to his students of the study of the Odes (the Chinese classic anthology). By so commending, adds Pound, Confucius was aiming at "a type of perception, a kind of transmission of knowledge obtainable only from such concrete manifestation." He then moves on to a juxtaposition of Confucius' views on music with Western notions of Pythagorean harmony. Then he abruptly stops and addresses the reader:

> Let the reader be patient. I am not being merely incoherent. I haven't "lost my thread" in the sense that I haven't just dropped one thread to pick up another of different shade. I need more than one string for a fabric. . . . I am trying to get a bracket for one kind of ideas, I mean

that will hold a whole set of ideas and keep them apart from another set.

The "bracket" is the arrangement of detail—facts or events—in such a way that they interact and affect each other. Pound then points to the tradition in Western thought in which knowledge was based on particulars and not on abstractions: Heraclitus and the pre-Socratics as the occidental counterparts of Confucius and Mencius and as the spiritual ancestors of modernism. It is foolish to suppose, writes Pound, that the pre-Socratics were not ideogrammic in their thinking and in their arriving at certain general statements (for example, "Everything flows"). Pound values their effort because they "*tried* to correlate their thought, to carry a principle through concrete and apparently disjunct phenomena and observe the leaves and/or fruits of causation." Pound wants to distinguish between ideas "in a species of vacuum" and "ideas which are intended to 'go into action,' or to guide action and serve us as rules (and/or measures) of conduct." Thus, in the beginning of the book Pound is concerned with establishing for the reader, all through particulars, his "ideograph of the good," which contains Confucius, Fenollosa, and the pre-Socratics. He is at all times dealing with and relying upon *facts*; he never abandons them for the sake of a logical extract or summation. The facts and their relation compose a new whole (a vortex or an ideogram), in much the same way that the rose-cherry juxtaposition operates: a quality or value emerges which is rooted in the individual "pattern units."

An even clearer example of the method can be found in the juxtapositions in the section between pages 63 and 75. In the first unit Pound reprints verbatim "Vortex Gaudier-Brzeska," in which Gaudier gives a condensed history of sculpture from the Stone Age to 1915. Gaudier proposes that the basic form of plastic expression was the sphere, from which the Egyptians, in their metaphysical aspirations, developed the art *vertically*, while the Semites of Mesopotamia "elevated the sphere" and created the *horizontal*. Gothic sculpture was a derivation of "hamito-semitic energies," and the mental energies of the "primitives" of Africa and Oceania pushed the sphere in a *convex* direction; the shape of their sculpture is that of the *cone*. Finally, the moderns (Gaudier himself as well as Epstein, Brancusi, Archipenko, Dunikowski, and Modigliani) "have crystallized the sphere into the cube," creating a combination of "all the possible shaped masses."

The second unit is the exposition of Pound's "great bass" theory of music, or rather musical pitch. According to this theory, "down below the lowest note synthesized by the ear and 'heard' there are slower vibrations. The ratio between these frequencies and those written to be executed by instruments is OBVIOUS in mathematics. The whole question of tempo, and of a main base in all musical structure resides in use of these frequencies."

In the next passage Pound discusses Leibniz and his "unsquashable monad" which, Pound admits, may be outdated by the new nuclear physics, but still "holds as a concept." It holds because it was the philosophic complement of the emerging empirical sciences based on observation.

Pound also says that Leibniz was the "last serious character" to have worried about the reconciliation of churches. His stumbling block—whether one should accept church authority when it conflicts with one's conscience—leads Pound to the fourth unit, Erigena, who said, "Authority comes from right reason." Pound writes that on the basis of this statement a reexamination of the case of Erigena would be beneficial to a renaissance of the Catholic church.

At this moment Pound, again nudging the inattentive reader, adds in italics: "*These disjunct paragraphs belong together, Gaudier, Great Bass, Leibniz, Erigena, are parts of one ideogram, they are not merely separate subjects.*" But *how* do they belong together? At first glance it would appear that the four subjects are united in the fashion of the "rose-cherry-iron rust-flamingo" ideogram. Yet here Pound is not juxtaposing overt *qualities* but is dealing with *essential relationships* within and between each subject. Each unit has two components in common with the rest: an attempt to establish a *basis* and a desire for *unification*. In Gaudier, the basis of sculpture and the form from which all other plastic expression stems is the sphere; all sculptural modes—vertical, horizontal, conic, cubic—are unified through this one basic principle. The "great bass" (or "base") is an unheard vibration below the heard; it is a foundation which, according to Pound, the great composers never neglected in constructing their "heard" compositions. In Leibniz the monad is again a basis, the ultimate unit present in everything in nature; it is the basis, among other things, of his syncretism. Erigena's *recta ratio* is that sound basis from which true *auctoritas* can issue forth. None of these basic forms are man-made; none of them—the sphere in a multitude of shapes, the monad in all things organic and inorganic, the great base in a Bach fugue, right reason in true authority—are visible. They are manifestations or integral parts of that "latent structure" which lies behind the vital and perceptible universe and which includes constructive human activity.

With the ideogram Pound intends to show that the plastic arts, music, philosophy, and religion have an essential basis in nature: they all derive from a deeper, unseen source. Pound singles out these four human endeavors and could have continued with other disciplines. But he found that for his statement on structure these interrelationships should suffice. The ideogram thus formed is a whole, but like Fenollosa's "things in motion, motion in things," it is open at both ends. It is a whole, but the individual components retain their uniqueness. It is a natural whole, not a purely logical or abstract whole. It is scientifically accurate, for the ideogram may be likened to a molecule which constitutes, according to a scientist's definition, "a larger functional whole which contains several atoms as subordinate wholes. Functionally, the atoms belong to the molecule-unit; but in this unit they do not altogether lose their individuality."[19] This quality of retaining individual properties while forming a larger conceptual unit, image, or ideogram is the basic quality of Pound's juxtapositions. The particulars stay in the mind, and general summaries of the preceding ideogram ("From the unseen structure grows the seen" or "From essence grows substance, from substance grows form") are weak and abstract if we let go of the occasion which gave rise to them. Since essence is invisible or "latent," Pound reverses the process by juxtaposing phenomena in order to *reveal* through their relations the invisible idea. He conveys this idea (much better) with a natural simile: from relations of the seen arises the unseen form, "the *forma*, the immortal *concetto*, the concept, the dynamic form which is like the rose pattern driven into the dead iron-filings by the magnet itself, but separate from the magnet. Cut off by the layer of glass, the dust and filings rise and spring into order."[20] The force of the magnet is akin to that force which orders sphere, great bass, monad, and right reason; the individual parts *contain* and in their juxtaposed union *affirm* the concept of nature's dynamism and nature's ceaseless transference of power.

The second definition of the ideogrammic method in *Guide to Kulchur* is more concerned with the method's psychological effect on the reader, its direction toward insight:

> At last a reviewer in a popular paper (or at least one with immense circulation) has had the decency to admit that I occasionally cause the reader "suddenly to see" or that I snap out a remark . . . "that reveals the whole subject from a new angle."
>
> That being the point of the writing. That being the reason for presenting first one facet and then another—I mean to say the purpose of the writing is to reveal the subject. The ideogrammic method consists of presenting one facet and then another until at some point one gets off the dead and desensitized surface of the reader's mind, onto a part that will register.
>
> The "new" angle being new to the reader who cannot always be the same reader. The newness of the angle being relative and the writer's aim, at least this writer's aim being revelation, a just revelation irrespective of newness or oldness.

The important point here, apart from the definition and authorial intention ("revelation"), is that the accumulated data will at one point cease to be just a "heap" of detail. As in a flash, the whole subject or phenomenon will appear, in the form of an image, in the reader's consciousness. What Pound avers here is that *revelation is a process*, the final stage of a cumulative agglomeration of detail. "All knowledge is built up from a rain of factual atoms,'' said Pound, a statement that Hugh Kenner restated and further il-luminated when he wrote, "The mind lays hold only on particular things. It can NOT know an abstraction it has not itself made."[21] The validity of these propositions on perceptions and the validity of the revelatory process is cor-roborated by the findings of psychologists, notably those of Jung and his followers. Jung himself has often been criticized for a lack of systematic presentation of his material. But as Dr. M.-L. von Franz, Jung's closest associate, adds, such critics ignore the fact that "the material itself is a living experience charged with emotion, by nature irrational and ever-changing, which does not lend itself to systematization except in the most superficial circumstances." And she further notes: "When we are dealing with statistical averages, a rational and systematic description of the facts is possi-ble. But when we are attempting to describe a single psychic event, we can do no more than *present an honest picture of it from as many angles as possible* (my emphasis).[22]

The rendering of a "psychic event" is structurally identical with that of a "poetic event." The process underlying the particular manifestations is the same in a host of cumulative events and experiences, whether internal or ex-ternal—in meditation or spiritual exercises, in a pilgrimage, in the recording of a *periplus*, in all happenings where intense individual participation, follow-ing natural modes and directions, is involved. The ancient Chinese ideogram is based on this principle, and so are the most characteristic methods of modern art: collage, montage, Poundian juxtaposition.

This type of juxtaposition in Pound's work I call the *cumulative ideogram*. The ideogram of Sigismondo Malatesta, amassed from his letters, belongs here, as does the Gaudier–Great Bass–Leibniz–Erigena juxtaposition in *Guide to Kulchur*. The variant of the cumulative ideogram is exemplified by the latter, perhaps the strongest type, because it is based on identity of struc-ture. One of the finest examples is in Canto IV, in which Pound juxtaposes certain mythological elements (such as the cannibalism in the story of Tereus and Philomela and the metamorphosis of Actaeon into a stag) with stories from Provence (the eating of Cabestan's heart and the "metamorphosis" of Peire Vidal into a wolf running through the forest). Again, in Pound's hands the individual values and characteristics of the "factual atoms" (ideogram-mic components, pattern units, sub-wholes) are not blurred or distorted in order to make them fit his scheme. Pound does not intervene subjectively to say (or to suggest) that "this *is* that" or one thing *is like* another thing. Pound establishes not analogies or similarities but relations, or *relations-in-process*, in a language "beyond metaphor." The "new angle" Pound aims at in his juxtapositions inheres in the changes and the metamorphoses mutually ef-fected by each particular unit, and these changes bring about the creation of a new whole which is simultaneously perceptual and conceptual.

The isomorphic-cumulative ideogram is almost invariably tied to myth, and through myth to fundamental processes of nature. It is an instrument to signal relations between such processes and recurrent events in history and the processes of growth in human individuals. These constitute the cornerstones of *The Cantos*, embodying Pound's main themes and motifs. For larger individual blocks Pound employs a variant of the method, which I call—still within the cumulative mode—qualitative-isomorphic. Here the material juxtaposed (as in the "rose-flamingo" or Malatesta ideograms) is based on fragmentary sub-wholes pertaining to a historical event or to an individual, and their identity of structure is not immediately apparent. This is the method Pound employs in synthesizing the images of such men as Confucius, Thomas Jefferson, John Adams, and others, or of historical periods such as the late Renaissance in Italy, the great dynasties of China, or the Tuscany of Leopold II. This method was also used in Pound's "Homage to Sextus Propertius," and J. P. Sullivan's description of it in that poem applies with equal force to *The Cantos*:

> All formal and grammatical connection may vanish in the interests of the harder poetic impact. But the juxtaposition of apparently unrelated subjects is a *significant* juxtaposition with its own logic. The new theme affects the preceding theme and modifies the effect of the whole. . . .[23]

This new "logic" of depiction does not follow causal, predetermined lines. As opposed to syllogistic "knowledge," it proceeds from the particular toward the general in accordance with natural perceptual processes. Our real knowledge of Confucius, for example, comes about through seeing Confucius engaged in a variety of actions (as Fenollosa would say, "Confucius is all that he does"), and these actions are depicted paratactically. It is as if we had met the master at different times and places. In Canto XIII Pound thrusts aside all the formal narrative unities. As in a film or collage, the "apparently unrelated" units form an organic whole irrespective of their origin. In the whole there are no "chief characteristics" and no "subordinates," for they are all functioning parts and at the same time individual entities within the larger organism. This idea lies behind Fenollosa's description of a painting in which a number of colors have been "mutually juxtaposed so that their multiple cross relations have only clarified and irradiated each other, then no one is cause and no one effect, for all is cause and all effect."[24] The "natural picture," or the new whole, is composed not of general comments or deductions but, as Pound says in Canto LXXIV, of a "sufficient phalanx of particulars."

The other main group of ideograms I would call the *contrastive* or antithetical juxtapositions. In comparing Noh drama (and the type of civilization it represents) with the state of Western Europe in the late nineteenth century, Pound, after a particularly vituperous outburst, adds (in italics): "*I am not merely taking a pot shot at something I, personally, loathe, I am contrasting the fine flower of a civilization with a species of rot and corruption.*"[25] The intention of such ideograms in *The Cantos* is basically ethical or moral; the method itself can appear in a number of formal arrangements of opposing sets of particulars. In the Hell Cantos (Cantos XIV and XV), for example, the accumulation of detail produces an image of unrelieved evil, and only the attitude of the speaker gives hints of an opposing set of values. In the next canto, Canto XVI, the image of hell is carried on, first from Dante's "Inferno" and then from the hell of World War I, but it is followed by data, objectively and unexpectedly juxtaposed, from the Russian revolution of 1917, which, if not exactly a foil or solution to the state of affairs in Europe, is seen as a step toward the establishment of some kind of order.

In Canto XLV the method is not the juxtaposition of larger narrative units but the creation of antithesis between lines and even within the lines. The unnatural, destructive force of *usura* invades all human activity. The elements are all chosen from different areas of human endeavor, yet they are all within one "field of reference," that of productive, creative activity. The peculiar rhetoric of the canto (it sounds less like a catalogue than a litany—cf. Litany of Loreto) allows for a variety of metaphoric expression, not just pure ideograms. The *usura* ideogram is composed of a set of images: *usura* is seen as an "unlawful law" preventing good building and good art, a "sin against nature," a negative force in commerce, a disease like cancer, a murderer, an impotent obstructor of natural pleasure and fertility, a paralyzing force affecting the craftsman and his craft, a pimp who desecrates the eternal mysteries, and a ghoulish master of ceremonies or Antichrist who "revives the dead" and destroys the living. Each separate image unit is indictment enough of the life-sapping nature of the usurious lending of money (or so Pound presents it). But only through their objective interaction can the true visage of *usura* be perceived.

The final image of *usura*, cohering from the heterogeneous active parts, is a "just revelation," emerging from the many angles Pound sees fit to show us: "*Usura* is all that it does." And the juxtaposition of the antithetical images (Pietro Lombardo, Duccio, Pier della Francesca, the churches of St. Trophime and St. Hilaire) reveal that *usura* is also what it *cannot* do. Similarly, in the other Usura Canto (Canto LI) the images of *usura* are juxtaposed with instructions on how to tie trout flies. A constructive human activity is set against the nihilism of *usura*. Thus, the ideogram is complete. That is, it is "complete" in the sense that any transmission of force is complete. Both *usura* and its opposites are only "meeting points" of a larger congeries of cosmic and human processes. The openness of the paratactic juxtapositions and the accumulation and clash of data confirm this. As M. L. Rosenthal observes,

The first effect of all these successive, varied breakings is not intended to be total intellectual understanding, any more than in real experience we "understand" situations upon first coming into them. But by and by the pattern shapes up and relationships clarify themselves, though always there remains an unresolved residue of potentiality for change, intractable and baffling.[26]

What remains "unresolved" is a partial aspect of the method's faithfulness to a kind of creation which proceeds in accordance with nature's creative movements and the way of human perception. But the "shaping up," the "clarifying" aspect, aims at attaining a perceptual-conceptual image, a vision which arises from the contemplation of dynamic relationships.

Another example of the contrastive ideogram can be seen in the Seven Lakes Canto (Canto XLIX). The text consists of an imagistic recreation of a Chinese manuscript book and collation of some notes by Fenollosa, with some lines added by Pound himself. The entire canto, including some words in Chinese transliteration and Pound's final lines, compose one large cumulative ideogram: a Chinese idyll and its roots embedded in natural production ("Sun up! work / sundown; to rest / dig well and drink of the water / dig field; eat of the grain"). But the leisurely pace of the images is suddenly, almost brutally interrupted after the serene line "A light moves on the south sky line":

> State by creating riches shd. thereby get into debt?
> This is infamy; this is Geryon.

After this the poem continues with the Chinese words, and winds up with Pound's two lines, "The fourth; the dimension of stillness. / And the power over wild beasts."

The two interrupting lines are not due to Pound's inability to sustain an image or merely to his giving vent to something he "personally loathes." The intruding rhetorical question and its amplification by the mythical reference disrupt the idyllic mood of the preceding and following lines, just as usurious practices disrupt the potential abundance of a society based on natural productivity. The idyll is deceptive, Pound implies. The human struggle toward equity and toward a harmonious existence has not changed since mythic times. In fact, whereas a superhuman Hercules was able to kill the three-bodied monster Geryon and thus gain access to the oxen (natural riches), in our age the multibodied monster Usura cannot be so easily destroyed. The "beast" Geryon is still with us, even if we do possess "power over wild beasts." But after the intrusion the poem resumes on a positive note, as if to indicate that nature's fertility is eternal and that human beings are part of that process. Geryon is unreal and unnatural, an "interruption," and not an integral component of the universe.

The aim here is not to provide a full explication of the ethical, economic, or cosmic implications of the ideogram, but to point to its form. The two lines appear alien in the body of the poem; in reality they *protrude* from it. This seemingly alien matter may in fact anger sensitive readers who were up to that moment enwrapped in a state of aesthetic pleasure, and they may try to dismiss it as an unwelcome sign of Pound's obsessiveness. But they cannot dismiss it, for the "cut" effected by the Geryon image changes the entire poem. Only through a contemplation of the relation of these lines can readers arrive at a true vision which is Pound's intention.

The size of the ideogrammic components varies in *The Cantos*. In the Seven Lakes Canto an extended image is juxtaposed with an image composed of one line and one word. The rapid associative patterns in some cantos, especially in the Pisan sequence and thereafter, are the result of the appositioning of micro-images charged with a variety of mythical, historical, religious, philosophical, artistic, and personal matter. Some images, contained in the isomorphic ideograms, recur throughout the poem, and their juxtaposition with new images in turn changes their influence within the particular ideogram. Such a method gave rise to the theory that the overall form of *The Cantos* is fugal, an idea reinforced by Pound himself when he tried to explain to his father the "main scheme" of the entire poem as "rather like, or unlike subject and response and countersubject in a fugue."

The observation, I think, is valid, and the fugal structure is one that Louis Zukofsky explicitly adopted for his long poem "*A*". The term "fugal" covers a particular type of composition (of verse, in our case) which is based on the asyndetic juxtaposition and variation of intellectual-emotional units. And in the case of *The Cantos*, as mentioned earlier, we could also talk about it as a "long vorticist poem," or one using the collage technique. But then the objection may be raised: Does this mean that *The Cantos* have no "main structure," that it is *formless*? As James E. Miller asks, "How can a poem have a form if it embodies or engages events unforeseeable when it was launched? how can a long poem be called an epic when it has no hero or narrative?"[27] In answer to Miller's first query, one must first determine what we mean by *form*. *The Cantos*, and all ideogrammic long poems, are "formless" if "form" denotes nothing but a logical assemblage of data, rationally structured and transitionally executed. But if we allow that *The Cantos* work out a new kind of form based on the juxtaposition of particulars and their various recombinations, then the poem most certainly has form. If "form" is not equated with "story line," then, again, *The Cantos* have a most clearly demonstrable form: it is composed of interconnected and mutually affective "units of design" working toward synthesis and revelation.

As to the second question, whether *The Cantos* (or any modern long poem, beginning with *Leaves of Grass*) may properly be called an "epic," it is echoed by the confusion of critics who, thirty years after Kenner's *The Poetry of Ezra*

Pound and over twenty years after Clark Emery's *Ideas into Action*, are still looking for the "key," the "scheme," the "structure" of Pound's poem. Clearly, the present study has aims other than correction or polemics. Yet, when confronted with the ingenuity and zeal of scholars to find the "scheme," it is disheartening to note that they neglect to consider the findings of seminal research such as the two works mentioned above. These scholars do almost everything—finding the rites of Eleusis as the structural key to *The Cantos*; reading the poem as postromantic "psychodrama"; labeling the work as an example of "stream of consciousness"—so as not to face the simple fact: *The Cantos* is an *ideogrammically structured modern epic*. The two terms are by no means mutually exclusive. Here is an excerpt in which an author presents the elements of epic structure:

> First of all, the data or the items without exception have to be stated as events in time. They are all time-conditioned. None of them can be cast into a syntax which shall be simply true for all situations and so timeless; each and all have to be worded in the language of the specific doing or the specific happening. Second they are remembered and frozen into the record as separate disjunct episodes each complete and satisfying in itself, in a series which is joined together paratactically. Action succeeds action in a kind of endless chain. The basic grammatical expression which would symbolise the link of event to event would simply be the phrase "and next. . . ." Thirdly, these independent items are so worded as to retain a high content of visual suggestion; they are brought alive as persons or as personified things acting out vividly before the mind's eye. In their separate and episodic independence from each other they are visualised sharply, passing along in an endless panorama.

The above may read as an unusually perceptive assessment of the form of *The Cantos*; yet it is a definition of the general character of *The Iliad* by Eric A. Havelock in *Preface to Plato*.[28] In this light the form of *The Cantos* is contemporary; it is also archaic. And this new form—with its imagistic clusters, its paratactic concatenation of particular events, its visual objectivity, the variety of its "time-conditioned" language, even down to its use of "and then" and "so that"—retains the essential properties of the ancient epic. The Greek poet George Seferis saw the virtues of *The Cantos* in similar terms: "The word epic loses its meaning of a form of literature in order to keep much closer to its original meaning of sentence, word, speech, and becomes the symbol of a liturgy which makes use of everything within the framework of a wider unity."[29]

Yet this epic is simultaneously, as Max Nänny so correctly noted, *the* poem for our electric and nuclear age, and it is most appropriate to estimate its structural qualities in the language of microphysics, as did Walter L. Fischer:

Pounds Ideogramme sind in moderner Terminologie mikroästhetische Textstücke, semantische Zellen, die meist aus mehreren Atomsätzen oder atomaren Sprachbestandteilen aufgebaut sind. Jeder dieser Atomsätze fungiert als semantischer Kern, in dem ein Geschehen, ein Zustand, ein Ereignis der geschichtlichen oder mythologischen Welt oder der Naturwirklichkeit formelhaft kondensiert ist.[30]

[Pound's ideograms, in more up-to-date terms, are micro-aesthetic textual particles, semantic cells, which are mostly built out of several micro-propositions or atomic speech components. Each of these micro-propositions acts as a semantic nucleus in which an occurrence, a situation, an event in the historical or mythological world, or in natural reality, is formally condensed.]

And since in the juxtapositions of the textual particles "all is cause and all effect," to quote Fenollosa again, a linear and logical structure is not only inconceivable, but its attempted introduction in the form of a "key" or "scheme" would effectively negate the force of the "poetic mobile" which constitutes *The Cantos*. The essence of Pound's method is not to fragment what was whole before, but to join in the manner of nature's joining that which was separate and alone. To the uninstructed eye, *The Cantos* may look fragmentary and static, especially from a nineteenth-century perspective. But, as Daniel Pearlman noted, "In the magical, wireless twentieth century, in the age of Freud, Picasso, and Planck, Pound's apparently static juxtapositions form dramatic continuities, his particles form waves, and the magnet of his artistry draws a paradisal rose out of a heap of iron filings."[31]

Pound's ideogrammic method is the culmination of his aesthetic research. His natural predilection for the paratactic or juxtapositional mode, his aim to reach "beyond metaphor" has been clarified and confirmed by Fenollosa's findings. The method, begun in his vorticist period, received its full practical implementation in *The Cantos* and its formal theoretical exposition in the thirties in *ABC of Reading* and *Guide to Kulchur*. His "misreading" brought about the hypostatization in poetry of that general *form of the mind* which was "in the air."

Critics will no doubt continue to dispute the validity of the ideogrammic method for Pound's work. One scholar argued, as recently as 1979, that *The Cantos* "cannot be read as an enormously extended imagist poem in which the more intellectually weighted ideogram has replaced the essentially emotional image."[32] Instead of dealing with the statement's obvious inaccuracies, both factual and substantive, I would like to conclude with a more positive example of the "romance of scholarship." At the end of *The Chinese Written Character* there are five plates of ideograms with Fenollosa's and Pound's interpretations. The interpretations contain a number of misreadings. The eminent sinologue Achilles Fang wanted to write an essay on the plates, with the intention of showing up the translators' errors. But, he admitted, "I soon found out that I would be levelling my gun at the id. method in the guise of scholarship. No, the value of the method is greater than sciolists surmise; greater than EP's own insistence." And Fang concluded: "It is easy enough to demolish the id. method philologically; by no means so when it comes to write on its operation on poetic levels where it works like a fugue."[33]

The scholars who have perceived the validity of the method are not numerous, but poets, particularly those Americans whose objective, like Pound's, had been to "make it new," saw its potential (fugal and beyond) and have used it in accordance with their individual needs, temperaments, and artistic vision.

Part Two
The Poem as Object

So sagt der Meister Eckhart nach einem Wort des
Dionysius Areopagita: diu minne ist der natur,
das zi den menschen wandelt in di dinc, di er
minnet.

—Martin Heidegger, "Das Ding,"
Vorträge und Aufsätze

4. Sincerity and Objectification

Fenollosa's essay on the Chinese written character was published and republished on at least five different occasions during Pound's lifetime, and Pound never ceased to commend it as a theoretical basis for fellow poets, critics, and students of literature. A typical directive is the one contained in a letter to C. K. Ogden: "I can't rewrite all Fenollosa's essay which is the most important item on my list of what you don't know."[1] There is evidence that the poets in the ideogrammic stream have all been familiar with the work, but it is equally important to realize that for them it was inextricably bound up with Pound's own poetics, and of interest mainly because Pound had derived his poetic method from it. By the twenties and thirties it was Pound's own critical and poetic output which had become a source for poets who intended to carry on in the direction set by the great modernists. His method was no longer a theory based on a rather obscure essay but a working tool present in his cantos and prose writings.

The growth of the work of William Carlos Williams runs parallel to that of Pound. Although he was Pound's senior by a couple of years and began writing poetry about the same time as Pound did, Williams had been, if not exactly a disciple, then the "younger man" in their relationship. Furthermore, while Pound's influence was already demonstrable in the first half of this century on a variety of poets (including Williams himself), Williams's merits as poet (and theorist) came to be recognized only after the publication in 1946 of Book One of *Paterson*. This work contained Williams's most often quoted phrase, "No ideas but in things," which was a kind of "open sesame" for some young poets (Olson, Duncan, Creeley, Ginsberg) to a valid and usable poetic *oeuvre*. These poets value Williams as the only modernist poet whose impact on the development of their art is comparable to Pound's.

But before discussing Williams's poetics, it is more appropriate (for chronological as well as thematic reasons) to treat a literary movement which preceded the emergence of Williams as an influential figure by some twenty years—a movement, moreover, in which Williams was not an initiator but a

relatively minor participant. This was the appearance in 1931 of the objectivists, whose chief organizer was Louis Zukofsky and whose ideas of "objectification and sincerity" were shared by the poets Basil Bunting, Carl
Rakosi, George Oppen, and Charles Reznikoff. In my dealing with the objectivists I shall concentrate on Zukofsky, Reznikoff, and Oppen, because of
their contribution to ideogrammic theory, and because their work has of late
begun to command respect and attention as a major contribution to modernist literature.

Almost from the start of his poetic career, Zukofsky was aware of Pound's
position as the major force in modernist poetry. In 1927, about the time he
began to correspond with Pound, Zukofsky embarked on the writing of a
long poem which he called *"A"*, a poem, in Robert Creeley's estimation,
"much akin in nature of purpose to Pound's *Cantos.*"[2] Zukofsky was also
among the very few sympathetic and incisive critics of *The Cantos*, and in his
critical pieces he tried to come to terms with the poem in accordance with the
creative principles operating in it, not just the ones operating in his own
mind. Pound, he wrote,

> has contented himself with a parsimony of adjective (about four adjec-
> tives to a folio page is almost an exaggerated estimate); with the com-
> mon speech meanings of nouns, their bareness their entire attraction;
> and primarily (thanks to his study of the Chinese ideograph) with im-
> plicit metaphor present in simple verbs and their modifiers.[3]

In a later article, in discussing Canto XVI, he noted, "That Pound,
previous to this presentation, chose to benefit along the lines of clarity and
intelligence by the study of Chinese written character and Confucius is merely an indication of the accurate scale he has constructed to measure his
values."[4] In the same review he quotes Pound's footnote from *The Chinese
Written Character* and applies it to Pound himself, saying that Pound is "intent
upon 'language not petrifying on his hands, preparing for new advances
along the lines of true metaphor, that is, interpretative metaphor, or image
as opposed to the ornamental.' " Zukofsky may be said to be Pound's first
"ideogrammic" critic, preceding John Drummond by at least two years and
Kenner by two decades. He recognized that the basic unit of *The Cantos* is the
image, and that the long poem is built up not transitionally or teleologically,
but through the interaction of the juxtaposed images. In 1930 Zukofsky
wrote, "In the last ten years Pound has not concerned himself merely with
isolation of the image—a cross-breeding between single words which are absolute symbols for things and textures . . . but with the poetic locus produced
by the passage from one image to another."[5] That "poetic locus" is the relation between images, a "thing" more important (as Zukofsky no doubt
knew from Fenollosa) than the images related.

The clarity and accuracy of Zukofsky's estimate of Pound do not merely signify unusually perceptive critical acumen; they also betray Zukofsky's own poetic intentions. He recognized that for the further development of modern poetry Pound was indispensable. He went so far as to say that Pound was "the only Xtian prophet,"[6] and he dedicated his *An "Objectivists" Anthology* to Pound, saying that he was "still for the poets of our time the most important." But Zukofsky was also aware of his own distinct poetic powers and the direction he wanted to take. Consequently, his attitude to Pound (as witnessed by their lively and voluminous correspondence) was never that of a deferential disciple. Pound, with his own unequaled ability to pick out promising new talent, in turn recognized Zukofsky's importance and used his considerable leverage with editors to advance Zukofsky's poetry. He was instrumental in getting published Zukofsky's most notable early work, "Poem beginning 'The' " and paved the way for the appearance of the "Objectivists" issue of *Poetry* which came out in February of 1931 under Zukofsky's guest editorship. After he succeeded in breaking down Harriet Monroe's defences and she agreed to let Zukofsky take over for one issue, Pound wrote to her, with obvious delight: "Waal, waal, my deah Harriet, I sho iz glad you let these young scrubs [i.e., Zukofsky's group] have the show to their selves, an ah does hope they dust out your office."[7] Although he expressed some fear that perhaps Zukofsky might prove to be too "prewdent," he was in general satisfied with the outcome. He was particularly pleased with Zukofsky's editing. He wrote to Harriet Monroe, "The zoning of different states of mind, so that one can see what they are, is good editing."[8]

Zukofsky presented to the readers of *Poetry* twenty-three poems by twenty writers, of whom the most important were, in order of appearance, Carl Rakosi, Zukofsky, Robert McAlmon, Charles Reznikoff, Kenneth Rexroth, George Oppen, Basil Bunting, and Williams. Zukofsky later insisted that the group did not really constitute a "movement," that he had invented the name "objectivists" at Monroe's insistence. Reminiscing nearly forty years after the event, Zukofsky said he found the invention of another "ism" abhorrent because "as soon as you do that, you start becoming a balloon instead of a person."[9] Nonetheless, when he got his contributions together, he appended a short theoretical postface entitled "Program: 'Objectivists' 1931," and when, a year later, he published *An "Objectivists" Anthology*, he prefaced it with a proper manifesto, " 'Recencies' in Poetry." Whether it was a movement in the strict sense of the word is perhaps not the issue. In retrospect it is more important that Zukofsky announced a *program* and that for certain poets in the group it determined, with individual variations, the direction of their work in a concrete way. To this day, Zukofsky, Oppen, Reznikoff, and Rakosi are still called "the objectivists."

Zukofsky, in the earlier essay which appeared in *Poetry*, used his theory of "sincerity and objectification" to explain Reznikoff's poetic technique. He defined sincerity as the writer's absolute fidelity to detail, "of thinking with the things as they exist." Zukofsky means the recognition of the particular, of the perceptibly real, of which the poet must build the artistic construct. "*Impossible* to communicate anything but particulars," he wrote in "'Recencies' in Poetry." And these particulars are "bound up with the events and contingencies," a slightly different version of Fenollosa's "things in motion, motion in things." "Thinking with the things as they exist" is for the poet the internalization of their wholeness, their self-contained unity —their *integritas*, to use Aquinas's term. As Zukofsky explained in a later interview: "I come into a room and I see a table. Obviously, I can't make it eat grass. I have delimited this thing, in a sense. I call it a table and I want to keep the word for its denotative sense—as solid as possible. The only way it will define itself further will be in a context."[10] Sincerity is the grasping of particulars; objectification, in Zukofsky's theory, is the next step which provides the structure of the artistic whole. It is "a rested totality"—a deliberate arrangement "into one apprehended unit, of minor units of sincerity—in other words, the resolving of words and their ideation into structure."[11] For Zukofsky, objectification means the creation of an *art object* out of carefully observed particulars, and the term does not carry with it the usual connotation of objectivity. As he says, "A personal structure of relations might be a definite object," just as an object may effectively bring about a set of personal relations.[12]

In "Recencies" Zukofsky identified the basis on which he built his poetics by expanding some lines in his poem *"A"* which read:

> The melody, the rest are accessory—
> . . . my one voice; my other . . .
> An objective—rays of the object brought to a focus,
> An objective—nature as creator—desire for what is objectively
>   perfect
> Inextricably the direction of historic and contemporary
>   particulars.[13]

The poetic "objective" is then a kind of lens through which the "historic and contemporary particulars" become focused. It is also a direction of the artist's will to create as nature creates. In the original poem (*"A"*-6) the above lines are preceded by a section which leads up to a statement on natural creation:

> Natura Naturans—
> Nature as creator,
> Natura Naturata—
> Nature as created.

> He who creates
> Is a mode of these inertial systems—
> The flower—leaf around leaf wrapped around the center
>   leaf, . . .[14]

The poet's creative act is seen as an internal part of the law of growth and generation operative in the cosmos; it recreates the "latent structure" in its form as the flower recreates it in its own. Zukofsky affirmed this law of nature throughout *"A"*; as he wrote in *"A"*-8:

> And the veins of the earth, and the veins of a leaf,
> And the ribs of the human body are like each other—[15]

He conceived of the work of art as an expression of this isomorphic reality:

> The order that rules music, the same
> controls the placing of the stars and
> the feathers in a bird's wing.[16]

Perceptual values take precedence over conceptual values, and particulars over universals and abstractions. Just as everything in nature is a unique individual thing and at the same time part of a process, so the creative act consists of the realization of particular wholes ("sincerity") and combining them into meaningful structures ("objectification"). Artists, Zukofsky believed, should rely on their senses, and he stated this directive in philosophical terms:

> If you know all the qualities of a thing
> You know the thing itself;
> Nothing remains but the fact
> The said thing exists without us;
> And when your senses have taught you that fact,
> You have grasped the last remnant of the thing in itself.[17]

Zukofsky confidently cuts through the seemingly unbridgeable gap of phenomenon and noumenon, the Kantian *Erscheinung* and *Ding an sich*: the thing is that which is perceived. Perceived reality is the totality of reality. Zukofsky's faithfulness to particulars (his "sincerity") is perhaps even more pronounced than Pound's, and whether his poetics stems from a more radically nominalistic world view may be further argued. At any rate, in the *Poetry* issue he edited Zukofsky included an essay by René Taupin. Among other things, Taupin gave a valuable description of the type of poetry Zukofsky and some of the other objectivists were writing, and he applied to their art the name "nominalistic" poetry. Zukofsky may not have agreed to the choice of the epithet, but he would have found little to argue with in Taupin's definition of it. "Nominalistic poetry," wrote Taupin, "is a synthesis of real detail similar to the art of the primitives. . . . The most direct contact [with the real] is obligatory, more striking than any metaphor tainted with impure interpretation."[18] Taupin's observations are valuable for at least two reasons: first, for his connecting the new poets' attention to "real detail" with modes existent in pre-logical times, thus pointing to one of the live traditions of modernism; second, for his dissociation of the modernists' reliance on true metaphor (in Fenollosa's and Pound's sense of the word) from conventional metaphoric composition. Zukofsky, as mentioned above, praised Pound for his "implicit" metaphors. Similarly he commended Reznikoff's concision in presenting his metaphors in one word. In Reznikoff's lines one should be aware, he wrote, of "the isolation of each noun so that in itself it is an image, the grouping of nouns so that they partake of the quality of things being together without violence to their individual intact natures."[19]

This last remark also describes Zukofsky's own poetic method, which is essentially ideogrammic in that the poet's aim is to place particulars in a working relationship where each will affect the other and establish conceptual links while preserving the sovereign identity of each functional unit. The poetic object, Zukofsky wrote, must be viewed as a process, a thing open, inclusive, and in motion. For the objectified artistic whole he used the word "context." He spoke of the artist's desire "to place everything —everything aptly, perfectly, belonging within, one with, a context." Whether the word stands for Zukofsky's own ideogrammic method or whether, as one critic phrased it, " 'context' seems to be the nominalist's means for arriving at the universal,"[20] the end result is the same. We are speaking about a method of poetic composition in which the realized whole, the art object, is constructed by a dynamic juxtaposition of particular details, where they are all cause and all effect. As Fenollosa and Pound did before him, Zukofsky pointed out the relationship between the method of poetic composition and the method of science. As he said, "A person would show little thought to say poetry is opposed to . . . science" and again,

> Good verse is determined by the poet's susceptibility involving a precise awareness of differences, forms, and possibilities of existence—words with their own attractions included. The poet, no less than the scientist, works on the assumption that inert and live things and relations hold enough interest to keep him alive as part of nature.[21]

The method thus inheres not in transitional, rational presentation but in ideogrammic juxtaposition. "As against transition," he said, the poets "oppose condensation. The transitions cut are implicit in the work, 3 or 4 things occur at a time making the difference between Aristotelian expansive unities and the concentrated locus which is the mind acting creatively upon the facts." Poets are interested only in particulars, he said. Thus "poems are only acts upon particulars, outside of them."[22]

Zukofsky conceived of his method of ideogrammic composition in explicitly musical terms. The juxtaposition and movement of objectified particles of sincerity he worked out in accordance with the contrapuntal development of the fugue. Guy Davenport noted that, especially in the middle and later sections of "*A*", Zukofsky succeeded in finding a way "to harmonize counterpointed themes . . . something like Pound's and Williams's imagistic gisting of English phrases into a Chinese aesthetic of terseness."[23] No doubt Zukofsky chose the structure of the fugue because it was the freest possible structure, and closest to the scientific method of "heaping together" the particular units. He did, in fact, write in "*A*"-6:

> The fugue a music heap
> only by the name's grace music.

The structure of the fugue is rather simple: it begins with a short phrase which is called the subject, after which another voice restates the subject in a different key (the response). During the response the first voice takes up a new motive, called the countersubject. Afterward the various voices repeat the subject in specific keys, interspersed with episodes, i.e., musical material different from the subject. When the subject is reintroduced in the original key, the fugue is brought to a close. But it is a notable feature of fugal structure that it is endless, that is, new material can always be brought in to complement and carry further the interplay of subject, response, and countersubject. Furthermore, the various voices can overlap in a *stretto*, in which the different voices sing different parts of the subject simultaneously.

The fugue, then, in Zukofsky's poetry—as I have noted it in connection with Pound's poetry—is a form of juxtaposing and repeating in amplified or metamorphosed fashion certain thematic units. I stress the fugal form in Zukofsky's case because he employs it much more consciously than Pound ever did and because he adheres to this mode of counterpointing much more rigorously. Also, Bach's music is one of the main *themes* of the entire poem "*A*" (which begins "A / Round of fiddles playing Bach"), and the text of the St. Matthew Passion is interwoven into the text of several parts. *Passion*, in all the connotations of the word—the passion of Christ, of humanity, of the artist, and of Zukofsky personally—is the subject of "*A*", with which an almost infinite variety of "historical and contemporary particulars" are constantly juxtaposed.

"*A*"-1 imagistically and dramatically starts with the "superposition" of two events: the performance of the St. Matthew Passion in Leipzig under Bach's own direction and a performance of the same work in New York 200 years later. Zukofsky states the subject thus:

> Black full dress of the audience,
> Dead century, where are your motley

> Country people in Leipzig,
> Easter,
> Matronly flounces, starched, heaving,
> Cheeks of the patrons of Leipzig—
> "Going to Church? Where's the baby?"
> "Ah, there's the Kapellmeister
>   in a terrible hurry—
> Johann Sebastian, twenty-two
>   children!"

The response follows immediately, the restatement of the subject in a different "key," which in this case is the twentieth-century recital in New York:

> The Passion According to Matthew,
> Composed seventeen twenty-nine,
> Rendered at Carnegie Hall,
> Nineteen twenty-eight,
> Thursday evening, the fifth of April.
> The autos parked, honking.

Just as we have seen Bach, the choirmaster, hurrying to church, we see the speaker of the poem (Zukofsky himself?) coming out of Carnegie Hall ("I lit a cigarette, and stepped free / Beyond the red light of the exit"). Then Zukofsky introduces the countersubject: after the fading face of an usher, the speaker's eyes focus on the face of a tramp in rags. The countersubject (poverty, destitution) is again answered by the idle chatter of the people who have been at the concert ("Patrons of poetry, business devotees of arts and letters, / Cornerstones of waste paper"). The theme introduced by the countersubject is again taken up, now amplified and explicit, by some workers gathering on the street and discussing a strike by Pennsylvanian miners, their whisperings ending on an ominous note: "the thing's becoming a mass movement." At that moment a part of the original subject, "Easter," is echoed by "It was also Passover."

Next we have an overlapping of the speaker on a train and the memory of the music, followed by a further rearrangement of the countersubject in the form of a powerful indictment of the American economic system in which the increasing number of roads and automobiles are contrasted with the growing number of unemployed workers who are not satisfied with the economists' explanations ("Production exceeds demand so we curtail employment"), and who cry out in reply, "Yeh, but why don't you give us more than a meal to increase the consumption!"

The progression of the countersubject has thus moved from the tramp to the worried group of sympathizers with the striking miners to the voices of protest of organized workers. In the same metamorphic progression the theme of the answer, from usher to idly chatting bourgeois concert-goers, is brought to a head in Zukofsky's introduction of a captain of industry, a certain Mr. Magnus. The industrialist of course has the "answer" (literally and as part of Zukofsky's musical structure) to the demands of the workers, for he knows how to deal with them: "We ran 'em in chain gangs, down in the Argentine," and then adds in the same breath: "Been fishin' all Easter / Nothin' like nature for hell-fire!" Mr. Magnus's Easter activity is a travesty of the real meaning of the feast as it is contrasted with the plight of the workers and with the true piety of the Leipzigers. "*A*"-1 ends with a quote from the libretto of the Passion, ironically echoing the industrialist's "hell-fire" with " 'Ye lightnings, ye thunders / In clouds are ye vanished? / Open, O fierce flaming pit!' "

This brief analysis of "*A*"-1 does not purport to have explored with any completeness the richness of the poem; it only presents the Zukofskian method of juxtaposition. The method may be described as *fugal metamorphosis*, based on an energy-transference concept akin to that of Pound and Fenollosa, in that it is a natural composition where the juxtaposed particulars "work out their own fate." Zukofsky called the form of "*A*" organic—"involved in history that has found by contrast to history something like perfection in the music of J. S. Bach."[24] Since Zukofsky, like Pound in *The Cantos* or like Williams in *Paterson*, works with a great assortment of borrowed material, he also characterizes "*A*" as a conglomeratum of "ready-mades" which act and react according to the relations established by their various proximities:

> The work then owns perhaps something of the look of found objects in late exhibits which arrange themselves, as it were, one object near another—roots that have become sculpture, wood that appears talisman . . .—they appear entirely *natural*.[25]

Natural, that is, in the sense that the active particulars change, grow, and evolve in the way of things in nature, involved with each other while preserving their individuality. Zukofsky's method is in line with his isomorphic vision of the cosmos, but his ideograms, his contexts, and his metamorphoses follow more faithfully the specific contrapuntal structuring of a Bach fugue than Pound's cumulative and contrastive ideograms. "*A*"-12, which apart from "*A*"-24 is the longest section of the poem, running to nearly 140 printed pages, is a monumental fugal metamorphosis in five parts. Zukofsky described its structure as follows:

> The form of "*A*"-12, as I intend it, is speech growing into song. I again take up the Bach material of previous parts. . . . The form is prompted by his Art of Fugue. The fourfold subject of words including

Bach's name announced on the first page of my poem is developed, augmented, combined in five principal sections, and then recapitulated in a stretto. The coda once more recalls the subject.[26]

The subject is about "making music," i.e., creating art by fusing shape, rhythm, and style. The musical theme begins with Bach and moves through Handel, Mozart, Chopin, Beethoven, and Schönberg to Bartók. The "response" is poetic creation, based on Shakespeare's *A Midsummer Night's Dream*, amplified and juxtaposed with Li Po, Ovid, and Whitman, among others. The countersubject is Zukofsky's personal history, from his father Paul through himself to his son Paul. The personal history is counterpointed by world history and the history of philosophy. The various materials are supplemented and contrasted with lyric passages, letters to Zukofsky copied verbatim (as in Williams's *Paterson*), and political material in the form of quotes and conversation. Zukofsky arranges his material in such a way that when the particular units appear and recur they enhance each other's affective power. The inclusiveness of the form allows for the bringing in, as G. S. Fraser noted, of "the most remote and intellectual ideas, if they are creative ideas, and the most personal anecdotes of a lifetime: prose, documents, anti-poetic detail. . . ."[27] As all organic and inorganic beings in nature, Zukofsky's poetry is alive with objectified particulars in ceaseless interaction.

Zukofsky defined poetry as "an order of words that as movement and tone (rhythm and pitch) approaches in varying degrees the wordless art of music."[28] "*A*"-12, as he intended, comes as close as possible for a poem to attain a musical structure, but Zukofsky intended to go beyond that. He was aware of Pound's interest in music (he wrote, "Imagism and music direct the composition of the *Cantos*") and shared Pound's conviction that "verse to be sung is something vastly worth reviving." His initial interest in Bach's music and his persistent adherence to a poetic structure evolved from that music predisposed him to attempt a wedding of words and music. This attempt is realized in "*A*"-24, the final part of his long poem. This section, the longest in the entire poem, is composed for music and voices. The musical background is Handel's *Pièces pour le clavecin*, against which speakers recite from Zukofsky's works, from his collected essays *Prepositions*, from different sections of "*A*", from his play *Arise, Arise*, and from *It Was*, a collection of short stories. The voices speak their various parts in contrapuntal unison, achieving a polyphonic effect singular in poetry (or music).

"*A*"-24 is perhaps the ultimate in sincerity and objectification (for Zukofsky, at any rate) as brought together in a total context where words and music play an equal part. It brings to a close, in a triumphant *stretto*, the entire fugal structure of "*A*"; but it is also a pioneering work in a new mode which subsequent poets (or musicians) may consult.

None of the other objectivist poets, with the possible exception of

Reznikoff, possessed Zukofsky's genius to conceive and execute something monumental. They were in the main interested in seizing significant detail and rendering it in terse and precise language. But apart from writing short poems of carefully observed particulars, they have all developed their own versions of paratactically juxtaposed smaller wholes.

In Reznikoff's case the influence of Chinese poetry is evident in the shorter poems, augmented by his admiration of Pound's work. Of the modernist poets, together with the later work of Gary Snyder, Reznikoff pursued most consistently the possibilities inherent in the haiku and in the Poundian superposition. He quotes with approval the statement of Wei T'ai, an eleventh-century Chinese poet: "Poetry presents the thing in order to convey the feeling. It should be precise about the thing and reticent about the feeling."[29] This definition could well be Reznikoff's *ars poetica*, for he said of his own poetic composition: "I see something and it moves me and I put it down as I see it. In the treatment of it, I abstain from comment."[30]

Reznikoff is a kind of Giacometti of poetry: in his most successful short pieces he has whittled down his material to the barest essentials, eliminating not only all ornament and decorative fillings but logical, transitional progression as well. Such poems are as memorable in their concision and exactness as any of Pound's similar imagistic compositions.

A close parallel to "In a Station of the Metro" is Reznikoff's three-line poem "Railway Station at Cleveland." After the first line ("Under cloud on cloud the lake is black"), the "wheeling locomotives" of the yard are seen pouring their smoke "into the crowded sky." As in Pound's poem, the title is an intrinsic part of the image Reznikoff wants to create; it presents the precise locus, or the "natural picture." In the first line the copula has no metaphoric role. It signifies nothing more than the actual color of the lake: the darkness of the water reflects the darkness of the cloud hanging over it. The verb "is" evokes a sensation of motionless tranquillity; the line is as static as the lake and the clouds are. It is contrasted strongly by the motion present in the adjacent railway yard: the locomotives are "wheeling," they "pour" their smoke. The puffs of smoke emitted by the engines are cloud-like. As opposed to nature's serene clouds they are active, dynamic, and the product of technology. It is their *addition* to the natural clouds (produced by the evaporated water of the lake) which *transforms* the color of the sky and is responsible for the lake's blackness. The poem is built on the juxtaposition of nature's handiwork, the natural cloud, and the result of technological skill, the smoke cloud.

I do not believe Reznikoff's juxtapositioned particulars can be reduced to a "meaning," like "Industry interferes with nature," or "Human technology upsets the harmony of nature," for the clouds remain clouds and the lake remains a lake, despite human intervention. The sky is already "crowded" with nature's things, so human beings do not destroy the balance, they only contribute to it. The contribution may not always be salutary, but in all events the human being is part of nature, just as smoke clouds merge with those in the sky. Of course, the above two "meanings" may also be part of the image, but its import is much more wide-ranging and inclusive. It has the capability to move the reader toward meditation, and in that it is like the natural scene it depicts. The unseen relations of the precise details produce in the attentive reader an insight, or a succession of insights and revelations, all having to do with the human being as participant in nature's processes. The poem is thus a "context" of particulars interacting in their own way. Reznikoff does not disturb their reality, but only presents them in their relations with one another.

The objectification of things is the strongest element in Reznikoff's work. Concepts such as transience and permanence are never described, but are evoked by the contrasted images, so that the reality of the actual particulars is wrought indelibly on the mind's eye. The superposed units are "only" themselves, undisturbed in their integrity. Their setting beside each other, their appearance-in-conjunction, releases their hidden power, which shows them bound together in an ordinarily unperceived secret union.

The poem is thus truly an "object," and Reznikoff's intention with his poetry is to illuminate the understanding. He does not mention the word "ideogram" in connection with his method, but he employs paratactic juxtapositions and uses strong simple verbs. On the other hand, he is quite explicit about his aversion to metaphor—not true metaphor in Pound's and Fenollosa's meaning (these Reznikoff employs fairly often, as for example, "The blue luminous sky furrowed into clouds; the clear air / crowded with rain—the dark harvest"), but the ornamental kind which dilutes the intrinsic and genuine reality of objects. In a discussion of Greek poetry, he said: "I'm not so sure that English poetry needs the use of metaphor. . . . There is a magnificent fragment by Archilochus in which there is simply a description of a girl walking, with her hair about her shoulders. I wouldn't want to see her compared to a hind or whatever."[31]

Such a statement by a poet is significant, especially for someone like Reznikoff, who among the objectivist poets was the least concerned with "theory" and "method." But he did have his own method, developed from his haikuesque juxtapositions, from what he learned from Pound and Zukofsky, and also from his own personal experience. Though he never practiced the profession, Reznikoff was a trained lawyer, and his own version of ideogrammic technique owes a great deal to his education in a law school and to his subsequent study of legal cases. He declared: "I am an 'objectivist' and I have my own 'formula' for writing," which he described in the following way:

By the term "objectivist" I suppose a writer may be meant who does *not* write directly about his feelings but about what he sees and hears; who is restricted almost to the testimony of a witness in a court of law, and who expresses his feelings indirectly by the selection of his subject-matter. . . . Now suppose in a court of law you are testifying in a negligence case. You cannot get up on the stand and say, "The man was negligent." That's a conclusion of fact. What you'd be compelled to say is how the man acted. . . . There is an analogy between testimony in the courts and the testimony of a poet.[32]

In his longer poems (*Testimony: The United States 1885–1890* and *Holocaust*) Reznikoff uses just such a method: his ideogrammic method is the paratactic placing of law reports and actual testimonies. As opposed to *The Cantos*, *"A"*, and *Paterson*, the persona of the poet is never present. The poet's presence is felt only through the mode of selection and the arrangement of the juxtaposed testimonies as a way to evoke emotion in the reader. "In *Testimony*," said Reznikoff, "the speakers whose words I use are all giving testimony about what they actually lived through."[33]

The poem is divided into four natural sections: "The South," "The North," "The West," and "The East." In each section Reznikoff organizes his material into clusters of phenomena and situations, repeated in the various major parts and laconically titled "Social Life," "Domestic Scenes," "Boys and Girls," "Machine Age," "Property," "Negroes." In certain sections he adds groups not included elsewhere, such as "Persons and Places," "Railroads," or "Stagecoaches." In the "Stagecoaches" cluster (in "The West" section) three events follow each other without comment or explication. In each episode there is "testimony" of mismanagement, carelessness, and lack of sensitivity when dealing with the most crucial element of a stagecoach operation, the horses. All the cases are scrupulously worded occurrences; no conclusions may be drawn except when viewing the entire group—when the unseen relations become apparent. Like Pound in his ideograms, Reznikoff presents one facet and then another and another until he feels his statement has been made—that is, until he can expect the reader to *see* the individual events in their uniqueness and then to see through them to their relations in a larger whole.

Holocaust is constructed in a similar way. As Reznikoff wrote in the preface, "All that follows is based on a United States government publication, *Trials of the Criminals before the Nuernberg Military Tribunal* and the records of the Eichmann trial in Jerusalem." Shortly before his death in 1975 Reznikoff was working on another long poem, *The Good Old Days* (as in all of his long works, Reznikoff gave it the subtitle "recitative"), which was based on early American texts such as *Winthrop's Journal* (1637) and Charles Fenno Hoffman's *A Winter in the West*. Reznikoff remarked: "In editing the following episodes I thought of myself as a kind of archeologist. I did not invent the

episodes but neither did the original writers''—which I take to mean that the
"original writers" worked from reality, from actual observation. Such research was part of Pound's creative work. It is also an activity Williams and
Olson have been engaged in. Reznikoff's great recitatives of testimony move
in a similar though much less cryptic way to Pound's Chinese history and
Adams cantos. The order he achieves by "heaping together" relevant detail
is like the archeologist's arrangement of artifacts.

The collage-like serials of objective particulars and testimonies (such are
Reznikoff's long poems) in their dynamic relations realize an image of the
United States in a certain period and of the horrors of the Nazi concentration
camps. Whether the image is an illumination as Reznikoff intends it, de-
pends on the individual reader. Reznikoff remarked: "A reviewer wrote that
when he read *Testimony* a second time he saw a world of horror and violence.
I didn't invent the world, but I felt it."[34] And having felt it, he recreated it in
its own image, in clear and precise language, so that we, too, can feel it in its
almost palpable reality.

George Oppen was likewise not interested in "inventing" the world, but
the poetic means with which he pursued his ends is markedly different from
Reznikoff's (or, for that matter, Zukofsky's). His humble statement, "I'm
just telling about what I encountered, what life was to me,"[35] suggests a
poetry of factual reportage which, however, accounts little for the complexity
of the poetry. Oppen is perhaps the most "philosophical" among the objectivists, not only because he lists Kierkegaard, Maritain, and Heidegger as
three of the most important influences on him, but also because his method
relies less on the disinterested presentation of units of "sincerity" than on an
intricate combination of perceptual data and emotional or intellectual
declaration. This is especially true of his later poetry. After his early poetic
output of the late twenties and early thirties (from which Zukofsky chose
selections for his objectivist anthologies), Oppen stopped writing poetry for
some twenty-five years, and his later writing departs in many ways from the
earlier work. In some of these later poems (more so in the 1968 volume *Of Being Numerous* than in the others) Oppen does not aim at inducing contemplation or meditation by his arrangement of particulars; in many instances the
meditation is right there on the page—it constitutes the poem.

Abstract statements, alone and without their imagistic counterparts, are
rare. Particularly in his latest poems (*Myth of the Blaze*, written between 1972
and 1975) Oppen manages to fuse overt intellectual announcements with
emotionally charged images to create constructs of great intensity. A number
of these poems ("The Speech at Soli," "Latitude, Longitude," "The Book
of Job and a Draft of a Poem to Praise the Paths of the Living") are at times
strongly reminiscent of Pound's late cantos, especially *Drafts and Fragments of
Cantos CX–CXVII*, where Pound powerfully juxtaposes particular details with
what Reznikoff would have termed "conclusions of fact" ("But the beauty is

not the madness" and "If love be not in the house there is nothing" in Canto CXVI; or "When one's friends hate each other / how can there be peace in the world?" in Canto CXV). In a poet such as Reznikoff these "conclusions" would undoubtedly blur the hard-edged contours of his "testimonies," but in Pound and Oppen they act not as commentaries or connectives but compressed units supplementing the images. For the philosophical meditations do not arise from the particulars immediately preceding them, nor are they followed, in a logical or rational manner, by other detail. The sequentiality is paratactic, and solely the relation of parts (including the meditative parts) can render up a "meaning."

From the beginning Oppen conceived of poetic creation in the form of series. His first book was called *Discrete Series*, and his later poetic sequences (the title poem in *Of Being Numerous*, the poem "Route," and the volume *Seascape: Needle's Eye*) are executed in a similar manner. Oppen began from imagism, and his earliest modernist influence, as he stated, was Pound. It was Pound's method that he wanted to carry further and not, as he said, "the sloppy American imagism descending out of Amy Lowell and a thousand others." Oppen was attempting "to construct meaning, to construct a method of thought from the imagist technique of poetry—from the imagist intensity of vision."[36] But this construction and handling of words required Oppen to overcome certain, for him very real, obstacles. Among the poets that make up the ideogrammic stream it was Oppen (and in some respects Creeley) for whom language itself posed enormous problems. In order to "build" meaning from words Oppen had to begin from an existential basis, from what he termed "an act of faith"—that is, the faith that language has a reality of its own and that it also refers definitely to things in the world. This "act of faith," he said, means that

> the nouns do refer to something; that it's there, that it's true, the whole implication of these nouns; that appearances represent reality, whether or not they misrepresent it; that this in which the thing takes place, this thing is here, and that these things do take place.[37]

This is Oppen's own restatement of the assertion (also voiced by Zukofsky) that perceptual reality *is* total reality; the things are *there*, even the smallest unitary particle is *out there*, except that in and through language it is not possible to grasp it. It remains, as he said, "absolutely impenetrable, absolutely inexplicable." This despair would mainly stem from the ineffectuality of logical discourse, for poets, in their constructions, are involved in a more hopeful enterprise: they put verbal objects in touch with one another according to nature's structure. In poetry, as he wrote in "A Narrative," "Parallel lines do not meet / And the compass does not spin," for this is an "interval" where relationships are more important than the things related:

. . . and events
Emerge on the bow like an island
. . . .
And the small trees
Above the tide line
And its lighthouse
Showing its whitewash in the daylight
In which things explain each other,
Not themselves.[38]

This is a central and crucial image of all ideogrammic poetry—the recording of inner and outer perceptual data as they appear successively to the navigator. In substance it is identical to Pound's image of the *periplus* and to Olson's "composition by field." Things perceived must be left undisturbed in their wholeness; they must be allowed to arrange themselves in a sequence, as with islands, trees, lighthouse on the horizon. The significance lies not in an a priori human ordering, but in the eventual natural order the objects create themselves in their interactions. In total isolation they are "impenetrable"; they can "explain themselves" only through their relations.

Oppen derived his poetics from imagism, but his organizational method of poetic series was implemented from another, personal source. What the Chinese ideogram was to Pound, the Bach fugue to Zukofsky, and the law report to Reznikoff, mathematics was to Oppen. This is how he explained the title of his first book *Discrete Series*, a term he took from mathematics:

A pure mathematical series would be one in which each term is derived from the preceding term by a rule. A discrete series is a series of terms each of which is empirically derived, each one of which is empirically true. . . . I was attempting to construct a meaning by empirical statements, by imagist statements.[39]

The underlying concept is thus not a progression like 1, 3, 5, 7, 9, etc., or 1, 2, 4, 8, 16, 32, etc. Oppen revealed to Hugh Kenner that he regretted not having printed the series 14, 23, 28, 33, 42 on the title page. These numbers refer to the names of the subway stations on New York's East Side. They are derived empirically, and not from each other. As Kenner writes, "They derive from a reality prior to number, the street grid of Manhattan (influenced by geology and commerce and history), and each gives access to a whole life."[40] The individual parts are separate wholes in themselves, yet they constitute a series, just as an island of rock, trees on the shore, and a lighthouse are joined as one image in the vision of the beholder. But the beholder—the poet—is not a passive onlooker who is somehow "above," by virtue of human consciousness, the things and events in nature. As Oppen wrote:

> There are things
> We live among "and to see them
> Is to know ourselves."

> Occurrence, a part
> Of an infinite series.[41]

We humans, Oppen implies, are just another "occurrence," a finite part of the infinite universe. For the human being to be a meaningful "term" in the discrete series of the world involves an act of volition, a will to participate in the process of the whole:

> The self is no mystery, the mystery is
> That there is something for us to stand on.
> We want to be here.
> The act of being, the act of being
> More than oneself.[42]

Oppen's "act of faith" means that the world is our home, and the poetic act is constructive in that it rises above the "shipwreck / Of the singular," and becomes "more than oneself," by pointing to the unseen relations which are the foundation and structure of our cosmic home. Oppen appears to have absorbed a number of Heidegger's ideas, particularly that of being *in* the world. In Heideggerian terms the human desire to be in the world, the will to "dwell" (*wohnen*) is coterminous with constructive activity (*bauen*) which includes the cultivation of the soil and the building of houses.[43] For Oppen the poet's work inheres in a like "building," in "objectification," i.e., in "making an object of the poem," an erection of a human habitation from the materials of the world. Like human beings in the world, the poem is an "occurrence," or a series of perceptual occurrences, put together "sincerely." In *Discrete Series*, as in the other serial sequences, there are no associative links whatever between the individual units. Unit one, for example, proposes the idea of boredom as being *of* the world, "weather-swept, with which one shares the century." Unit two is a geometric image, "the red globe" moving from the "underarm of T" as part of the world's "round / Shiny fixed / Alternatives." Next comes an image of a restaurant, a series of "private acts" behind which looms the world of "big-Business." Things are seen and recorded in their functional reality as they elliptically converge upon one another, illuminating not themselves but each other in the infinite series which is the world. Things are what they *do*, as Oppen affirms in unit ten:

> Closed car—closed in glass—
> At the curb,
> Unapplied and empty:
> A thing among others

Over which clouds pass and the alteration of lighting,
. . . .
Moving in traffic
This thing is less strange. . . .

All things in nature, when they are "unapplied and empty," are abstract and unreal; they can only be known when they are in "context," as parts of an assemblage of individual objects. For Oppen the poetic—objectifying, constructive—act is *epiphanic* in that it is a "showing forth" of the discrete, by themselves unrelated, particulars in the world. This conception of art is implicit in the Greek term *techné*—which, as Heidegger pointed out, does not mean craft or "art" *per se ipsum*, but to *make appear*, to show the reality of something. Oppen's central poetic purpose, as he wrote in *Of Being Numerous*, is

Not to reduce the thing to nothing—

I might at the top of my ability stand at a window
and say, look out; out there is the world.

He *might* say it, yet he does not, for it would mean the negation of all the discrete things which *make up* what we conveniently name "the world." As one critic said about Oppen, such an attitude may be a form of nominalism in which "appreciation of the existence of an object, in its tangibility or luminosity, is the primary poetic feeling."[44] But beyond that there is another emotion—love. And in a rare moment Oppen confessed that he is in love with things: "With the streets and the square slabs of pavement." This most *human* of the human emotions sustains Oppen's "faith" in continuing to dwell and build in the world.

Oppen does not conceive of seriality only in spatial terms. For him, as for Pound, "all ages are contemporaneous." As may be gathered from his method, Oppen feels as close an affinity with the archaic as his modernist confreres; it is an integral part of his artistic intention of "showing forth" occurrences in a continuum of time and space:

They made small objects
Of wood and the bones of fish
And of stone. They talked,
They gathered in council
And spoke, carrying objects.
They were credulous,
Their things shone in the forest.
They were patient
With the world.
This will never return, never,
Unless having reached their limits

They will begin over, that is,
Over and over.[45]

This "patience with the world" connotes an absence of predatory aims to possess the knowable universe and deform it in accordance with our reason and intellect. Oppen in his poetry of series exhibits such patience, a deep respect for "small things" and "small words," for in them the world, otherwise a bewildering abstraction, is made real.

The objectivists were the first group of American poets who attempted to make use of Pound's theories and who proved that his aesthetics offered new possibilities in poetic composition. But their work, significant though it is, has not received the attention it deserves. It fell to the "last" of the objectivists, William Carlos Williams, to assure the continuity of the mainstream of modernism that Ezra Pound began.

5. Dr. Williams: Ideas in Things

By its sheer size alone William Carlos Williams's *oeuvre* (some forty volumes of poetry, fiction, essays, interviews, autobiography, and letters) is one of the most impressive in twentieth-century American letters. But the importance of his work can be gauged with any accuracy only if we keep in mind that this author throughout his creative life was an uncompromising modernist, at times even a one-man avant-garde. His aesthetics is as wide-ranging as the media in which he worked. It touches all aspects of the art of poetry, from a new theory of the imagination to a new poetic diction to a new prosody—his idea of the "variable foot." These significant innovations have begun to receive, in the last decade and a half, well-earned critical recognition. In these pages I shall mainly be concerned with outlining Williams's contribution to the ideogrammic method, or more exactly, giving an account of his method of composition, which stands as a definite expansion of the nontransitional, paratactic mode of poetic expression.

Much has also been written about Williams's association and personal friendship with Pound, which began in 1902 and lasted until Williams's death in 1963. Particularly for the young Williams, Pound's advice and criticism was invaluable. As Williams himself admitted later in life, "meeting Ezra Pound is like B.C. and A.D."[1] Williams was an imagist and later an objectivist; he "followed Pound's instructions, his famous 'Don'ts,' eschewing inversions of the phrase," and other directives.[2] But it is important to remember that Williams's art developed the way it did not only because he took Pound's advice in certain matters but also because of his very staunch opposition to some of Pound's notions about poetry. From the very beginning Williams felt that if there was going to be a renewal of American verse, so that it might recreate a faithful image of modern life, it must start *in* America, *from* American material. While never denying Pound's singular position as *the* pioneer of modernism, at the same time he resented both Pound's living outside America and his Provençal, Italian, and Chinese "archeology." Only late in life did he acknowledge that Pound's "digging" was not a snob's way of filling his poems with quaint subject matter, but that in his own way, roundabout though it may have been, Pound had enriched American poetry just as he had done. As he said in a 1950 interview, the two of them wanted "to uproot poetry and start it on its own, on its proper tracks in this country," i.e., in America. But he never for a moment abandoned his conviction that his own place could never be anywhere else than in America, on the East coast, in Rutherford, New Jersey. He could not conceive of his poetry other than as a form of the imagination arising from the reality of his surroundings.

Williams's modernism, his own method of nonlogical composition, grew from a philosophical basis which he already had firmly in mind before he wrote his first important book, *Kora in Hell: Improvisations*. It was, of course, no formal philosophy; it was "merely" the distillation of his own experience and of the people and events around him. To find "a local assertion" was his ideal, the "rediscovery of a primal impetus, the elementary principle of all art, in the local conditions."[3] But this closeness to the local and the recognition of its primacy did not mean a simple-minded collection of particular data. As with Pound and the other ideogrammic poets, their virtue lay in being raw material for the imagination and its peculiar power to realize through them the immortal concept, the idea of a certain place or an era. The imagination must proceed from knowledge, but that knowledge must be based on evidence gathered by perception. These notions Williams saw confirmed by contemporary philosophy ("formal" philosophy), in his case the work of John Dewey. Dewey's 1920 essay "Americanism and Localism," with its axiom "The locality is the only universal, upon that all art builds," gave Williams added impetus to continue on the road he set upon. In the rise of the new sciences he saw a similar direction, as did Pound, and said, "[What] all our most complex philosophies (and mathematics) have finally come to mean to us is that we cannot begin to go beyond the evidence of our senses."[4] But this evidence must be transfused, blown out to its full potential: the artistic act involves a metamorphosis of the particular elements into a larger perceptual-conceptual form. Williams wrote:

> General ideas, if they are to be living and valid, to some extent depend . . . on local cultures. It is in the wide range of the local only that the general can be tested for its one unique quality, its universality. The flow must originate from the local to the general as a river to the sea and then back to the local from the sea in rain.[5]

Williams thus views the human cognitive process as essentially isomorphic to natural process. Therefore the poet's task cannot be a *copying* of nature but an *imitation* of its movements and actions. Williams sharply distinguishes between the two activities. Imitation for him is "active invention," paralleling the separate but apposed reality of the objectively perceptible universe. As an example of the aesthetics of copying, Williams picks out and attacks

Shakespeare's (or Hamlet's) advice "to hold the mirror up to nature" as a representative mode of occidental art. As its opposite, he gives imitation. Though he does not mention Fenollosa or the method of oriental poetry, the implications of his phrasing, I believe, implicitly point to them: "To imitate nature involves the verb to do. To copy is merely to reflect something already there, inertly; Shakespeare's mirror is all that is needed for it. But by imitation we enlarge nature itself, we become nature or we discover in ourselves nature's active part."[6]

Imitation through imagination means the creation of art objects, to be set beside the natural objects of the world. The method of artistic creation and the shape of the object created are the specifically human realizations of the universal creative forces present in nature. It is the force of the imagination through which we can feel ourselves related sympathetically to the larger, "latent" force of the cosmos. In creating new objects with the aid of the imagination, the artist, Williams asserts, does not desert reality by constructing things alien and unnatural. Imagination "does not tamper with the world but moves it," in accordance with nature:

> Imagination . . . affirms reality most powerfully and therefore, since reality needs no personal support but exists free from human action, as proven by science in the indestructibility of matter and of force, it creates a new object, a play, a dance which is not a mirror up to nature but—
> As birds' wings beat the solid air without which none could fly so words freed by the imagination affirm reality by their flight.[7]

Also, birds cannot fly without periodically descending to the earth to draw sustenance for their flights, just as the flight of the imagination must receive its sustenance from the actual presence of real detail, its only source of nutrition. This means that the poet, in order to create an art object that is "consonant with his day" cannot withdraw into a kind of ivory tower but must be actively involved in the reality around him.

In Williams's case one factor has been continually underrated: the influence his medical practice exerted on his poetic activity, particularly his poetics and method. But in fact it was his daily work as a general practitioner which nourished his artistic imagination. Medicine, he wrote,

> was my very food and drink, the very thing which made it possible for me to write. Was I not interested in man? There the thing was, right in front of me. I could touch it, smell it. It was myself, naked, just as it was, without a lie telling itself to me in its own terms. . . . It was giving me terms, basic terms with which I could spell out matters as profound as I cared to think of.[8]

From day to day he observed human beings "just as they were," in their uniqueness and individuality, discovering details of an entire community's way of living, thinking, and feeling in the world. He saw the poet's business as minutely knowing and seeing the material, "not to talk in vague categories but to write particularly, as a physician works, upon a patient, upon the thing before him, in the particular to discover the universal."[9] The endless procession of patients before him did not conform to any predetermined set of rules; it was undifferentiated as reality itself. The insight of Pound's theoretical statement, that the science of medicine "leaves off" where art begins, is corroborated by Williams's own daily existence. And just as "the unselected nature of the material," one case followed by another, allows the doctor to intimate the larger meanings of reality, present though unseen in the world, so the poet cannot proceed otherwise than to construct the art object by a natural juxtaposition of particulars. Every day in the life of a physician is a "series," naturally composed of discrete human beings with their ailments and complaints. These cases may seem unrelated, yet there is nothing accidental about their contiguity, for they add up, or a representative sample of the cases adds up, to a "picture" of the state of health in the community. For Williams the method the artist uses in dealing with imaginative material must be essentially identical to the ways in which the doctor deals with human material. The two activities overlap, and Williams formulated his poetic method accordingly: "Art can be made of anything," he said, "provided it be seen, smelt, touched, apprehended and understood to be what it is—the flesh of a constantly repeated permanence."[10]

The data gathered by the senses—this intimate, received knowledge—is unified by the imagination without doing violence either to the process or to the things' integrity. The imaginative "welding" process does not follow the path of reason and logic, and Williams was just as much against what he called the "paralysing vulgarity of logic" as Pound and Fenollosa were. (As he advised a young poet, "You know yourself that a poem is not a thought but a composition. The thought does not have to follow any logical order but can come in any way that the making of the poem orders."[11]) The mind amasses perceptual data and makes "sense" out of them. In turn, the imagination unifies in a similar, nonlogical manner:

> The imagination goes from one thing to another. Given many things of nearly totally divergent natures but possessing one-thousandth part of a quality in common, provided that be new, distinguished, these things belong in an imaginative category and not in a gross natural array,[12]

that is, not in a collection of data arrived at by mere copying. The above statement, significant though it is, is a more general version of Fenollosa's theory of metaphoric overtones. Williams at this stage does not yet allow for the juxtaposition of wholly unrelated material.

At least not in theory, for the above passage is a quote from the prologue to *Kora in Hell: Improvisations*, Williams's first ideogrammic work where more often than not even "one-thousandth part of a quality in common" is hard to locate in the texts juxtaposed. Robert Creeley's description of Williams's mode of composition can be applied to *Kora in Hell* as well as to the later *Spring and All* and *Paterson*. In a Williams poem, wrote Creeley, "you get apparent juxtapositions . . . that would not be understandable unless one were to take it literally as the context in which the mind has shifted to another point of contact in the very writing. There is no unity of view . . . in the more classical sense."[13] Each observed particular—inner happening or outside event—requires a corresponding emotion, and in the final imaginative object these abrupt changes of emotional patterns are faithfully recorded.

Kora in Hell, as Williams related in his brief poetic autobiography *I Wanted to Write a Poem*, is an assembly of notebook entries Williams jotted down during a period of one year. They were reflections of what happened during the day, how Williams responded to them, and in general anything that came into his mind. Later, when thinking about publication, he realized that some of the entries, too private in nature, would be totally incomprehensible to the reader. Taking an example from a book left in his house by Pound (by the Italian poet Pietro Metastasio), Williams decided to append interpretations to some parts of the text. The explications rarely solidify or enclose the text; that is, they do not act as suddenly switched on lamps in a dim room. Rather, they are themselves separate, adjoining rooms, somewhat more brightly lit than the first rooms which they then partially illuminate. Here is an example, the first improvisation in group XXIV (the book is composed of twenty-seven groups):

> I like the boy. It's years back I began to draw him to me—or he was pushed my way by the others. And what if there's no sleep because the bed's burning; is that a reason to send a chap to Greystone! Greystone! There's a name if you've any tatter of mind left in you. It's the long back, narrowing that way at the waist perhaps whets the chisel in me. How the flanks flutter and the heart races. Imagination! That's the worm in the apple. What if it run to paralyses and blind fires, here's sense loose in the world set on foundations. Blame buzzards for the eyes they have.

Then, separated by a line and set in italics, comes the "interpretation":

> *Buzzards, granted their disgusting habit in regard to meat, have eyes of power equal to that of eagles.*

The interpretation throws only a faint light on a certain aspect—which is seemingly the least in need of an interpretation—of the unit, and for this reason it is the least expected. The effect is neither cumulative nor contrastive; it is what I would call *reflective* or *quasi-reflective* juxtaposition within one sub-whole. The explication is not a new particle, for it is connected to the previous part, though not logically; yet it lights it up and makes us see it from a different angle. The enlarged buzzard image presents an objective picture of the bird's duality—it has a "disgusting habit," i.e., it is necrophagous, but it also possesses the eyesight of the most noble of birds —and allows us to perceive a tenuous link between it and another ambivalent image in the improvisation proper: that of the imagination. Its virtue is vision, but this vision is fraught with dangers, for the imagination also seeks to absorb and transform the object of its attention, in this case the unique reality of the boy. Of course the light of the reflective interpretation can penetrate the first particle only up to a certain point, just as the chisel of the imagination can only partially realize, through verbal means, the total complexity of that being who is the speaker's object of affection. The imagination, shorn of its predatory aspect, is nonetheless capable of showing relations, a context within which the objects may interact and reveal each other.

The second improvisation and interpretation in the same group offer a further meditation on the imagination:

> Five miscarriages since January is a considerable record Emily dear—but hearken to me: The Pleiades—that small cluster of lights in the sky there—. You'd better go on in the house before you catch cold. Go on now!

> Carelessness of heart is a virtue akin to the small lights of the stars. But it is sad to see virtues in those who have not the gift of the imagination to value them.

In this case the interpretation is a fully developed discursive sub-unit in its own right, to be set beside the image of the improvisation. But here it is the imagistic part that lights up the "conclusion" of the interpretation, or rather, they are mutually reflective. Williams's startling assertion that carelessness of heart is not a fault but a virtue gains its momentum from the actual event recreated in the improvisation. In the particular context it is a virtue, i.e., it is the natural extension of the girl's being, of her natural sexuality and fertility, akin to the light of the stars, an emanation of their being. The functioning parts of the juxtaposition may be diagrammed as follows:

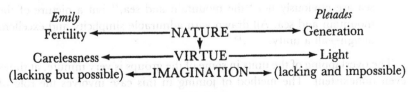

SPEAKER

While Williams establishes a relation between the girl and the stars, for both of them are motivated by natural forces, he does not blur their identities together, but points to the unique human ability of the imagination which could justify "carelessness of heart."

Each of the two units I have briefly looked at in group XXIV puts forward a facet of the imagination in a wholly individual context. In the first part the poet presents it as part of the creative act where it can be both beneficial and destructive; in the second its absence prevents the meaningful, fully human exercising of natural faculties. In the third part, which is given without interpretation, Williams shows it in its positive fullness as a play and dance. Here the image is self-contained because the imagination takes delight in its own creative powers; it needs no additive or illumination. The three units compose a delicately balanced whole, an interrelated visual-conceptual object.

The improvisations in *Kora in Hell* are made up of mutually illuminating units of design, which are random, almost dadaistic, and rooted in the experience and imagination of the poet. They have a strong pictorial quality, demonstrating Williams's interest in the works of modernist painters (Duchamp, Demuth, Arensberg, Man Ray) and their influence on his juxtapositional technique. His major influence, though, was Cézanne, whom he valued above all because he was a "designer," and he saw in Cézanne's method an early manifestation of the form which characterized modernism in all the arts. Cézanne, wrote Williams, created his pictures

> so that there would be a meaning without saying anything at all. Just the relation of the parts to themselves. In considering a poem, I don't care whether it's finished or not; if it's put down with a good relation to the parts, it becomes a poem. And the meaning of the poem can be grasped by attention to the design.[14]

The partially overlapping, reflexive juxtapositions of *Kora in Hell* may also owe something to the compositional technique of the cubists, especially Braque and Juan Gris, the latter of whom Williams particularly admired. The cubists, Williams noted, did away with creating an "illusion" of reality on the canvas. In a picture constructed of the recognizable shapes of a window shutter, a guitar, the sea and the mountains, for instance,

> one thing laps over on the other, the cloud laps over the shutter, the bunch of grapes is part of the handle of the guitar, the mountain and sea are obviously not "the mountain and sea," but a picture of the mountain and sea. All drawn with admirable simplicity and excellent design—all a unity. . . .[15]

The overlapping of the units in some of the groups is very minute, at times even nonexistent. The method of joining in this case involves the role of *chance*, a factor whose significance Williams, along with Marcel Duchamp, Arp, and Tzara, was one of the first to recognize. Also, the juxtaposition of distinct particulars does not result in a blurring of their distinctness, just as in music the simultaneously sounded instruments do not obliterate each other but rather emphasize the "perfections" of each in their interplay.[16] Their notes blend harmoniously precisely because they retain their individuality. As Williams constantly and untiringly kept pointing out, imaginative wholes are different from natural wholes in substance, though not in essence—for the poetic act recreates with its own "materials" a process both visible and hidden in the processes of nature.

Spring and All, Williams's second ideogrammic book, operates on the principles of the collage. The poet brings together without logical transitions textual units of every conceivable kind: poems, parts of manifestos, critical observations, autobiographical information in diary fragments, paragraphs that look like unfinished short stories. The book as a whole is unclassifiable, unless we say that it is ideogrammic, but this is no classification in the ordinary sense of the word. Williams reiterates in the book that he does not intend to copy nature; rather, he has put nothing down in it which is not "of a piece" with nature—he intends to give an image of "the common thing which is anomalously about us."[17] He also points to the tendency of the modernist artist to reach back to the poets of the archaic world, reaffirming that "the work the two-thousand-year-old poet did and that we do are one piece." He specifically mentions Homer and the creator of the *Arabian Nights* as his forebears: "Their compositions have as their excellence an identity with life since they are as actual, as sappy as the leaf of the tree which never moves from one spot."[18] The so-called primitives, he said, "are not back in some remote age." They are with us, in that their attitudes in recreating the universe parallel those of the modernists—their mistrust of logic, their grounding of cognition in the dispersed and heterogeneous particulars that they find all around them, unifying them into imaginative categories.

Readers do not do injustice to *Spring and All* (or that other ideogrammic work in a like vein, *The Descent of Winter*) if they make no attempt to bridge the obvious gulfs between the parts. They may rearrange the chapters at will, since they are numbered out of order anyway. But the parts, at least at certain points, are definitely *in place*, the prose reinforcing the poem and vice versa. Again, the effect is not cumulative in the sense of the Poundian ideogram or the conscious fugal development of Zukofsky. Yet the theoretical, "conclusive" statements receive "proof" from their adjacent imaginative counterparts and in that they are consubstantial though materially different.

In these juxtapositions the abstract statement does not remain a mere shell, but is filled with the imagined substance of the poem, giving it life and validity. It is possible to suppose that Williams's main interest in writing *Spring and All* is basically theoretical, though here again we need not make an attempt to view it as a whole. But if we go along with this notion for the sake of argument, it becomes clear that just as Pound could not conceive of writing a theoretical book without filling it with "exhibits," Williams likewise felt compelled, out of his faith in the primacy of particulars, to complement and infuse with imaginative reality his arguments on aesthetics. The poem is an objectification of experience; the poet does not tamper with it, attempt to interpret it, or remake it in his own image. He does not copy it but recreates its structure, leaving intact its essential quality: its mystery.

Williams does not believe that either poets or scientists can logically explain the world. The world is composed of things, and even scientists can at best only give an image of things as they formulate a law based on observation. Poets also gather their material together but can deal with it when suddenly things reveal themselves as part of an unseen "latent" reality, when, as Williams writes, "that underground current can be tapped and the secret spring of all our lives sends up its pure water."[19] It has always been Williams's purpose as an artist to create poems in which the individual components establish relationships, the poem being "an assertion, always, of a new and total culture, the lifting of an environment to expression," the poet vivifying the current age "exactly as Hellas lived in the *Iliad*." The form itself must bespeak the era which gave it birth. As he wrote in 1939,

> An 8th century form, that is, *means* in some measure the whole conceptual world of the 8th century which invented it and to which it is fitted, whereas a 20th century form should embody, if possible, something of the astrophysical, chemical, sociological make-up of its own day.[20]

During this time he was already engaged on a project in which this aim was to be realized. The project was *Paterson*.

The form of *Paterson* shows a development of the organizational methods of the earlier ideogrammic books. Williams extends the reflexive or overlapping juxtaposition, and the introduction of certain types of material influences the relationship of each succeeding part. He uses "ready-mades," unretouched segments of documentary prose gleaned from his reading and research, from books published by historical societies, from original records he found in libraries in Paterson, New Jersey, and from medical records available to him from hospitals. He even includes several letters with no deletions, written to himself by various people, among them Pound, Ginsberg, and the often desperate poet Marcia Nardi. The technique of dealing with documents in this manner was foreshadowed by his 1925 book *In the American Grain*, in which Williams inserted documents by American statesmen and writers. "I copied and used the original writings," he said, "as in the Cotton Mather chapter, the Benjamin Franklin chapter and in the Paul Jones chapter, of which no word is my own." Williams arranged the texts in such a way that they fitted into his scheme "perfectly, leaving not a seam."[21]

Such was not Williams's aim in *Paterson*, for here the "seams" in the great "patchwork" of the poem not only show; they are in fact emphasized by having the documentary parts printed in different, smaller type to distinguish them from other, more overtly "poetic" original passages. Williams said, "I used documentary prose to break up the poetry, to help shape the form of the poem,"[22] for it was the creation of a new form that was of paramount concern to him prior to and during the writing of the work. He realized that it was not a traditional, "finished" form, yet at the same time he was aware that the poem was not formless either. In the end he "let form take care of itself," that is, instead of imposing a predetermined order or structure on his material, he allowed the material to establish an organic form through relations and reciprocal action.

Critics have pointed out the affinities between *Paterson* and *The Cantos*, though more in general terms than by actual comparison. Resemblances are there certainly, for both poems represent in language "heaps" or clusters of historic, mythic, contemporary, and personal events paratactically juxtaposed. As Williams himself said, *Paterson* is "a hodgepodge, the American version of Pound's more famous 'ragbag.' "[23] The remark is not to be glossed over because of Williams's brand of self-deprecating humor, but the differences are just as important. The form of *Paterson* grows from Williams's earlier experiments in *Kora in Hell* and *Spring and All* as inevitably as Pound's cantos derive from his Provençal studies and his imagist and vorticist periods. The apparent ease and sureness of hand with which Williams assembles his disparate material are in no small way due to his having mastered his personal ideogrammic method during the previous two decades.

In *Paterson* Williams shows a much less free hand in the rearrangement and editing of his adopted material than Pound does in *The Cantos*. Facts, he said, "appear in very much the same form as they appeared in the documents,"[24] but the facts also include his own creative "documents." As in the earlier works, theoretical pronouncements are an integral part of *Paterson*, and Williams is quick to state the central philosophical premise which informs his poem. He does so at the very beginning of Book I, where he first presents the "hero" of the poem, a combination of the real-life Jersey patriot N. F. Paterson, a personification of Paterson the city, and the poet's persona:

> Say it! No ideas but in things. Mr.
> Paterson has gone away
> to rest and write. Inside the bus one sees
> his thoughts sitting and standing. His
> thoughts alight and scatter—.

The metaphor (sitting and standing thoughts) indicates that the materials with which the poet is going to construct his work are not abstractions but people, events, and facts having a verifiable existence and a perceptual reality. The poem is to have imaginative-natural form:

> a mass of detail
> to interrelate on a new ground, difficultly;
> an assonance, a homologue
>   triple piled
> pulling the disparate together to clarify
> and compress.

From one-line images to documents several pages long Williams weaves together a tapestry of varying emotional-intellectual units, where the units retain their individuality, only clarifying and illuminating one another through their relations. These relations, as in the world, are complex, both obvious and latent. The poem is constructed in such a way that the active participation of the reader is indispensable. The reader must deal with each emerging discrete object, as when perceiving real objects. As James E. Breslin wrote,

> Not given a surface network of articulated connections, the reader is forced to suspend each block of material in his mind until he gets to the end, when the entire poetic field has been defined. Hence, relations among parts are fluid, and they must be uncovered by the imaginative activity of the reader.[25]

Williams conceives his work as a series of imaginative objects, outlining his material in the epigraph of the poem: "a local pride; spring, summer, fall and the sea; a confession; a basket; a column; a reply to Greek and Latin with the bare hands; a gathering up; a celebration." More than anything, it is a "gathering up," a heaping together, and not a subjectively unified progression of ideas. Rather than fitting the world's phenomena to his ego and to his conception of them, Williams must begin with "sincerity," with a regard to the actuality of things as he finds them. And so *Paterson* begins:

> To make a start,
> Out of particulars
> and make them general, rolling
> up the sum, by defective means—
> Sniffing the trees,
> just another dog
> among a lot of dogs. What
> else is there? And to do?

The poet is just another creature among all the others. The unique power of the imagination does not make the poet a demigod justified in ordering and reordering things, events, and experiences contrary to their objective reality. This is why the art of poetry has been abused in the past, "subverted by thought," breaking the oneness of the universe. The poet can only show the natural overlapping of human being and world, "an / interpenetration, both ways." This is how the world exists; this is how the poet must recreate it through the imagination. And this is how the reader must deal with the poem—as another object among the many, as a process of nature.

Book II, bearing the title "Sunday in the Park," is a large poetic field of interpenetrative detail where Williams's method can be observed particularly well. It begins with Dr. Paterson's (Williams's) credo as he joins the crowds of a Sunday afternoon picnic:

> Outside
> > outside myself
> > > there is a world
> he rumbled, subject to my incursions
> —a world
> > (to me) at rest,
> > > which I approach
> concretely—
> > The scene's the Park
> > upon the rock,
> > > female to the city
> —upon whose body Paterson instructs his thoughts
> (concretely).

His ruminations are interrupted by the shouts and laughter of the people around him; all the while he is conscious of the elemental activity he is engaged in: walking—separate yet together with the others, noting the ground, the bushes, trees, and rocks as *parts* of his movements. Juxtaposed to this reality Williams offers a dry, "logical" description of the act of walking taken straight from a book on physiology:

> The body is tilted slightly forward from the basic standing position and the weight thrown on the ball of the foot, while the other thigh is lifted and the leg and opposite arm are swung forward (fig. 6B). Various muscles, aided.

Without transition but in small type there follows an excerpt from a frustrated young poet's letter to Dr. Paterson, a terrain as difficult to "walk on" as the real ground under his feet. This is interrupted by the voices of the picnickers and Paterson's own thoughts as he hears the distant roar of the waterfall. A newspaper report follows, again in small type, about another picnic, one in 1880, when a man was murdered and the happy crowd turned into "a great beast" in trying to lynch the murderer. This juxtaposition of crowds, their potential violence lurking behind the placid exterior, is metamorphosed into a flock of birds as Paterson resumes his walking: "He is led forward by their announcing wings." The young poet also resumes her lamentations of her (imagined or real) rejection by Paterson. Her pain and longing and the previous image of the birds ("couriers to the ceremonial of love") overlap in a meditation on love by Paterson, in whose imagination love assumes the image of "a stone endlessly in flight."

Another news story follows: in 1878 a couple of officers of the law tried to shoot or club to death a little mink that appeared in the town. No moralizing is attempted by Paterson, but the ensuing poetic sequence counters the senseless act with the sense of poetic creation, of making it new:

> Without invention nothing is well spaced,
> unless the mind change, unless
> the stars are new measured,
> . . . .
> without invention the line
> will never again take on its ancient
> divisions when the word, a supple word,
> lived in it, crumbled now to chalk.

Invention, the concretization of the imagination, can truly emerge from a respect for nature in all its manifestations, from a love encompassing all beings. The world is not ours alone; we must coexist and interact with all other "objects," recognizing their inviolability. Accordingly, the imagistic resumption of Paterson's observation of the people in the park begins in this spirit: "—a park, devoted to pleasure : devoted to . grasshoppers!"

An echo of the mindless "fun" of the mink-chasing policemen is sounded in the group of girls Paterson encounters, "their laughter wild, flagellant." As a counterpoint, the birds return, and a faint image of Indians, the disinherited inhabitants of the land, closes the sequence.

Paterson continues walking and comes upon a man combing a dog. The next document is a letter addressed to "B." by a neighbor who was supposed to look after B.'s female dog and protect her from other (male) dogs while the bitch was in heat. But "tragedy" occurred: the dog is pregnant, and the neighbor is overtaken by excessive remorse and despair.

"And still the picnickers come on," continues Paterson. After a great "gathering up" of the detail he sees about him, he ends the first part as he reaches the summit with the transcription of the imposing sign:

NO DOGS ALLOWED AT LARGE IN THIS PARK.

The second and third parts of Book II do not logically develop the themes introduced in the first part. But as Paterson encounters new scenes and comes upon additional characters in the park, they evoke other objects and documents which illuminate their reality in space and time. The specious haranguing of a preacher on how he abandoned worldly riches ("This is a Protestant! protesting—as / though the world were his own") is juxtaposed with the machinations of Alexander Hamilton and his attempts to exploit the natural resources of the waterfall to enrich not the people but the state. The struggle of the preacher for his listeners' souls and Hamilton's struggle for assumption of the national debt by the federal government (empowering the banks to control and issue money) overlap in a continuous intercutting. Thus Paterson's description of the preacher applies equally well to Hamilton:

> —with monotonous insistence
> the falls of his harangue hung featureless
> upon the ear, yet with a certain strangeness
> as if arrested in space.

Book II ends with the finale of the young poet's letter (an excerpt over eight pages long), giving an image of monumental self-pity "created" by a lost soul. The pity is a kind of creation, but her habit of seeing and interpreting the world solely through her subjectivity, condemning the world for not conforming to her own ideas about how it *should* be, is diametrically opposed to Paterson's (and Williams's) state of being in, and dealing with, the world. Like the preacher and Hamilton, she acts as though the world were her own. Their failure—seeing the three of them in their relations—is a common failure and a just one. Their predatory attitude toward nature as a subordinate and not a coequal lies at the bottom of their undoing.

Williams never violates the particularity of the units he presents. The park, the animals, the picnickers, the young poet, the preacher, and Hamilton appear in their unadulterated reality. But in their "interpenetration" and relations the reader may see universal implications and general truths as they arise from the collisions of their scrupulously observed individuality. Only by juxtaposing the preacher with Hamilton do we perceive their reality, in what each *does*, as functioning parts of an overlapping process. Only by seeing the young poet's text interact with that of Paterson do we realize the falsity of her actions. For she proceeds to condemn Paterson (and with him, the world) by starting out from preconceived ideas, disregarding him and the world in their particularness. Thus, she ends in despair and nihilism. Paterson begins with particulars and proceeds from them to a vision of their relations. He begins with and ends in love, an affirmation of the world as it is.

For Williams imaginative invention does not mean a creation *ex nihilo*. As the Latin root verb *invenire* ("to come upon") suggests, the act is a gradual "gathering up" of things in language. The things of the world and the world itself are mute. Through imagination the poet releases their hidden identity so that we may know them and thus know ourselves. The desired objective of poetic invention is the acquisition by the reader of such knowledge—a realization of nature's "latent structure," of which each particular existent thing is a living proof. The poem is a construct; in Williams's definition, it is "a small (or large) machine made of words," and its proper function is to impart that knowledge. As he wrote,

> When a man makes a poem, makes it, mind you, he takes words as he finds them interrelated about him and composes them—without distortion which would mar their exact significances—into an intense expression of his perceptions and ardors that they may constitute a revelation in the speech that he uses.[26]

Williams is using the word "revelation" with the same connotation as Pound did. And if it still retains an overtone of the word's usual application to mystical vision, then one may perhaps say that both poets, and all ideogrammic poets to varying extent, are *mystics of the particular*. But Williams's poems proved revelatory in another way as well. The younger poets, those few for whom modernism was not an anomaly or aberration but a real poetic heritage to be carried on, found in Williams's work a precedent that was to fortify their intentions and aims. The modernist stream among the various poetic rivulets still flowing in America today would be far thinner and shallower without his contribution.

Part Three
The Open Field

Our intention is to affirm this life, not to bring
order out of chaos nor to suggest improvements in
creation, but simply to wake up to the very life
we're living which is so excellent once one gets
one's mind and one's desires out of its way and
lets it act of its own accord.

—John Cage, *Silence*

6. Projective Verse I: The Hieroglyphs of Olson

In 1945, barely thirty years after the launching of the modernist movement in the arts, the kind of poetry initiated by Pound seemed a historical curiosity, a relic of the past. Those poets who had kept alive and expanded the Poundian brand of modernism—Williams and the objectivists—were little known, and Pound was in prison, awaiting trial on charges of treason. Pound's works carried the stigma of their maker's political errors. Furthermore, they were "loose," without real form or proper structure. The poetic ideals of the time were the criteria set up by the New Critics of the late thirties and early forties (René Wellek, Cleanth Brooks, Allen Tate, John Crowe Ransom, and Robert Penn Warren). These criteria consisted of complexity and coherence, wit and irony, and intellectual hardness. But it was not Pound's hardness or Williams's toughness. (As Williams put it, "A poem is tough by no quality it borrows from a logical recital of events nor from the events themselves but solely from that attenuated power which draws perhaps many broken things into a dance giving them thus a full being."[1] Here was clearly an ideogrammic definition as alien to the aesthetic of wit and paradox as could be found.) No, the hardness in the poetry of the new traditionalists, or antimodernists, came partly from Eliot—not the Eliot of *The Waste Land* but the imperious critic and arbiter. The revival of logical composition was in no small measure due to Eliot's rediscovery of the metaphysical poets of the early seventeenth century. Some of Ransom's and Tate's "strong lines" vie with the extreme metaphoric density of Lord Herbert or Richard Crashaw. Richard Kostelanetz has summarized the established style in poetry around 1945 as "intricate in meter, approximately regular in length of line, ironic and elegant and sometimes aphoristic, controlled in texture and restricting in form. . . ."[2] The accepted measure again became the metronome, as opposed to the musical phrase. In general, the standard of composition was normative, and organic structure was frowned upon by the new reactionaries.

But modernism, all appearances to the contrary, was not dead. One of the first "outsiders" to gain access to Pound while he was awaiting a preliminary hearing in Washington was Charles Olson, ostensibly on an assignment for the *Partisan Review*. Olson was thirty-five at the time and unpublished. But two years later he published a book on Melville, *Call Me Ishmael*, whose structure was not logical but ideogrammic, and five years later there appeared his manifesto "Projective Verse," the first positive restatement of modernist poetics since Zukofsky's objectivist proclamation. In the year *Call Me Ishmael* came out another young unknown, Robert Duncan, hitchhiked to Saint Elizabeth's to see Pound—his "Good Teacher," as Duncan called Pound. A few years later, Allen Ginsberg heard Williams reciting some of his poetry, which came as a revelation and altered completely Ginsberg's attitude to the art. And Gary Snyder, inspired by Pound, was studying Chinese and Japanese and translating archaic Chinese poetry into modern American English. Modernism was not dead, but the "third generation" of the movement (the second being the objectivists) had to assert itself by fighting its own battle against the prevailing conservative tendencies in literature, just as the generation of 1914 had had to do.

   The center of the new modernist revolt was Olson, for it was he who laid down its theoretical foundation in the essay "Projective Verse." Olson's links to Pound are obvious. He was a self-confessed Poundian and considered the elder poet's work the indispensable source for the renewal of modernism (he called this renewal "postmodernism"). But his estimate of Williams was equally high, both for his poetic achievement and for his accessibility as a person. As he said, "Bill never faked, and that's why he has been of such use to all us young men who grew up after him. There he was in Rutherford to be gone to and seen, a clean animal, the only one we had on the ground, right here in the States."[3]

   With the publication of "Projective Verse," this admiration was reciprocated. Williams wrote to Robert Creeley in 1950: "I share your excitement, it is as if the whole area lifted. It's the sort of thing we are after and must have. . . . Everything in it leans on action, on the verb: one thing *leads* to another which is thereby activated."[4] It is more than simple coincidence that Williams praises Olson's manifesto in terms of Fenollosa's crucial notions of power transference and verbal action. Olson himself makes specific references to Fenollosa's essay in "Projective Verse." Like Fenollosa, he was concerned about formulating a basic statement for poetics, to be used profitably by his young contemporaries. Through Williams, Pound, and Fenollosa, he goes back to archaic, pre-Platonic modes of thought to define and redefine the use and usefulness, the role and importance, of the poet in the modern world. He regards the poet as the one creative being whose fundamental intention and raison d'être is, and must be, the "restoration of the human house."

   "Projective Verse" is central to Olson's work. His poetry, particularly *The Maximus Poems*, is the practical application of the theory contained in it.

And it grows naturally out of the earlier book, *Call Me Ishmael*. The essay is not merely derivative, a consolidation of what he learned from Pound and Williams. It is a step forward, even beyond the two indisputable masters whose influence Olson readily acknowledged. For there was still work to be done. "If I think," wrote Olson, "EP gave any of us the methodological clue: the RAGBAG; bill gave us the lead on the LOCAL. Or put it that pat: EP the verb, BILL the NOUN problem. To do. And who, to do. Neither of them: WHAT."[5] Even if this is a willed oversimplification, it is remarkably succinct and clearly registers Olson's own interest and direction toward the *object* of his poetic search. That object, the "what" of his doing, he defined in *Call Me Ishmael* as *space*, the central American fact. He saw Melville as a precursor in that Melville aimed at reaching back to the primacy of space which to him was "the First, before time, earth, man." "It is space," he wrote of Melville, "and its feeding on man, that is the essence of his vision."[6] Melville's search for space, Olson believed, was an archaic, mythic gesture, to reestablish the true coordinates of the relationship between human being and cosmos in nonanthropocentric terms. In Olson's perception, Melville's intentions coincided with those of his own, and generally with the modernist thrust to recapture the mythic, pre-logical heritage. Thus Olson claimed him as a premodernist on modernist premises:

> Logic and classification had led civilization toward man, away from space. Melville went to space to probe and find man. Early man did the same: poetry, language and the care of myth, as Fenollosa says, grew up together. . . . In place of Zeus, Odysseus, Olympus we have had Caesar, Faust, the City. The shift was from man as a group to individual man. Now, . . . the swing is out and back. Melville is one who began it.[7]

The "shift back" means a redefining of human beings in terms of space, and not space (the real, observable universe) in terms of human beings. Such a new shift in perception and art entails the poet's awareness of the new science, which has dislodged us as the unmoving center and fulcrum of the universe. In a later lecture on Melville Olson called attention to non-Newtonian physics as the basis of a more accurate world view. He specifically mentioned Whitehead and the theory that physical quantities are not scalar (i.e., possessing mass but not movement) but vector, both matter and motion, a corroboration of Fenollosa's insight of "things in motion, motion in things." Olson immediately placed the vector theory in context, for after quoting Whitehead he added: "So one gets the restoration of Heraclitus' flux translated as, All things are vectors. Or put it, All that matters moves!"[8] By this definition the human being is also a vector among vectors in ceaseless motion, growth, and metamorphosis.

The poetic act cannot but recognize, and re-create, this basic fact of the universe. The classical unities of artistic form as given by Aristotle (in Olson's punning, "Hairystottle") and all his followers are as obsolete as they are artificial, and Olson reaffirms the necessity of organic form, as did Pound and Fenollosa before him, in line with the archaic tradition:

> PROCESS—what Heraclitus tried on as "flux"—is reality; therefore, means or method is going toward and will become the object of its attention. . . . The object is changed because it is revealed to itself as much a part of process as it is of being. So the poles, then, are not quite such fixed terminals as they appear but are also developing and continuous things as is process or method.[9]

Poetic method cannot be divorced from the process of nature and from our relationship to it, which is a vector among vectors. "If there is any absolute," said Olson, "it is never more than this one, you, this instant, in action."[10] Logic and classification, on which a transitional, beginning-middle-end kind of composition is based, interfere with the human being as a "bundle of functions," the medium becoming more an end in itself than a fitting image of process and action. The method of juxtaposition, on the other hand, is not following a single logical thread but projecting a multiplicity of relations among functioning objects. Thus, it is more truthful to the actual motions of nature; it even approximates our relation to the space around us and to the events in which we take part: "For any of us," said Olson, "at any instant, are juxtaposed to any experience, even an overwhelming single one, on several more planes than the arbitrary and discursive which we inherit can declare."[11] Alluding to Fenollosa, Olson declared, "The harmony of the universe, and I include man, is not logical." So the method of poetry, if it wants to be truly relevant, must shift away from the general toward the particular. Logical discourse deals with universals and symbols. It *describes*, and it

> does not come to grips with what really matters: that a thing, any thing, impinges on us by a more important fact, its self-existence, without reference to any other thing, in short, the very character of it which calls our attention to it, which wants us to know more about it, its particularity.[12]

Olson's fundamental axiom is that "Art does not seek to describe but to enact." "Enact" is his equivalent to Pound's "create" and Williams's "invent." This is an accurate method the artist can use to deal with the live things in the universe, to reenact its process in linguistic form.

The theories of "Projective Verse" grow out of fundamental ideas laid down by Olson in his book and lecture on Melville and in his other essays, one of the most important being "Human Universe." The "Projective Verse" manifesto is unique in that it is the only document of modernist poetics which utilizes the precepts of *The Chinese Written Character as a Medium for Poetry* with as much consistency as Pound's aesthetics. Olson sets up projective verse ("projectile," "percussive," and "prospective" are his other epithets) in opposition to the nonprojective, i.e., closed form, "inherited line, stanza," the old form of logical verse structure. Projective is *open*; it is a "composition by field." It achieves a natural form which corresponds to the position of things perceived in space and the situation of events in time.

Under separate subheadings Olson treats the three aspects of projective composition; its kinetics, its principle, and its process. The poem, like all interactions in nature, is a transference of power: "A poem is energy transferred from where the poet got it (he will have some several causations), by way of the poem itself, all the way over to, the reader."[13] Then, the poem must be "a high energy-construct and, at all points, an energy discharge." The "energy" or poetic impact of the poem comes from the juxtaposing of mutually affective perceptual data. The poet can proceed by no other direction than what the material demands. The poem as vector has its own "push," but, Olson adds, "it is much more, for example, this push, than simply such a one as Pound put, so wisely, to get us started: 'the musical phrase,' go by it, boys, rather than by, the metronome."[14] To Olson even the musical phrase may in certain situations be restrictive, and the nature of the things or events to be reenacted may "push" the poet to get hold of other, more appropriate forms.

The principle of open composition follows from the above imperative, which Olson defines, in a phrase borrowed from Creeley, as "FORM IS NEVER MORE THAN AN EXTENSION OF CONTENT."[15] Olson adds that "right form" is the sole extension which it is possible for the material to take. In other words, just as any object of nature obeys natural laws in its growth toward a full realization of itself as form (the acorn grows into an oak tree; the semen of a stallion and the ovum of a mare bring forth a horse, not an alligator), so the poet must aid the particulars under consideration to assume their proper, organically determined form.

The process whereby the authentic form of objects and experiences is realized need not, therefore, be made to conform to a preconceived pattern dictated by logic and reason. In Olson's formulation, "ONE PERCEPTION MUST IMMEDIATELY AND DIRECTLY LEAD TO A FURTHER PERCEPTION." The "heaping together" of perceptual units as they follow each other in natural succession achieves the shape of the open poem, a shape commensurate with the shape and order of the things perceived. The structure of such poetic process is identical to the structure of natural processes. As Olson writes,

> Every element in an open poem (the syllable, the line, as well as the image, the sound, the sense) must be taken up as participants in the

kinetic of the poem just as solidly as we are accustomed to take what we call objects of reality; and that these elements are to be seen as creating the tensions of a poem just as totally as do those other objects create what we know as the world.[16]

The projective poem is held together by the tension of its juxtaposed particulars. It may properly be called a "field," where "all the syllables and all the lines must be managed in their relation to each other." The units of speech which contain the perceptual data are not isolated things but—as Fenollosa said—meeting points of actions in a process in which there is no completion. The poem as field is thus a natural development of Fenollosa's thought. But it is also paralleled by the theories of field physics, according to which an electron in an electromagnetic field is not regarded as an independent unit, but as a "limit-point" in the entire context of the field. The poem is a field, but it is also a meeting point, a transference of power, between poet and reader. As a field, it contains its own "limit-points" in the form of lines and syntactical units. These points Olson sees as enactments of natural energy transfers—a fact, he says, "of what Fenollosa is so right about, in syntax, the sentence as first act of nature, as lightning, as passage of force from subject to object."[17] It is from these smaller units as they are materialized into lines (where, Olson says, "the shaping takes place") that the poem grows and expands into its natural form and acts as energy construct/energy discharge.

The regulator of the shape of the line is not the metronome or musical phrase; it is the natural breath of the poet. The line for Olson is a kind of intellectual-emotional complex, in which the intellect (the "head") through aural perception shapes the syllables, and emotion ("heart") via breath orders the syllables into a line. In Olson's definition, "the HEAD, by way of the EAR, to the SYLLABLE, the HEART, by way of the BREATH, to the LINE." It follows, then, that the projective poets must constantly be listening to their own speech, listening to the shapes of syllables so that they may adequately store the perceptions which crowd in through the senses. The measure of the line should vary according to the nature of the perceptions and the emotions they arouse in the poet. They may be stately and calm or choppy and nervous as dictated by the heart. The composition of the poem on the page is aided by the use of the typewriter whereby the poet can indicate length of breath, pause, phrase, and "the juxtapositions even of parts of phrases," as the composer would transcribe a musical composition. Since the projective poem is not for the silent perusal of the eye but is "scored" for oral delivery, the ear is as much a measuring apparatus as the eye is; in fact it is more important. The typewriter, with its possibilities of exact spacing and various signs, is seen and used by Olson as an active participant in the realization of the form the poem must take in order to enact the natural process or event under the poet's attention.

The aesthetic of composition by field Olson called "objectism," to distinguish it from objectivism, although his method is really a further clarification and extension of the earlier method. Objectism means

> the kind of relation of man to experience which a poet might state as the necessity of a line or a work to be as wood is, to be as clean as wood is as it issues from the hand of nature, to be shaped as wood can be when a man has had his hand to it.[18]

This restatement of organicism has the added significance of attempting to restitute the individual's proper relationship to space by "getting rid of the lyrical interference of the individual as ego"—the presumptuousness through which human beings have succeeded in alienating themselves from what they are: creatures of nature, objects among others, a part of the vital universe. Olson often quotes Heraclitus's saying, "Man is estranged from that with which he is most familiar," to wit, from his immediate natural surroundings and his own body. Olson reaffirms that a man is what he does: "The use of a man, by himself and thus by others, lies in how he conceives his relation to nature, that force to which he owes his somewhat small existence." By setting himself above the natural scheme of things and giving himself metaphysical attributes, he will perforce fall back upon his ego and subjectivity and picture the world as nothing but a reflection of his subjective self. The artistic forms he creates will bear the signs of his artificial relation to reality. They will be artificial and estranged from his true identity. On the other hand, says Olson, "If he stays inside himself, if he is contained within his nature as he is participant in the larger force, he will be able to listen, and his hearing through himself will give him secrets objects share."

It is from nature that human beings got their "projective size," their organizing ability, their language. If they see themselves only as thinking and speaking subjects, they relinquish their claim to wholeness, for they are also hearing objects and listening objects, a meeting point of energies in a total field. For us to thus come to terms with ourselves requires humility. We must get rid of our habitual arrogance and adopt an attitude of "Pull down thy vanity." We did not invent the world but only dwell in it, and during the past two and a half millennia we have managed to get farther and farther away from our true dwelling place. Olson's contention is that projective verse brings poet and reader a step closer to that "human house," for it aims at a reinstatement of our proper relation to nature.

Since the projective poem enacts the larger process of space, it is *about* that process, but it is also a process in its own right. Olson's poetry has thus been criticized as "shapeless." However, the remark that *The Maximus Poems* is a book "without much rendering, ordering, or assimilation," and that it has "neither beginning nor end; it is all middle"[19] Olson would have accepted as a compliment, an insightful critique which recognized the essential message of "Projective Verse" and its realization in poetic form. Olson's poems are all "middle," in a sense incomplete because he attempts to turn to nature, not to human logic, for principles of organization. And he finds, as Fenollosa did, that in nature there is no completion. Poetic language must free itself from restrictive forms. As he said, "We have lived long in a generalizing time," with the result that

> Logos, or discourse, for example, has, in that time, so worked its abstractions into our concept and use of language that language's other function, speech, seems so in need of restoration that several of us go back to hieroglyphs or to ideograms to right the balance.[20]

The inspiration Pound received from ideograms Olson got from his Mayan studies. He spent some eight months in Yucatan in 1950 and 1951, actually doing field work among Mayan ruins and digging up and deciphering hieroglyphs. Fenollosa and Pound saw poetry in the Chinese ideogram; so did Olson in the writing of the Mayas, who, he wrote, "invented a system of written record, now called hieroglyphs, which, on its very face, is verse, the signs were so clearly and densely chosen that, cut in stone, they retain the power of the objects of which they are the images."[21] The hieroglyphs depict, as did ideograms to Fenollosa and Pound, operations of nature in the order they actually occur. The theses posited in "Projective Verse" are seen to be corroborated by Olson's Mayan exploration and his examination of hieroglyphs, for here also perception is followed immediately by another perception, not in accordance with logic but as dictated by nature.

Olson recorded his Mexican experiences in a series of letters to Robert Creeley, later published as *Mayan Letters*. These letters constitute a "basis for aesthetics" as much as Fenollosa's essay does. They are a companion piece to Olson's theory of objectism and composition by field, which assume a different and much more positive reality in the light of Olson's findings. He observed that the Mayas' hieroglyphic reenactment of nature assigns each object its proportionate "weight" as they exist in the world. In the relationship of objects of nature human beings do not "weigh" more than other "objects": each of us is "as object in field of force declaring self as force because is force in exactly such relation."[22] Western thought has gotten away from such nonhierarchical involvement with nature, with its disproportionate idealization (and idolatry) of the human being and its resultant anthropomorphism in art, science, philosophy, and religion. In the perspective afforded by the Mayan hieroglyph Olson finds even *The Odyssey* and its modern equivalent, *Moby Dick*, wanting, for they are borderline works, one signaling the entry of humanism, the other the exit. On the subject of a model for the projective poet, Olson makes this suggestion to Creeley:

> A Sumer poem or Maya glyph is more pertinent to our purposes than anything else, because each of these people & their workers had forms which unfolded directly from content (sd content itself a disposition toward reality which understood man as only force in field of force containing multiple other expressions.[23]

Olson's world view and method are in a sense based on a method of science: he had a theory and he tested it by empirical evidence which bore it out. But Olson, the modernist poet who speaks of vectors and nuclear physics and fields of force, felt "at home" among the pre-Columbian relics. He is at the same time a "savage" as Wyndham Lewis had applied the term to the modern artist. More precisely, he is a "modern savage," not a pale, nostalgic replica of the pre-logical primitive, but the bearer of a new, *postlogical* consciousness. It is this syncretism which Creeley noted in Olson:

> In "Mayan Letters" we have unequivocal evidence of a *kind* of intelligence which cannot propose the assumption of content prior to its experience of that content, which *looks*, out of its *own* eyes. This does not mean that conjecture is to be absent, insofar as *jacio* means "throw" and *con*, "together"—however simply this may note the actual process. It is a consistent fact with Olson that he does use his legs, and does depend on what his own instincts and intelligence can discover for him. In this way he *throws together* all he has come to possess.[24]

Olson's poems, particularly his magnum opus *The Maximus Poems*, are just such a "throwing-together," a ragbag of American hieroglyphs continually enacting objects and events.

The topos of the poem, placed between the huge spaces of the sea and the American continent, is Gloucester, Massachusetts. The "hero" is Maximus, who writes letters, mainly to Gloucester, which are about Gloucester and its relation to Maximus. ("In *Maximus*," writes Olson in one of the letters, "local relations are nominalized.") In another (Letter 5), he says "Limits / are what any of us / are inside of." Maximus is *inside* Gloucester as Olson is *inside* the poems. But these limits are natural ones, and as such, never final. They are points of contact between inner and outer forces affecting each other. The letters compose a series, and each unit in the series accentuates through its individual form the perceptual matter in which it originates. Some letters work in the way of Pound's contrastive ideograms. In others Olson presents the history of an entire sequence of events, interspersed with other historical, autobiographical, and anthropological data.

In the continuation of the poem (*Maximus Poems IV, V, VI*) there is a more pronounced emphasis on typographical arrangement of the text on the page. Some parts follow the natural unfolding of a day's happenings: a few lines jotted down in the morning are juxtaposed to densely filled pages written in the afternoon or evening of the same day. It is always the particular "shape" of the experience which shapes Olson's breath and in turn shapes the poem.

In Letter 19, for instance, certain values of human behavior are presented through the enactment of a real event. Olson's ironical subtitle for the poem is "A Pastoral Letter," for it is about a minister. First Maximus introduces the pastor: he has friendly manners, is polite, and wears "(besides his automobile) / good clothes. / And a pink face." The telling image reveals that the minister "wears" his face as he wears his clothes and car—it is "put on" like his other paraphernalia.

The image is followed by another, more dramatic event, an encounter between the minister and Maximus, during which the mask comes off. The minister asks, "Pardon me, but / what church / do you belong to, / may I ask?" The moment the question is put, Maximus envisions an eclipse of the sun affecting the entire continent—a sardonic vision of the "man of God" concerned not with diffusing the light of the Creator, but merely with sectarian formality, which in effect blots out that light:

> And the whole street, the town, the cities, the nation
> blinked, in the afternoon sun, at the gun
> was held at them.

The minister's words metamorphose into a gun, a weapon of the unnatural forces, the forces of darkness. Maximus wavers over whether to give in or somehow restore order. He opts for the latter:

> I sd, you may sir.
> He sd, what, sir.
> I sd, none,
> sir.
>
> And the light was back.

The extremely short lines render the quickness and sharpness of the exchange. And as the light comes back, the minister vanishes, leaving Maximus with the thought that he was able to make his stand because of his independence ("for I am no merchant"). He concludes with a rather uncomplimentary image: that in the minister he had glimpsed not God's face but his backside.

In the personal battle Maximus has succeeded in preserving his own face, without donning a mask, though he did waver for an instant. The poem ends with an image of a third face, which is neither a travesty of God's visage nor subject to doubts and hesitation: the appearance of his baby daughter. She is singing in unison with a bird, all pure and natural, for "she wears her own face / as we do not." The child is a creature among the other creatures of nature, in harmony with things, *inside* herself. Letter 19, then, juxtaposes different "faces," all aspects of the hidden face of God, and their varying relations to it and to each other. The minister's face is the farthest from that hidden perfection and the child's is the closest to it. Maximus, knowing both, in conflict with the former and admiring the latter, is in between, in a state of becoming. The images of the three are reenacted in that natural order: they all grow out of God's "perfection" and are located at increasing distances from it.

Letter 5 shows Maximus involved in a different struggle. In nine sections, plus a proem, he recounts the vicissitudes of creating and maintaining a literary magazine of quality in Gloucester. The letter is addressed both to Gloucester and to Ferrini, the editor, and attempts to answer questions about what sort of publication the town can absorb and appreciate, and how an editor ought to edit something so that it will be read. In the proem Maximus stresses that a magazine cannot (and should not) compete with local newspapers; what they offer in the way of news stories, obituaries, reports of scandal and gossip, advertisements of sales, and so forth satisfies a certain demand which pertains to people's lives. This requirement is juxtaposed with the ideas of the "culture mongers" as to what people should read. They are based on an attitude which regards the people en masse as children, to be spoon-fed with "culture" that has nothing to do with them. After a scathing attack on the current issue of the magazine in the first section, Maximus begins a series of juxtapositions of the magazine with facts and events that are peculiar to Gloucester. First, he admonishes Ferrini, "It is not the many but the few who care / who keep alive what you set out to do," and these few cannot be fooled. The poems and stories in the magazine do not have the freshness and innocence of budding writers or local talent that the editor sought out. Nor is it "what it ought to seek to be": a "catch" of such expertise and seriousness comparable to the haul of Gloucester fishermen. To illustrate their expertise, Olson cites his own father, Carl Olsen: "a peak of the ocean floor he knew so well (the care he gave his trade, his listening." The content of the magazine should be "as good as fish is," says Maximus in section 3, "its stories / as good as any of us are." Maximus is not dissatisfied because he would like the journal to be filled with a kind of pedestrian localism. As he says to Ferrini, "Nor assuage yrself I use the local as a stick to beat you." His aim is to have something as whole and as fully realized as nature is: "as fine as fins are."

Part 4 is still concerned with knowledge; but this time it is not knowledge of the sea but of the land, which Maximus knows so intimately but Ferrini knows hardly at all. Maximus harks "back to an older polis." To him a single word can bring back a host of real events in which he participated, as when he says, with quiet pride: "I am not named Maximus / for no cause / when blueberries. . . ." The word "blueberries" evokes not a happy day of picking but the day when a construction company that was contracted to hire local help satisfied the letter of the law by hiring local workers and then fired them after twelve hours. It is such deep knowledge of the place that Maximus possesses, and he offers to put this knowledge, his active help, at Ferrini's disposal, so that the magazine could "come home a winner (as the Bluenose so often did." But Maximus does not use the past as another "stick" with which to beat Ferrini. As he says in section 5, "I'd not urge anyone back. Back is no value as better. . . . Back is only for those who do not move. . . ."

Maximus demonstrates his readiness to "move": he will still try to meet with Ferrini, even though he realizes, in a biting pun on "editor," that Ferrini is "adither" of the future which the magazine should *project*. He adds a warning: "The mind, Ferrini, / is as much of a labor / as to lift an arm / flawlessly." He concludes with an appropriate nautical image: "know, if you are a skipper, the position of the ship you are commanding."

The next section shows Maximus's mixed feelings about the possibility of his meeting with Ferrini, but his zeal overrides his frustration. In section 8 he even suggests possible names for the magazine, so that it will "have something at least which belongs to the truth of the place." Then he again takes up the matter of content, mentioning specifically a play that appeared in the issue in question, a play "with God as the Master of / a Ship." And he indignantly sweeps away this allegorical nonsense:

> In Gloucester-town
> you publish it, where men
> have cause to know where god is
> when wooden ships or steel ships,
> with sail or power,
> are out on men's business
>
> on waters which are tides, Ferrini,
> are not gods.

Finally Maximus admits defeat: "There is no place we can meet," for Ferrini has left Gloucester. The ending is not a logical outcome of structure but an outcome of events, and the structure would (could) have taken a different turn had the events occurred differently. Each section begins with a hope of a meeting and continues with an instruction intended for Ferrini. Through all the various aspects of the art of editing that Maximus brings up, there emerges the overall image, the projective ideogram of a totality of concerns and associations. It is rooted in the reality of Gloucester, the topos between land and sea, determining relations and providing soil for the roots of the people and their ideas.

Olson freely admits that he wants to make "no strict personal order" of the objects and events which he inherited from Gloucester, from the "space" of America. No predetermined order is feasible or advisable in the work he is engaged in, for

> An American
> is a complex of occasions
> themselves a geometry
> of spatial nature[25]

The individual is an object of force in the field of force. The poem, an enactment-in-language of these "complexes of occasions," cannot but adhere to the form they themselves "push" into being by their actions. And the work Olson sets out to do stems equally from his own person and his relation to his topos:

> I have this sense
> that I am one
> with my skin
>   Plus this—plus this:
> that forever the geography
> which leans in
> on me I compell
> backwards I compell Gloucester
> to yield, to
> change
>   Polis
> is this.[26]

Like Williams's Paterson, Gloucester is Olson's "local," in its particularity containing the universal *polis*. But Olson's sweep encompasses a wider field than does Williams's. He reaches deeper into the past and *projects* farther into the future. He believes himself to be standing at the threshold of a new era, which he sees as posthumanist, postlogical, posthistorical and postmodern. In his method and practice he proclaims that this era has already arrived:

> This is the morning, after the dispersion, and the work of the morning is methodology: how to use oneself, and on what. That is my profession. I am an archeologist of morning. And the writing and acts which I find bear on the present job are (I) from Homer back, not forward: and (II) from Melville on, particularly himself. . . .[23]

This poet of the morning is a digger who presents his hieroglyphs in the order of his natural perceptions, to be *used* by other humans as nuggets of reality and experience and as affirmation of process. As Olson puts it in Letter 6,

There are no hierarchies, no infinite, no such many as mass, there
    are only
eyes in all heads,
to be looked out of.

7. Projective Verse II:
Duncan's Collages, Creeley's Pieces

Olson's influence, as theorist and practicing poet, was a significant factor in the postwar revival of modernism in America. But his influence was augmented by a third aspect of his activities, perhaps equal in importance to the other two: his influence as a teacher. In 1948 he received an appointment to teach at Black Mountain College in North Carolina, which at that time was under the rectorship of Josef Albers, the abstract painter. (Before coming to America, Albers had been on the teaching staff of the Weimar and Dessau Bauhaus.) After Albers's departure in 1951, Olson became rector under very difficult circumstances and held that position until the college was forced to close down in 1956. The college's curriculum was as unconventional and innovative in the literary arts as the Bauhaus had been in the fields of fine arts, crafts, and architecture. Attracted by its relaxed, unacademic atmosphere, a number of avant-garde artists and writers came there to teach, among them Franz Kline, John Cage, and Paul Goodman. Robert Creeley and Robert Duncan both taught at the college, and Creeley edited the short-lived but influential *Black Mountain Review*. The magazine launched the careers of several talented poets, many of them students at the college. Edward Dorn, Paul Blackburn, Denise Levertov, and Joel Oppenheimer, along with Olson, Duncan, and Creeley, eventually became associated with the college and the magazine, and were later named "the Black Mountain poets."

The Black Mountain group of poets may be considered a movement in the sense that Zukofsky's objectivist group had been one. That is, it was a gathering of poets holding different views on what a poem is and how one should proceed to write it. But just as Zukofsky's ideas of objectification and sincerity were shared by Oppen and Reznikoff, the Black Mountain poets also had a central theory, Olson's projective verse, shared to varying degrees by Duncan and Creeley. The poetics and art of these two poets also constitute an advance on Olson's theory and on the ideogrammic method in general. They have both produced a body of work which, after Olson's death in 1970, occupies a prominent place in the modernist line of contemporary American poetry.

Duncan's output, perhaps more than that of any other modernist poet, defies easy classification. This may in part be due to his being the most "derivative" poet in American literature since Pound—a characteristic Duncan himself admits to. Translation, in various forms, has been an integral part of his poetic activity; but also, like Pound, he fills his poems with lines and fragments from the most heterogeneous sources. Incorporation of foreign matter is basically an ideogrammic act, Duncan's variant of the method, which he conceives of as collage. But it is, in a larger sense, a *projective* act, for Duncan includes among the objects of perception the forms and artistic wholes created by other writers, as was the case with Williams. For Duncan, composition by field means that the field contains all objects, both physical and mental; and their "use" by the poet is determined by the exigencies of the poet's particular view of this field. As Olson remarked, "Duncan never has any trouble stealing because he has a visional experience which prompts him to reach out for just what he knows he wants."[1] Taking the phrase from Gestalt psychology, Duncan defines the "field" of *composition by field* as "a geography of requiredness," which he expands to "a cosmos of requiredness." This field contains all objects the poet may apprehend as a whole, and poetic composition consists in working with these objects. In the process the poet may include or omit them—not in accordance with a subjective ordering or reordering, but with the way the various objects establish (or reject) relations between each other. The poet does not stand outside of but is part of the field. As Duncan explains,

> there is an immense difference between the context in which requiredness arises for the poem where the poet thinks of himself as a personality, or as a voice of the gods, or as a culture hero, or as a shamanistic culture traveler, or as a magician, and the poem that arises where the poet is taken to be a creative locality of the cosmos.[2]

Duncan refuses to impose a hierarchy on the objects in the field; they all coexist as forces whose energies are there to be tapped by the artist, whether they are flowers, streets, animals, or poems by Baudelaire or Blake.

The other unique characteristic of Duncan's versemaking, stemming from this vision of a total field, is its incorporating all possible poetic forms, projective as well as nonprojective. Duncan has been an ardent Poundian since the age of eighteen, and Olson's essay "Projective Verse" has had a profound effect on him—this despite the fact that he has never stopped writing in traditional forms. His open sequences, "Structure of Rime," and, even more, the series called "Passages" show the novel application of the ideogrammic method and composition by field. Yet Duncan, who has shown himself a master of closed form even in his early work (as witnessed by the collection *The Years as Catches*), has never disowned his nonprojective past. He in fact continues to write in what Olson would call "imposed" form. But for

Duncan even the traditional meters and rhymes are not "imposed"; for him the field is absolute, and that is why he rejects Olson's division of projective and nonprojective:

> I want to keep the whole thing going, so although I'm not going to take Charles's alternatives, I'm not going to take closed form versus the open form because I want both, and I'll make open forms that have closed forms in them and closed forms that are open. . . . I really do not work on a positive-negative yes-no system . . . because here I think there is a field. And if there is a field of poetry, then this is all in one.[3]

For Duncan a division exists elsewhere, between what he termed *periodic* and *aperiodic* form. The former presents a poetic stance where the poet is outside the field and controls, or attempts to control, the apperceptual objects within it. Duncan calls the forms of control "conventional," "regular," or "periodic," in that they repeat the same structure again and again, as do the molecules of a crystal. The opposite is aperiodic structure, which does not seek to control but follows the processes of nature like the structures of organic matter in which atoms and molecules are part of a larger entity and yet play individual roles. Of course, aperiodic structure is what Olson's projective poems are built on, and this is how Duncan views *The Maximus Poems*, where "structure is not given but emerges from the cooperation of many events in syllable, in word, in phrase, to be satisfied only as their complex interrelations are fulfilled."[4]

But in Duncan's theory even a so-called traditional poem can assume aperiodic structure if it is achieved as an extension of the perceptions of the poet and not simply imposed beforehand. This seems to be a rather dubious point, for it is very difficult (and perhaps unprofitable) for the reader to try to determine whether the sestina or sonnet emerged *naturally* from the poet's content, or whether the content was made to fit it a priori. In any event, a closed form is a closed form, however the poet came by it. The interesting thing in Duncan's case is that in many instances a "sonnet" resembles a traditional sonnet only in name, and other examples of closed form, particularly quantitatively measured lines, always appear in juxtaposition with prose or lines shaped by Duncan's breath. There are also occasions when the particular field of the poem at hand *requires* the inclusion of rhyme and metre; so they are not imposed but are rather extensions of the content.

Duncan contends that certain attributes of poetic speech ought not to be discarded just because in the past they were made to serve and express an outmoded world view. Such devices—which include Duncan's frequent use of a rhapsodic, elegiac tone, a high rhetoric similar to Ginsberg's but eschewed by Williams and Olson—are employed by Duncan not simply for ironic contrast, but because they carry emotional values *as objects* in the "cosmos of requiredness." As Duncan says, "My Heraclitean feeling is that old feelings must be kept alive in the structure of what you do," so the "old rhetoric" may serve certain purposes if used projectively. In short, Duncan's poetics is dogmatic in that it will not abide any dogma, just as the universe appears to have the one fixed law that there are no fixed laws and that "all flows." Duncan has said he reads Heraclitus "all the time," and he envisages his aesthetic and practice along the lines of the all-encompassing vision of the philosopher:

> You find a cosmos that's perennial and that's destroyed—the law constantly *destroys* the law, which is not a dogma but a thing devouring itself and undoing itself, and you will find that in my poetry I undo my propositions.[5]

This constant undoing and renewal which Duncan sees operating in the universe is the basis of his own poetic process. The poet is a creative force within the cosmic order which flows ceaselessly in accordance with the law of plenitude, containing beings extinct, now alive, and beings to come. All beings or objects possess manifest form. They are all sovereign and unique, and since they are a vector and not inert, they compose a total field through their relations. The form and structure of the poetic field cannot be otherwise. So Duncan declares, "My concept of form is the co-inherence of all parts and all other parts . . . so a poem is discovering the actuality of the form it is anyway, it is the consciousness in its composition, the indwelling in and discovering the form that's there."[6] Thus in Duncan's rephrasing of the principle of projective verse, form is a discovery of content, an unfolding, a letting-appear. As he writes in *The Opening of the Field*, "There is no greater wrong / than to force the song." But Duncan's method goes beyond organicism. As James Mersmann noted,

> It not only claims that the poem unfolds according to its own law, but envisions a compatible cosmology in which it may do so. It is not the poem alone that must grow as freely as the plant: the life of the person, the state, the species, and indeed the cosmos itself follows a parallel law.[7]

This is the central law operating in all growing and co-inhering things in the cosmos, as insisted on by Fenollosa, and which the ideogrammic poets saw confirmed in archaic art and myth, as well as in contemporary science. Evidence of this cosmic view (*vision* would be more appropriate) can be found scattered in Duncan's writings. He most emphatically asserts it in his first serial poem, "The Structure of Rime," as the basis of his work in progress: "The structure of rime is in the rigorous trees repeated that take on the swirl visible of the coast winds and the outcroppings, the upraised and bared granites that define sentences of force and instrument."[8]

The Middle English spelling of "rime," carrying all connotations of the word, from the Anglo-Saxon *rim* ("number") to archaic Greek *rhythmos* ("measured motion") signifies the *being* of poetry as force within a field of force, identical in structure to an actual field of relations in nature—the trees as they are "shaped" by the wind, and as the wind in turn is formed by the configurations of the coastal crags. And in the same way, since the vector objects in nature draw in, transform, and emit power, they are "sentences," agent-verb-object continua, a language in which the "latent" law becomes manifest. The law is unnameable. So Duncan in the introduction to *Bending the Bow* calls it *It*, but *It* is only conceivable through the perceivable particulars of the world:

> *It* is striving to come into existence in these things, or, all striving to come into existence is It—in this realm of men's languages a poetry of all poetries, *grand collage*, I name It, having only the immediate event of words to speak for it. . . . The gnostics and magicians claim to know or would know Its real nature, which they believe to be miswritten or cryptically written in the text of the actual world. But Williams is right in his *no ideas but in things*; for It has only the actual universe in which to realize itself. We ourselves in our actuality, as the poem in its actuality, its thingness, are facts, factors, in which It makes Itself real.[9]

This remarkable statement, then—unifying Heraclitean, gnostic, pantheistic, nominalistic ideas and their modern (and modernist) equivalents—is the basis of Duncan's aesthetic. Essence and existence, phenomenon and noumenon coexist in an inseparable unity: *It* grows into the *grand collage* of the universe, and the *grand collage* manifests *It*. So the poem as collage is an enactment of the process and structure of that universal juxtaposition.

Duncan's aim, like Pound's and the ideogrammic poets', is revelation: "We do not make things meaningful," he wrote, "but in our making we work towards an awareness of meaning; poetry reveals itself to us as we obey the orders that appear in our work."[10] This obedience at the same time also means the freedom to utilize all points in the field of language according to the poem's "cosmos of requiredness."

Duncan's syncretism has been called eclecticism and obscurantism that results in a field of hieroglyphs which is all but undecipherable. He has repeatedly stressed the opposite: for him a poem "is not a field of the irrational, but a field of ratios in which events appear in language." True, he believes that a poem is "an occult document, a body awaiting vivisection, analysis, X-rays," but this simply means that the poem, like the Chinese or Egyptian characters, is a shorthand script of the processes of nature, fused into compactness by the poet's perceptions. It is for this reason that he links his own method and that of the projective poets with Pound's poetics: "We see the importance of the ideogram for Pound, for it is his route towards that 'pictographic script'—the *condensare* of the dream or poem." And in a revealing note to Charles Olson: "And we've, both of us, got Grandpa [i.e., Pound] to thank for our way station of the ideogram."[11] He stated this significant point even more fully in his essay on "Grandpa." Pound, he wrote,

> remains for me a primary—the master of his craft, yes; but also, in the art at large the creator of a mode, projecting beyond his work new considerations of the meaning of form (as, indeed, our idea of sidereal orders, of cosmos, is no longer that of a creation by paradigm but of a creation in process, and our own experience thereof an ideogram).[12]

Such statements reveal, beyond the confirmation of the tradition and the significance of that tradition in which Duncan continues to work, that he is not interested in chaos and disintegration of form. Rather, he proposes *true form*: obeying the process by which elements join and separate as components of a mobile, taking part in a multiplicity of linguistic and spiritual relationships.

Duncan's collage technique, extending from his vision of the *grand collage* and from Pound's ideograms, is reinforced by his interest in modern art, in cubist and surrealist collage, and by the specific influence of the San Francisco artist Jess Collins, Duncan's companion since 1951. Jess (for he exhibits and publishes under his first name only) has expanded (and if possible, improved upon) the collage method of Max Ernst, particularly Ernst's "novels," in which segments from catalogues, magazines, and newspapers are "seamlessly" pasted together to make a completely new composition. In his compositions Jess also makes use of all possible art techniques and media: photographs, crayon drawings, lithographs, oil, and actual three-dimensional objects are juxtaposed, so that all of them together create a new field of vision and enigmatic associations. Duncan has written a number of prefaces to Jess's "picture books," the most significant being his introduction "Iconographical Extensions" to Jess's *Translation*.[13] The essay is as much about Jess's aesthetic as it is about Duncan's own. The pictorial objects are "translations" from their original contexts. They, with other "translations," participate in a new whole, yet they still retain vestiges of their primary locus. As Duncan writes, "Translation leads to and from translation. But there are no established orders here, every order in the order of another order appears significantly disordered." Emblems, hieroglyphs, images, and symbols appear "thrown together" in the visual (or linguistic) field, "giving rise to possibilities in relationship of continuity and discontinuity." Jess's view of his art shows striking resemblance to Fenollosa's theory of the picture as the dynamic interaction of colors, where all colors are cause and all effect. As Jess puts it, "Every point of color is autonomous, but still it is within the total relationship, the total network of color." Contemporary painters aim at an intensity of color; in contrast, Jess says that he is "concerned not with the intensity but with the identity of the color in the total; it may be intense, but it may be dim or ambiguous, seeming to change in relationships with different other points of color." It is the unique individual qualities of the particulars in their mutual interlockings and separations that "make" the picture what it is; this co-inherence is its "meaning."

Duncan's serial collage poems show a similar aesthetic intention. As an ideogrammic artist he is not concerned with meaning as such, for "making things meaningful" in a poem is prompted by a "humanist" arrogance alien to his mode of seeing the world and the function of the poet in it. "The order man may contrive or impose upon the things about him," he writes, "or upon his own language is trivial beside the divine order or natural order he may discover in them."[14] The parts of "The Structure of Rime" are such discoveries of the matter of which they are made, the poetic-linguistic realizations carrying in their form the shapes of the perceptions. The entire sequence is about writing, about language and the presence of the language-maker *within* language, and their metamorphic relations. In Part I Duncan announces the theme of his journey, much as Pound did in Canto I and Zukofsky in *"A"*-1:

> I ask the unyielding Sentence that shows itself forth
> in the language as I make it,
>   Speak! For I name myself your master, who come to serve.
>   Writing is first a search in obedience.[15]

The poet thus submits his creative will to the law of *It* implicit in the *grand collage* of language and of the world. His "shaping" is not a selfish imposition or distortion but a loving enactment of *It*.

In the twenty-five parts of the poem Duncan evokes "the Master of Rime" in various guises ("Outrider," "Lion," "Fish," primitive kings and gods)—all manifestations of *It*. Each is filled out according to the particular field of requiredness. In Part III Duncan addresses the "Glare-eyed Challenger! serpent-skin-coated / accumulus of my days! / Swung in your arms, I grow old." The image of the Challenger is ambiguous; it is at once a snake-like apparition and a protector. From the two elements of the third line grows a new perception of the speaker: "The numbers swing me." The phrase also recalls the "days" of the second line, so that he is no longer "swung" by the Challenger but by its aspect: time, the "dervish-invisible" of the second stanza. The final query of the stanza ("My time is up?") echoes faintly the laconic statement of the first ("I grow old"). The speaker's own time-bound fate immediately focuses upon the unit which is all about him, without which he is not a full being: his activity as a creative force within the larger field of time. So he begins the third stanza, "Period by period the sentences are bound," by the same law which binds him. The apposition of this line to the previous ones is not logical but perceptual. It does not "follow" from them, but from the particular position of the speaker involved in his own area of requiredness. In the next two lines of the third stanza it is the fate of his sentences that engages his attention, again in relation to time. They are seen as "Fragments delivered up / to what celestial timekeeper?"

With the fourth stanza a new phase begins, signified by a change in tense. In it the snake reappears in its reality, viewed objectively, in total contrast to the first-person ejaculations of the first three stanzas. The serpent's color is orange; it "spread its hood, cobra-wise." "Wise" is being used in a double sense, for the snake accepts its "fate" as bound by nature, and even though it knows its brilliant color will not hold, it relies on the recuperative powers of the process—for "Summer advances / preparing new orange." The cobra-wisdom is at once contrasted with its human equivalent in the next three lines: "The human hood spread orange in time, / fixation of relentless color / —character, scaly-feathered presumption." The "hood" of the human ego attempts to extend beyond nature's boundaries; it is colored by its own presumption, in attempting to fix itself as permanent, above the other particles in the universe's grand design. However, it is in truth one unit among the many, and like them, "scaly-feathered."

The following section deals with the actuality of the human body as the speaker looks at himself in the mirror after a shower. The mirror "shows the body spreading, orange in time." It is not outside the law but in fact the incarnation of *It*, a revelation of the speaker's own process. It is the body and its "accumulations" (recalling the "accumulus" of the first stanza) that the speaker brings up to his time, shedding the false color of presumption, "whatever the pretense," "to this / rearing up / this / snake stance." In the end the speaker identifies with the "wise" creature of nature. His stance is "snake stance," and the more or less regularly spaced lines of the earlier parts accordingly metamorphose into "projective" ordering, based on the poet's breath and on the extension of his physiology. The last line swings back to the first one: the "Challenger" is also the body, his own physical being, just as it is the image of poetry as well as the reality of the snake.

Duncan's collages show an affinity with Pound's isomorphic ideograms, and there are devices reminiscent of Zukofsky's verbal echoes and reverberations as well as Olson's and Williams's heaping up of perceptual data. It is a unique feature of "The Structure of Rime" and of his other open-sequence work, "Passages," that the different parts, though numbered in order, do not appear consecutively in separate volumes, as do *The Cantos*, *Paterson*, or *The Maximus Poems*. Rather, they are dispersed in various books among other poems ("The Structure of Rime," for instance, spreads over three books, *The Opening of the Field*, *Roots and Branches*, and *Bending the Bow*). With this device Duncan wishes to underline the fact that these serial works are not "wholes"; they are fragments, meeting points in a process which is larger than any subjective ordering, and the junctures of the parts with other poems not belonging to the series are just as significant as their juxtapositions with each other. He *could* of course put the parts in regular sequence, but it is not a question of will in Duncan's case, a will made subservient to reason. If will enters into it at all, it is the will to discover the process in its disjointedness and in its unyielding reality; it is the will to assume a "snake stance" instead. For this reason, as A. K. Weatherhead notes, Duncan "will not write the perfect lyric, but must corrupt the linear melody for the strategy of the collage, break up the unity with elements recalcitrant and untamed."[16] Whether the correct term is "corrupt" is open to questions. At any rate Duncan himself would disapprove of it, for in his poetics it is precisely the linear logic, the "reaching after facts and reason" which corrupts the objects and events that the poem by its very function is called upon to enact. The design is never preordained by the poet, but is achieved by the accumulation of particulars in a field according to their own inner and outer reality.

"Passages," begun in *Bending the Bow* and continued in *Tribunals*, is Duncan's most ambitious undertaking, comparable to *The Cantos* in its scope and invention. In its structure it is even more aperiodic than "The Structure of Rime," and as the poem progresses, it draws in an ever increasing conglomeration of detail. As Duncan writes in Passages 33, "Not one but many energies shape the field. It is a vortex." Words, images, signs, and phrases are continually mixed, joined, and separated to bring about a multiplicity of active relations. For example, in Passages 6, titled "The Collage," process is enacted as process, each potent element touching and igniting the rest, stopping only when the content requires a stop, the naming of the source: "the life-door, the cunt."

Adjoining to this first "passage," there is a brief interpretation, as in Williams's *Kora in Hell*, but it is also poetry in its own right, taking farther the content it explicates. The theme of initiation, only hinted at in the first part, is taken up in the following section, juxtaposed to a slightly altered version of Heraclitus's fragment, in Duncan's words, "The way below is the way above." The poet, the poem, the reader's perceptions advance together as the particles of the poem gradually establish their unified field, as "the body of the poem" becomes "aroused."

The bold period employed by Duncan throughout the poem is a sign calling for extended pause, which Duncan explains in the introduction as "a beat syncopating the time at rest; as if there were a stress in silence." In the next part the poet's intentions emerge in their form. His concern is to bend the parts of speech (consonants, vowels) "to imitate juices, excretions, the body's / spit." A picture of a building block appears, this time with the letter "E," "for elephant," as on a child's toy. Duncan thus takes up again and reinforces the collage technique introduced in the beginning. The final section enters into the tripartite reality of the poem, "the language, the sea, the

body," of which it is made. The three active elements converge and inter-
mingle with each other. The body of the poet, moving among the particulars
of nature's *grand collage*, enacts both itself and nature's interactions via the
collage of language.

Duncan's collage ideograms are not strictly cumulative, contrastive, fugal,
or overlapping, though they contain traces and elements of each. They are
cyclical or rather *spherical*, each point within the global field faintly or strongly connected to every other. The final part of a "passage" often returns to
the first part (as in Passages 5, 11, 13), not in the same form, but showing its
usage and the signs of its journey. Duncan began and continues his voyage
with and through "Passages" without following any preconceived plan. He
is fully aware of his ideogrammic predecessors and the fate of their work: for
even though Pound envisaged a long poem of "some one hundred cantos,"
and Williams planned *Paterson* to have only four books, neither of them could
terminate their projects according to a preconceived design. Duncan in his
ongoing "Passages" remains faithful to the epigraph he has chosen for his
poem, a passage from a hymn by the Emperor Julian: "For the even is
bounded, but the uneven is without bounds and there is no way through or
out of it." The only way out is through death. But while the poet is still a
creative "bundle of functions" within the larger creative force field of the
grand collage, he will continue to delight in his senses, in the voyage of
discovery he has undertaken, registering the areas of his discovery as he
comes upon them, even if they seem jumbled, thrown-together, or out of
order. For his experience tells him that "all orders have their justification
finally in an order of orders only our faith as we work addresses."[17]

Duncan is fairly secure in this faith; consequently he is mainly interested
in moving ahead into uncharted regions of reality, language, and poetry,
without relying on the compass of rationality. In his method the process is re-
created, the process which is experimental, unlimited, and not subject to
human logic. So Duncan affirms: "Praise then the interruption of our com-
posure, the image that comes to fit we cannot account for, the juncture in the
music that appears discordant."[18] The chasms, shifts, enigmatic juxtapositions, silences, and disharmonies of Duncan's method are not willfully
directed against "reason" in the name of "unreason." Their requiredness
arises from the topography the voyager traverses.

In the external appearance of the poems, typography follows topography.
"With 'Passages,' " says Duncan, "I have come more and more to feel my
original writing of the poem in my notebooks as a sketch, . . . a preliminary
version subject to new developments when I come to work with the typewriter and its own special spacings and relationships on the page."[19] A
similar concern is paramount in the writing of Robert Creeley, though in his
case the purely pictorial can never obscure the basically oral intention. As
Creeley writes, "The typographical context of poetry is still simply the issue

of how to score—in the musical sense to indicate how I want the poem to be read.''[20] The actual circumstances, the physical dimensions of the poet's surroundings, however, play an unusually important role in the way the poem grows and gets written. Unlike Duncan, Creeley uses no diaries and notebooks but composes directly on the typewriter; though he uses only two fingers, his typing speed approximates the speed with which he speaks. Creeley's very strict writing habits came about through force of circumstance, which were later entrenched and perpetuated by Creeley himself. Creeley felt confined by the room where he wrote, and further confined by the limits of the actual page, the $8^{1}/_{2}$-by-11-inch yellow sheet he used for his writing. In consequence, the Creeley poem is brief, made up of short lines and short phrases; it rarely extends beyond one page. Creeley can write only in almost total isolation; the poems, like their maker, are closed-in, withdrawn, inhibited. The poet bastions himself off from external intrusion of any kind that might disturb his concentration, and this self-imposed confinement leaves its mark on the poem. As Creeley says,

> . . . when you've got the fort, like all the guns mounted and ready to blast until you're utterly safe, and you let out this little, agonized thing . . . it skips around the room, you know, and you're embarrassed, you hear someone move in the kitchen, think O my God they're *coming* . . . no wonder the poems are so short! I'm amazed that there are any at all.[21]

In spite of the restrictiveness of such working conditions, Creeley insists that it is imperative for him to secure a "congenial physical context" in which to work, for such contexts directly bear on the kind of poems he will be able to produce. Some critics object that Creeley's poetic method is projective on the surface only: in reality, it is extremely self-conscious, resulting in a form which is more "closed" than a sonnet or a minuet. The distinction to be made, however, is that Creeley's final form never originates in a prior imposition of closed form. His creation of a safe environment *is* a self-conscious act, but it is set up so that the poet may escape from self-consciousness in the act of writing. And whatever confinedness or coercion the reader may sense in the Creeley poem stems not from a predetermined closed form but from the locus—the "space"—of the writing itself. "I am not anticipating any content before it occurs," says Creeley;[22] and neither is he anticipating any form for the particulars of his contents except as shaped by their own movements and requirements and as given by the poet's "physical context." The addition of the latter and the dependence on it of the poem's form is the peculiar quality of Creeley's verse, though as he slowly discards the remnants of his New England upbringing, he is coming to rely less and less on the cramping though necessary "fort" of his contexts. In *Pieces* he abandons the regularly iterated two- and three-line stanzas which characterize his early poems for a much looser and less austere form which corresponds more faithfully to the reality of the objects perceived and to the poet's emotions.

Creeley's projective poetry, prior to *Pieces*, demonstrates a different attitude, a markedly contrary tendency and activity from the practice of Olson, and particularly of Duncan. As opposed to the *inclusiveness* of these poets—their belief that the poetic field by its nature may contain everything within the poet's perceptual field—Creeley's method has rather been *exclusive*. His writing is an act of delimiting the field by a scrupulous selectiveness. Yet the apparent sparseness and rigor does not lead to a closed, traditional writing. In Creeley's sense it is *free* composition, in accordance with his own idea of freedom, and he explains his own *vers libre* in this manner:

> If one thinks of the literal root of the word verse, "a line, furrow, turning—vertere, to turn," he will come to a sense of "free verse" as that instance of writing in poetry which "turns" upon an occasion intimate with, in fact, the issue of, its own nature rather than to an abstract decision of "form" taken from a prior instance.[23]   •

He has further clarified his writing by a revealing analogy to driving: "The road, as it were, is creating itself momently on one's attention to it, there, visibly, in front of the car. There is no reason it should go on forever, and if one does so assume it, it very often disappears all too actually."[24] Thus for Creeley the experience of writing is not involved in an unlimited field extending in all directions; it is more like a finite road, with its own tortuous bends, hairpin curves, or occasional straight laps. Creeley's "turnings" from word to word and line to line in the poem follow the road of his perceptions. As Warren Tallman writes, "When Creeley crosses over into the writing world he continues to move just as in the everyday world, one step, street, or party at a time," but at his own speed and in his own fashion, so that in the finished poem the reader experiences "a checked stride, a containment or build-up of whatever energy is involved, emotional, perceptional, or intellectual."[25] For him poems are "intense seizures," "absolutely centered," and as soon as the particular "center" has exhausted its own potential, the poem is finished and the road has come to its end. Creeley's poetic practice may thus be labeled "minimalist," as Joyce Carol Oates describes it, a process of "ascetic" elimination of matter from his "imagined landscape."[26] But it is minimalist in the sense that Pound understood poetic composition ("Dichten = Condensare"), and as understood by both objectivist and projective poets. The method of the ideogram is *eo ipso* based on condensation. And even though in Creeley's case his own "physical context" is determinative as to how he proceeds on his "road" toward the poem, he follows no prescribed route, given either by others or his own will or intellect. "I am more interested," he wrote, "in what is *given* to me to write apart from what I might intend."[27]

The reality of the given world is very much at the core of Creeley's poetic activity, centering in the belief, shared by all ideogrammic poets, that "one proceeds from the immediate and particular—this is where the universal is to be embodied, if anywhere."[28] He considers himself squarely in the modernist tradition, the primary source of which he sees to be Pound and his ideogrammic method. He values Pound as the originator of a *form* of poetry, a kind of artistic *doing* which Pound himself could only partially exploit. And he compares Pound's impact to that of Chaucer for his "setting a mode in the technical performance of the craft that stays for all the time subsequent." Creeley is strongly cognizant of the continuity of Pound's influence. In answering an interviewer's question, whether he feels the modernist movement has "broken down," Creeley said that even though the poetry between the two wars was antimodernist, tending to "block off, not to smother but to cover" the actual tradition, it was still kept alive by Zukofsky, Reznikoff, and Oppen, just as the work of the projective poets, as well as the Beats, constitute a new development of the kind of poetry initiated by Pound. So, in effect, says Creeley, "the continuity is there, suffers no break, keeps going."[29] Creeley also admits the decisive influence on his own poetics of Olson, Duncan, and Ginsberg, all three in some way responsible for a widening of the horizons of his poetic field, his breaking into a more open projective composition.

Creeley's first attempt at serial writing resulted not in a poem but a novel, *The Island*. Though he subjected the procedure of the writing, its economics, to certain limitations (five pages to a chapter, five chapters to each part, four parts to the entire novel), he likened these limits to a painter's buying a "particular size canvas," and the method he followed had little consideration for plot, character development, or unified action. He was more interested in a form which "could go on," an enlarged context in which the materials would direct and organize themselves. It was the problematic of phasing and balance which intrigued him, not to write a book "about" life. "The novel isn't so much *about* life," he said. "Either it's manifestation of the possibilities of life, either it's life itself, or else it's something that I certainly don't want to carry like baggage along with me."[30] The method itself he saw in terms of the montage technique of the cinema, where the "phasing of the relation of images" is juxtaposed in a one-two, one-two-three, etc. sequence until the pattern of the different takes achieves the intended effect. The reality of his "physical context" obviated the necessity of falling back on traditional novelistic devices. It in fact released the energies that would have been bogged down in any formal exercise. Creeley simply went ahead and wrote sequences of "takes," and forgot that he was writing a novel. But then as he got deeper and deeper into it, he reached a stage where he began to experience the "interworking" of his takes. And when the book was done and he read it through, he was amazed to find that it had "all this interweaving" which he had not intended but which came about by the relations of the particulars he juxtaposed.

This respect for the actual shows throughout Creeley's work, so that poetic form cannot be anything else than the realization of the actuality of each object in the field, or along the "road." His definition that form is nothing more than an extension of content, which became the cornerstone of projective verse via Olson, Creeley later modified to suggest an added emphasis on the active, dynamic aspect of the process: "Form is what happens." Any deviation from a respect for the individuality of an object leads to a blurring of its reality, and in this respect Creeley is as much an "antihumanist" as Olson is. "Even the most sympathetic ordering of human effects and intelligence leads to unavoidable assumptions," he said. The modern *anschauung* starts out from the reality of "one's quite literal being," which does not order things and their relations rationally, but in fact "denies any investment of reality prior to its fact."[31] It is for this reason, out of his reverence for the reality of things, that Creeley shrinks from abstractions and quotes approvingly Pound's statement: "Any tendency to abstract general statement is a greased slide." In his own words,

> *Abstract* means removed from its condition, removed from its own term—to drag away, literally, as with a tractor. That kind of abstraction I've always felt a great uneasiness about; but when the situation of something, be it emotion or actual potato, is left to exist in its own intensity and in its own organization, then I don't feel an abstraction is involved.[32]

This fidelity to the actual is akin to the "sincerity" of the objectivists, to Williams's "In the particular is the radiance,"[33] and to Olson's "Conception cannot be abstracted from doing."[34] It is perhaps needless to point out that in each of the poets the fidelity engenders different emotions and priorities, but the channeling of the emotions and perceptions toward form follows an analogous method.

Creeley realized that in order to be able to write a more open kind of poem, he would have to alter the context of his writing. He admits that he greatly admired Olson's and Duncan's works-in-progress (*The Maximus Poems* and "Passages") and was attracted by the possibilities and range of poetic statement that was available to them through their method. At the same time he was dissatisfied with the creative environment he had built for himself: "I really had a hunger for something that would give me a far more various emotional state, that is, the ability to enter it," and the method he naturally entered into was a kind of diary writing, somewhat similar to

Williams's method in *Kora in Hell*, though less improvisational. Still, Creeley says, "I simply let the writing continue almost as a journal might."[35] The accumulated "takes" of each day simply took their place chronologically in the flow of the larger context.

The poems are fragments, or pieces (hence the title given to the collection). *Pieces* is, in the words of one critic, "the record of the poet's consciousness and its interaction with the 'pieces' of the world around him."[36] Some of the pieces are extremely short, but at all times they are as faithful as Creeley could make them to the original experience, the actual detail of perception or vision. He separates the pieces of one day from those of another by three dots, and the individual pieces within one day by a single dot. Sometimes the daily compilation makes one ideogram, in others it extends over the accumulation of several days. In contrast to Duncan's method, echoes and references to previous images or perceptions are absent. It is as if Creeley is at all times concentrating on what is happening at the moment it is taking place, without looking back, without knitting the past events and objects into a map by a kind of intellectual hindsight. The reader's impressions are similar: each piece or group of pieces comes as a new and fresh experience, and only after a second or third reading (when the "terrain" has become familiar to us) do we see the interworking of the poetic particulars and their relations as a field. Even so, the compiled pieces are never "of a piece," just as the day may contain contrary or unexpected events, and yet they all still "belong" to the total reality of that one day. The only limitations Creeley accepts are the ones prescribed by nature—his own particular "space" where he actually is, and the limits of his physical being. He is less interested in imaginative categories than factual ones, and in this respect he is perhaps the most "puritanical" of all the ideogrammic poets. His imagination is firmly rooted in his specific space and in his body.

This does not mean a poverty of the imagination or a lack of insight, and even less does it mean a kind of resignation on Creeley's part to "copy" nature. His pieces are self-contained wholes like the segments of Oppen's series, yet they are not totally closed despite the sharpness of their contours. They project a portion of their energies to the succeeding piece, and that, in turn, to the next one, as the actual "pieces" in a day's series of events do. "Reality is continuous, not separable," says Creeley.[37] His pieces, and even the individual lines, sentences, and phrases composing them are "meeting points" of forces in a larger field. He states, "The sentence itself—as Fenollosa had proposed in *The Chinese Written Character as a Medium for Poetry*, and Olson reasserts, has become 'an exchange of force' in no way a 'completed thought,' since such 'completion' is impossible in the context of the real. . . ."[38] The pieces are not copies but condensed re-formations in language of ongoing sets of events and objects, the poet's attention being focused not on appearance but on transformation.

Here are the pieces of one day:

Having to—
what do I think
to say now.

Nothing but
comes and goes
in a moment.

Cup.
Bowl.
Saucer.
Full.

The way into the form,
the way out of the room—

The door, the hat,
the chair, the fact.

Sitting, waves on the beach,
or else, clouds in the sky,

a road, going by
cars, a truck, animals, in crowds.[39]

Each piece is a miniature process in itself, in each there is a movement
toward the fullness of facts and of reality. The poet begins with the conscious
imperative of "having to" impose his thoughts on the world, but he stops
himself, and accepts working with the materials of the world as they are
"given" to him. The second piece is a general statement of the brevity and
simplicity of objects interacting as functional parts in an event; by implication a poem must be such a metamorphosis of separate details into a coherent whole. The implication is materialized in the third piece, and the ef-
fective antithetical juxtaposition of "moving into" form and "moving out
of" a room throws light on the structural identity of both processes, a stepping into a larger context but through the reality of facts. A similar identity is

observed in the movement of waves, clouds, and objects on the road. They are each single phenomena, yet they tend toward a completeness and a fullness which is realized only momentarily and never absolutely. But the force is there since all these events and objects are not static but vectors. The pathways their forces cut may seem materially various, yet in reality they obey the same law.

In another group the pieces re-create occurrences somewhat differently:

> The car
> moving
> the hill
> down
> which yellow
> leaves
> light forms
> declare.

> .

> Car coughing moves with
> a jerked energy forward.

> .

> Sit. Eat
> a doughnut.

> Love's consistency
> favors me.

> .

> A big crow on the
> top of the tree's
> form more stripped
> with leaves gone
> overweights it.

The images are short "takes" of an action: the speaker (presumably) is driving a car up a hill; his attention is caught up by the noise the car makes; he arrives and eats; and then he looks out the window. But this is the surface only. The real action is highlighted by a single strong verb in each piece: the leaves on the hill *declare* light forms; the car *moves* with a jerked energy;

love's consistency *favors* the poet; the crow *overweights* the bare tree. These verbs function as the "language beyond metaphor" of Arnaut Daniel, as defined by Pound, functions. They are compressed "natural pictures," holding each piece together like magnets. Coming up the hill is "heavy going," but the leaves reveal (the meaning of "declare") a light form as they blanket the bulk of the hill; only the car is not deceived. By contrast, the absence of leaves on the tree makes even the crow seem heavy, "overweighting" the stripped branches. Amid these apparent inconsistencies of appearance and reality, presence and absence, the poet finds one secure ground in "love's consistency." This makes him a "favored" creature among all the other creatures of nature, for these latter have the capacity to interact, but only human beings can love. The pieces in the group, therefore, comprise a whole, not merely on the level of action but, more important, on account of the "beyond-metaphoric" inner action suffused in the verbs.

The components in the pieces and the larger units in *Pieces* are distinct, perceptual entities, but they invite the power of the imagination to bridge the gaps between them. The process always begins with an action, from a fidelity to the event-objects, whose images the poet carries over into language and thought. From these the "active transformation" can issue forth, a divination of universal truths and "meanings"—a revelation, "initial and eternal," as Creeley affirms. However modest the approach ("driving a car"), however persistent, even dogged, the fidelity to spatial and physiological contexts, Creeley's pieces still possess the capacity to point to a larger context beyond themselves. But as in Duncan's *grand collage*, the larger context exists only in the pieces and in their relation, for it (*It*) cannot be separated from them.

8. Ellipsis and Riprap: The Ideograms of Ginsberg and Snyder

Allen Ginsberg's early poetry, particularly his poem "Howl," has become synonymous with the Beat movement that included writers such as Jack Kerouac, Philip Lamantia, Gregory Corso, Philip Whalen, Michael Mc-Clure, and Gary Snyder. This stereotyping, partly the result of Ginsberg's public image of prophet and minstrel, has tended to obscure the artistry and serious theoretical foundation of his work, and, specifically, the impact of the Pound-Williams tradition of modernism on his poetic development.

Ginsberg started writing when he was still a high-school student in Paterson, New Jersey, and continued it as an undergraduate at Columbia. In college, he recalls, John Crowe Ransom and Allen Tate were the "supreme literary touchstones," but Ginsberg was not impressed. So he turned to imitating sixteenth- and seventeenth-century poets like Wyatt and Marvell. After his expulsion from Columbia he continued to write in this vein, and in 1948 sent a half-dozen of his poems to William Carlos Williams, who sent them back with the stern verdict, "In this mode, perfection is basic, and these are not perfect."[1] Then Ginsberg began to read Williams's poetry, and he tried to rearrange his lines as he saw them in Williams, according to emotional and breath patterns. He began to concentrate on "more detail, more minute particulars, less ideas, more things,—'icebox, cabinet, toasters, stove'—*presenting* material, rather than recombining symbols that I had appropriated from Yeats or Blake or Marvell."[2] The result pleased Williams, but the real turn in Ginsberg's poetry came when he *heard* Williams read for the first time at the Museum of Modern Art:

> I suddenly realized he [Williams] was hearing with raw ears. The sound, pure sound and rhythm—as it was spoken around him, and he was trying to adapt his poetry rhythms out of the actual talk rhythms he heard in the place that he was, rather than metronome or sing-song archaic literary rhythms he would hear in a place inside his head from having read other writings.[3]

He grasped that Williams's form was identical to his content; it *was* the content as it is uttered in daily life. The poem ("The Clouds") ended in mid-sentence, not as formally constructed poems do, but as a piece of conversation might end in reality. This was completely new and exhilarating to Ginsberg:

> . . . to arrive at a poetry that really means what it says, a poetry with a meaning which is identical with its form, with a rhythm identical with the arrangement of the words on the page, and the words on the page arranged identically with what you want to say and how you want to say it, was like a revelation of absolute common sense in my entire universe of complete bullshit.[4]

Ginsberg literally learned to speak as a poet from Williams, and his poems in *Empty Mirror*, published with Williams's foreword, attest to his amalgamation of Williams's lessons. But there is also another aspect to be noted there: Ginsberg is not proposing to merely reproduce faithfully what he observes; he aims at an imaginative transfusion of things, as can be seen in "A Poem on America." In this poem a seemingly photographic reproduction of industrial desolation is juxtaposed to an image from Dostoevski's *The Possessed*. The effect is not quite ideogrammic, for the poem begins with a "conclusion of fact," as Reznikoff would say, which in fact it would be the reader's task to arrive at after having meditated on the sequence of particulars. But the absence of logical connection between the lines "and dreamed of classical pictures" and "The alleys, the dye works" is an indication that Ginsberg was already on the lookout for nonlogical modes of poetic expression.

In the early 1950s the influences multiplied. Most important among them, pertaining to form, were Whitman, Kerouac, and the Japanese haiku. After having experimented with Williams's terse line patterns, Ginsberg turned his attention to the problem of how to sustain a long line in poetry without lapsing into prose. The example was Whitman's long line, ignored for more than a century as an uncontrolled and uncontrollable prosaic outpouring, and Ginsberg saw its potential as a vehicle that could carry his own "Hebraic-Melvillian bardic breath"—the kind of total expression he wanted to put in poetic form. Ginsberg's fastening on Whitman's line as a valid precedent was precipitated by the realization that his speech, his "breath," was different from Williams's; it was longer, more ecstatic and excited. Interestingly, breath length as organizer of the line came to him not from Olson but from Kerouac, who in turn was influenced by jazz musicians, particularly saxophone players like Lester Young and Charlie Parker. As Kerouac noted, the saxophone player, especially when improvising, is "drawing in a breath and blowing a phrase on his saxophone, till he runs out of breath, and when he does, his sentence, his statement's been made."[5] Similarly, Ginsberg's long lines in "Howl" and his other poems written in the middle and late fifties were organized according to his long breath, which became the unit for the line—"one physical and mental inspiration of thought contained in the elastic of breath."[6]

But the organization of the long line and breath, the "how" of sustaining it, came from a different source. Shortly before writing "Howl" Ginsberg read R. H. Blyth's collection of haikus and promptly began to compose in that form. He wrote some twenty-odd pieces in a brief period of time, only a few of which are successful. The majority are not strictly haiku but spontaneous juxtapositions, records of Ginsberg's actual flow of mind. The long line, then, is supported by seemingly incongruous, antithetical images:

> It is natural inspiration of the moment that keeps it moving, disparate thinks put down together, shorthand notations of visual imagery, juxtapositions of hydrogen jukebox—abstract *haikus* sustain the mystery and put iron poetry back into the line. . . .[7]

"Hydrogen jukebox" is a memorable image from "Howl," one of several elliptical juxtapositions which Ginsberg crammed into his lines in Part I—such as "stale beer afternoon," "unshaven rooms," "angry fix," and "heterosexual dollar." Just as Whitman's long line was an example of his own long breath, the haiku excited Ginsberg because in it he saw a precedent of his own naturally elliptical habits or patterns of speech. After his experiments with haiku and his own individual use of them in "Howl," he discovered that "all my talk is haiku"; that is, any conversation like "I need a spoon to eat soup" is "bridging Ellipse," filling up the gaps between essential facts with connectives, which he would normally omit from his hurried talk of telescoped, heaped-together perceptions. The study of the "primary forms of ellipse," Ginsberg concluded, is "useful for advancement of practice of western metaphor," toward a kind of "naked haiku" like his "hydrogen jukebox." Ginsberg's conception of "advancement" on metaphor can be seen from his description of his understanding of haiku:

> Haiku = objective images written down outside mind the result is inevitable mind sensation of relations. Never try to write of relations themselves, just the images which are all that can be written down on the subject.[8]

Ginsberg's phrase is clearly an echo of Fenollosa's "Relations are more important than the things they relate," which may also indicate the direction of his search: from metaphor toward ideogram, or, in his word, the "ellipse."

In feeling his way toward a theory of the ellipse, Ginsberg received corroboration of his experience with haiku from another source: the paintings of Paul Cézanne. As had Williams before him, Ginsberg noticed that in Cézanne's works visual structuring is not based on perspective—"it's just juxtaposition of one color against another color." So the idea came to him that "by the unexplainable, unexplained non-perspective line, that is, juxtaposition of one *word* against another, a *gap* between two words" would be created "which the mind would fill in with the sensation of experience."[9] While many of the ellipses in Part I of "Howl" are ironic in their incongruity (Plotinus, Poe, and St. John of the Cross are mentioned in the same breath with Kansas, Idaho with "visionary indian angels," Baltimore is seen gleaming in "supernatural ecstasy"), the elliptical juxtapositions of Part III are more arcane and the gaps between the images are wider. The rhetorical connectives "I'm with you in Rockland" are a form of parallelism, but they do not logically link up the lines. The images remain as they are, unrelated to one another, and they have relevance because the poet and Solomon are *related*. Ginsberg's imaginative juxtapositions are as condensed as those of Creeley, but of a different order. They are not scrupulous compressions of factual data taken from nature but, as Ginsberg says, "verbal constructions which express the true gaiety & excess of Freedom . . . by means of spontaneous irrational juxtaposition of sublimely related fact."[10] The juxtapositions in the above lines, and in several other places in "Howl," seem to be influenced less by Cézanne than by the method of the surrealists, and not so much the painters as the poets. During his "Howl" period Ginsberg was immersed in surrealist poetry and poetics, and saw Kerouac's advocation of spontaneity reinforced by the basic tenets of this important European literary movement. Spontaneity corresponded to the surrealists' automatic writing, and Ginsberg's juxtapositions of "hydrogen jukebox," "nitroglycerin shrieks," and "catatonic piano" are reminiscent of Eluard's *"nuit hermaphrodite"* and Breton's *"coqs de roche"* and *"revolver à cheveux blancs."* In "At Apollinaire's Grave" Ginsberg paid homage to the forefather of surrealism and acknowledged its influence:

> I've eaten the blue carrots you sent out of the grave and Van
>   Gogh's ear and maniac peyote of Artaud
> and will walk down the streets of New York in the black cloak of
>   French poetry.

Automatism meant a total disregard for logical and rational ordering of experience, because the experience the surrealists were interested in recording had to do with the inner, not the external, world. This setting a higher value on dreams, reveries, and hallucinations struck a sympathetic chord in Ginsberg because he was also interested in finding a way to re-create the unimpeded flow of his mind, and he experimented with various means of expanding consciousness by drugs, meditation, or mantra chanting. By releasing the forces of the unconscious he was attempting to reach a state of higher consciousness, or cosmic consciousness, an attainment of mystical illumination. Poetry, then, had to deal with the transmission of such spiritual/physical enlightenment, with what Kerouac termed "the unspeakable visions of the individual." The self is the center from which true knowledge is to emanate, and it is not difficult to see that Ginsberg took over from Whitman much more than the long line. Whitman had put his faith in the supremacy of the self, and poetry for him could not be anything else but "the outcropping of my own emotional and other personal nature, an attempt, from first to last, to put a *Person*, a human being (myself, in the latter half of the Nineteenth Century, in America) freely, fully, and truly on record."[11] Accordingly, Ginsberg saw the poet as prophet and visionary, and however he disordered his consciousness, and by whatever means, the sublime fact remained that it was *his* consciousness, and it was his duty to register its fluctuations.

Such a view of the function of poetry and poet obviously goes against the grain of Poundian modernism and the ideogrammic method proper. It is on these themes, the subjects of self and spontaneity, that the later ideogrammic poets show the greatest divergence from Pound's ideas, or, more precisely, his attitudes vis-à-vis Whitman and surrealism. Pound's ambivalence to Whitman is well known, and so is his coolness toward the surrealists, in spite of some initial enthusiasm. It is also a fact that this champion of all types of avant-garde artists had, in the 1930s and 1940s, begun to view with suspicion the work of even the greatest experimenters, such as James Joyce and Gertrude Stein. Because of his economic, political, and historical preoccupations during that period, Pound simply lost touch with contemporary currents in the arts—hence his oft-repeated lament to Olson during his confinement at St. Elizabeth's: "Thirty years behind the time."[12]

Yet the conceptual basis of surrealism is not markedly different from that of the ideogrammic stream in American poetry, and this accounts in part for the positive attitude of Williams, Duncan, and Ginsberg to the aims of the movement. One of these crucial notions is that the human being is not the apex of being in this, or any other, universe. As Breton put it in *Arcane 17*:

> En tête des erreurs initiales qui nous demeurent les plus préjudiciables figure l'idée que l'univers n'a de sens appréciable que pour l'homme, alors qu'il en manque, par exemple, pour les animaux. L'homme se targue d'être le grand élu de la création.[13]

> [At the top of the old delusions still with us and the most detrimental stands the notion that the universe has appreciable meaning only for man, while lacking any, for example, for animals. Man boasts of being the great elect of creation.]

Small wonder, then, that this essentially antihumanist attitude, coupled with the creative and imaginative freedom afforded by actual poetic practice, made surrealism attractive to Ginsberg.

But it is important to note that Ginsberg did not become a committed or dogmatic surrealist. In his search for a nonlogical, "elliptical" mode of expression, he utilized all possible manifestations of the form, whether found in haiku, Williams, Cézanne, or surrealism. Like Provence or Fenollosa for Pound, surrealism for Ginsberg had been just one area among many to be "dug up" and the findings integrated into the large process of discovering form, *his* form. And while his affinity to Whitman was genuine and pervasive, his beliefs in the self and the importance of the poetic personality were never held exclusive of other ideas. They were in fact continually complemented and balanced by his own brand of "sincerity and objectification," his concern for perceptual detail *outside* the subjective consciousness—the space of America and the material world. Ginsberg's poetics can actually be seen as an attempt at synthesis, at unifying the divergent traditions of American poetry, what Roy Harvey Pearce termed "Adamic" and "mythic." It is through the ellipse, his personal variant of the ideogrammic method, that Ginsberg sought to integrate self and space in a unified theory.

Absorbing and benefiting from the variety of nontransitional methods, Ginsberg in the 1960s arrived at his own poetics. He put them to use in an open sequence, begun in the volume *Planet News* and continued in *The Fall of America*. Ginsberg came to the realization that the mind is not all-powerful; it did not invent the world, but in fact it owes its being *to* the world. But by this same token the flow of consciousness cannot be essentially different from nature's flow, and if consciousness is permitted to stream forth unobstructed, it will realize both itself and the cosmos. Poetry, therefore, fulfills its function if it re-creates the mind's movement, which is no longer a law unto itself but a counterpart of the larger mind of nature. Poetry, Ginsberg affirmed, is "a Composition of Elements," the elements being discrete words, and words are "solid objects"; in the same way, "life itself is a composition of elements outside words." The mind does not think in rigid patterns, so artificial forms in poetry cannot be justified. "We think in blocks of sensation & images," said Ginsberg. Ginsberg's oft-quoted axiom follows from this: "IF THE POET'S MIND IS SHAPELY, HIS ART WILL BE SHAPELY." He goes on to explain that "the page will have an original but rhythmic shape —inevitable thought to inevitable thought, lines dropping inevitably on the page, making subtle infinitely varied rhythmic SHAPE."[14] Ginsberg does not elucidate further what he means by a "shapely" mind. One could perhaps say that in a dream or in a drug-induced state the mind still has a "shape," though quite different from the one it has when its attention is fastened on the particulars of the world. Shut off from the world, the mind feeds on itself, on its accumulated bits of reality which it rearranges just as subjectively as the purely rational mind does: both reorder the world in their own image. Ginsberg in his syncretic theory attempts to avoid the pitfalls of either. He does not relegate poetry to a kind of substitute therapy, and whatever evidence of such use there may have been in "Howl" and "Kaddish," they are definitely not present in his long poem *The Fall of America*.

The mind acquires its particular shapeliness in that sequence from the variegated shapes and turns and breaks of American reality, both spatial and temporal, and from its own relation to that space-time entity, a relation which is not just physical but moral as well. The form arises from this relationship; it is an open, ideogrammic, or projective form, the basis of which Ginsberg clarified for himself well before he started writing the poem, during his trip to India. This basic statement on form he put down in *Indian Journals*:

> Interest in the awkwardness
> accidents
> rhythm
> jump of perception from one thing to another breaking
> syntactical order
> punctuation order
> logical orders
> old narrative order
> meaning order.
> Notations of process of mind
> & relative natural process
> Uncensored by
> grammar
> syntax
> order
> because these Conventions
> we find not a
> rational ordering of
> experience
> but an attempt to
> censor experience
> & keep out certain
> facts which embarrass
> & throw doubt on
> whole of previously
> accepted
> Human
> Humanistic
> rational
> Reality.[15]

The poem is thus a union of "mind flow" and the *relative* natural process, "with space jumps to indicate gaps & relationships." *The Fall of America*, subtitled "Poems of These States," is not the record of a mental trip, but of actual criss-crossings of the entire continent. In these poems Ginsberg goes beyond the "hydrogen jukebox" type of elliptical juxtaposition. As in *The*

Cantos and *Paterson*, larger blocks of material, ostensibly unrelated, are placed side by side to enact the complex reality of America.

Ginsberg had read some of Pound's poetry before embarking on his long journey, and, as he later said, for his own elliptical method he was "drawing from Pound's discovery and interpretation of Chinese," both through Williams and Pound himself. During a side trip to Europe in 1967 he visited Pound and spent several days with the aged poet, who was already sunk in a deep depression and a silence he rarely broke. Ginsberg was undaunted, however, and told Pound that his perceptions had been "strengthened by the series of practical exact language models scattered through *The Cantos* like stepping stones."[16] His own long poem, which he continued with renewed vigor after his meeting with Pound, is an epic in the vein of *The Cantos*, "a poem containing history," of which Ginsberg was already conscious in 1967. He had said in an earlier interview that in the fabric of his poem he wanted to include

> all contemporary history, newspaper headlines and all the pop art of Stalinism and Hitler and Johnson and Kennedy and Vietnam and Congo and Lumumba and South Africa and Sacco and Vanzetti —whatever floated into one's personal field of consciousness and contact. And then compose like a basket—like weave a basket, basket-weaving out of all those materials.[17]

In order to be even more faithful to "mind-flow," Ginsberg in some of the poems composed directly and spontaneously not on the typewriter but on the tape recorder, signaling the end of a breath-perception unit with a click on the microphone for transcription of the poem onto the page. The "basket-weaving" is the abrupt juxtaposition of (1) perceptions—newspaper and radio reports put down either verbatim or compacted by Ginsberg; (2) related mental associations—memories and spontaneous responses answering or advancing the external material; (3) observational detail of immediate happenings during the journey, to fix the floating of the mind to the actuality and specificity of space. The various elliptical passages make up incidental, not consciously pre-planned, ideograms or groups of related units around a central theme and place which touch and overlap in the manner of Williams's juxtapositions in *Paterson*. Yet Ginsberg did not abandon his compressed elliptical juxtapositions of seemingly incompatible material, particularly adjective-noun pairs or series of adjectives. But instead of simply baffling the reader's mind, these juxtapositions are now made to function like sudden electrical discharges, jolting the mind to grasp relations where there seemed to be none before, or which were obscure until Ginsberg's projective act illuminated them.

In "Wichita Vortex Sutra," perhaps the most important among the "Poems of These States," the second part is a huge ideogram of language, its use and abuse in America during the Vietnam war. It begins with Ginsberg's sitting in the car, as it moves through the bleak winter scenery of the Kansas prairie, and taking down images of the passing landscape. These images are interspersed with his running commentary on the language of government dispatches, television news reports, magazine articles, and the declarations of the president, senators, and generals. Certain elements are repeated, at times rhythmically, at other times unexpectedly, in a new and different context. One such recurring element is Defense Secretary McNamara's "bad guess" as to who the *real* enemy is in Vietnam.

The other fact which reappears in various places in the poem is the number of Viet Cong losses per month as announced by the U.S. government. Ginsberg first presents it in the context of the manipulated media:

> Put it this way on the radio
> Put it this way in television language
> > Use the words
> > language language:
> > "A bad guess"
>
> . . . .
>
> Put it *this* way
> > Declared McNamara   speaking language
> > Asserted Maxwell Taylor
> > General, Consultant to the White House
> Vietcong losses leveling up three five zero sero
> > per month
>
> . . . .
>
> the latest quotation in the human meat market—
> > Father I cannot tell a lie!

Set among the other headlines, General Taylor's assertion is just another piece of news, but this added unit is not merely cumulative or contrastive—it is both. Washington's apocryphal statement at the end of the section is at once ironic and antithetical to the previous linguistic abuse, and it is also Ginsberg's own declaration of poetic truth-telling. By inference it is he who carries on and embodies the ideals of the founding fathers. The "father" he calls on, though, is not Washington, but Whitman, the author of *Democratic Vistas*, the "national expresser" of "adhesiveness," of "fervid comradeship." (The epigraph to *The Fall of America* is an extended quotation from *Democratic Vistas*.)

Washington's words are later echoed by the seemingly unequivocal statement of another president: "We will negotiate anywhere anytime," to which Ginsberg juxtaposes a newspaper report based on an Associated Press dispatch to the effect that the Americans do not encourage the South

Vietnamese to negotiate with the Viet Cong. "The last week's paper is Amnesia," comments Ginsberg, and in contrast to the mendacities and travesties of language he builds another section containing a different regard for language:

> Headline language poetry, nine decades after Democratic
> Vistas
>   and the prophecy of the Good Grey Poet
> . . . .
>
>   Ezra Pound the Chinese Written Character for truth
>   defined as man standing by his word. . . .

Whitman, Pound, Fenollosa, and the Chinese word for truth are Ginsberg's "ideogram of the good," which is "different from a bad guess," the "black magic" of the manipulators and distorters of language. The intrusion of the line, "Ham Steak please waitress," has a double-edged quality. It serves to pinpoint the actual circumstance, the "space" where the poet "lives" his imaginative particulars. But it is also a reminder of Ginsberg's position in the larger framework of American reality: he, the Buddhist, the advocate of vegetarianism, is caught up in the world-wide slaughter and eats not merely meat but, as he knows, the flesh of once-alive fellow creatures. In spite of his heightened moral sense he is not above the flow of the present, of the space and time of history. He is in it and of it, exerting his poetic force in the force field of language.

Ginsberg's synthesizing act in language enacts the parallel progress of individual consciousness and universal consciousness through the method of the ellipse. He knows that elliptical or paratactic composition is not an enemy of continuity but in fact a *real* way in which the ongoing process can be re-created and revealed. The contingent aspect of elliptical poetry, as in the Homeric and all other archaic poems, is its oral dimension, and one of Ginsberg's preoccupations has always been to bring to fruition Pound's ideas about the unity of words and music. Most of the ideogrammic poetry is written for the human voice and not for the eye, for silent reading. But Ginsberg's lines, as they come fully formed by his own voice during oral composition, are made to be chanted and even sung. In his work subsequent to *The Fall of America*, he has even experimented with writing songs, mainly influenced by the blues and Bob Dylan's compositions. With Ginsberg's poetics and oral-elliptical method the ancient art of poetry comes full circle. His works are at once the synthesis of ideogrammic modernism and Whitman's heritage, and a revival of the archaic oral tradition within the context of authentic, modern poetic expression.

A different cycle is completed in the poetry of another "Beat," Gary

Snyder, and on more than one level. Of all the poets who have maintained and carried forward the kind of modernism Pound initiated, Snyder is the one who has returned, both in the mental as well as the physical sense, to the Orient, that important source which, through Fenollosa, furnished Pound with the concept of a new creative method. The archaic has been a determining factor in the poetics and practice of all ideogrammic poets, but it is Gary Snyder who has not only adopted and revitalized archaic modes of expression, but refashioned his thinking and life-style to such an extent that they all but exclude *in toto* the values and achievements of Western civilization. He has taken Olson's "archeology of morning" one step further: Snyder not only writes and feels and thinks, but actually *lives* as if he existed after a true "dispersion," as if the whole of Western culture and way of life had already crumbled to dust. The "space" of America for him is "Turtle Island," the ancient Indian name for the continent, not expressible in the concentrated actuality of a Gloucester or a Paterson, but only as raw nature, the "wilderness." The community that alone is real to him is the group of people who live outside the norms and structures of postindustrial consumer society—the "tribe" of the new "primitives" living in harmony with nature. Within the nonhierarchic framework of the tribe the function of the poet is equivalent to the shaman, an essentially magical and heuristic activity. The shaman's unique ability gives form to archetypal strata of consciousness. Snyder defines shamanistic poetry as "the skilled and inspired use of the voice and language to embody rare and powerful states of mind that are in immediate origin personal to the singer, but at deep levels common to all who listen."[18] Such a poetic role stems from a vision which stands in complete opposition to the overbearing, rapacious, possessive kind of mentality which characterizes *homo technologicus*, and to the uncontrolled abuse and exploitation of nature and its resources. The vision demands a new (or postlogical) respect and love for nature, which Snyder calls "ecological conscience": "a new definition of humanism that would include the nonhuman." His poetry is the voice of this new "posthumanism," a revivification of discarded though enduring qualities and achievements:

> As poet I hold the most archaic values on earth. They go back to the late Paleolithic: the fertility of the soil; the magic of animals, the power-vision of solitude, the terrifying initiation and re-birth, the love and ecstasy of the dance, the common work of the tribe. I try to hold both history and wilderness in mind, that my poems may approach the true measure of things and stand against the unbalance and ignorance of our times.[19]

Snyder's archaism is far removed from an illusory, nostalgic "return to the soil." He is astute, sophisticated, learned, and much more. As Thomas

Parkinson puts it, "If there has been a San Francisco Renaissance, Snyder is its Renaissance man: scholar, woodsman, guru, artist, creatively maladjusted, accessible, open, and full of fun."[20] Other critics have called him the Thoreau of the Beat Generation, an influential force in the poetic community of the fifties and sixties, directing attention not only to sensible, ecology-conscious living but, through his first-hand study of Chinese and Japanese poetry, to poetic techniques best suited to embody the new consciousness. Not surprisingly, Snyder's models for composition included Pound and imagism, Fenollosa and the ideogram. But these influences have been supplemented by his direct study of oriental poetry (Snyder is fluent in Japanese and reads Chinese, and has spent several years in a Kyoto monastery studying Zen Buddhism). He has translated a good deal of poetry into English, chiefly from the work of the T'ang poet Han Shan and the modern Japanese poet Kenji Miyazawa—renderings which utilize and expand Pound's pioneering techniques in *Cathay* and *The Confucian Odes*.

Snyder—scholar, translator, *poeta doctus*—is an heir and continuator of modernism. In one critic's view, he "derives mainly from the Pound/Williams/Projectivist line," i.e., the ideogrammic tradition, and is "the subtlest craftsman of his generation."[21] Yet his method, his own version of ideogrammic composition, does not "derive" solely from his literary masters and predecessors. As with all the poets in the ideogrammic line, the method is equally the fruit of personal experiences and research. In Snyder's case, it characteristically comes from *work*, physical work, into which he threw himself with as much zest, concentration, and perseverance (he was a railroad brakeman, logger, and fire lookout, among others) as into his varied intellectual and artistic endeavors. The method was already at the base of his first published book of poems, *Riprap*, which Snyder has described vividly:

> *Riprap* is really a class of poems I wrote under the influence of the geology of the Sierra Nevada and the daily trail-crew work of picking up and placing granite stones in tight cobble pattern on hard slab. "What are you doing?" I asked old Roy Marchbanks.—"Riprapping," he said. His selection of natural rocks was perfect—the result looked like dressed stone fitting to hair-edge cracks. Walking, climbing, placing with the hands. I tried writing poems of tough, simple, short words, with the complexity far beneath the surface texture. In part the line was influenced by the five and seven-character line Chinese poems I'd been reading, which work like sharp blows on the mind.[22]

In poetry, "riprapping" is the re-creation of an ongoing, ceaselessly unfolding movement of things and events, more correctly, "thing-events," an act of conscious and intuitive participation in the universal scheme of eternal change. The fitting together of perceptual blocks involves both a freedom and an order within which they arrange themselves. But it is an order not predesigned by the intellect—it comes into being from the requirements, the actual direction of energies in each objective particular as it presents itself to the senses. Neither does the imagination soar unbounded; it is held in check by the real presence of the material gathered by the senses. Snyder's method is a realization of process, and the process of riprapping is analogous to Creeley's method of driving. It is a form of proceeding which, as Robert Kern observed, means "moving freely through unknown territory so that not only the form but the very language of the journey will emerge directly from the 'rough terrain' encountered," as opposed to a kind of movement which is self-conscious and follows a prescribed pathway.[23] The very term "riprap" onomatopoeically and morphologically suggests the close juxtaposition of things which are at once different and similar. In certain of their material manifestations, in individual structure and substance they may show a distinct unlikeness to each other, yet they all infuse and diffuse energies according to natural law. The title poem of *Riprap* is Snyder's *ars poetica* where he imagistically sets out the characteristic features of his poetic method. In the poem Snyder makes a notable distinction: the act of riprapping is a laying down of words *before* the mind and not *after* the mind itself has laid down its own rules, a blueprint which the words are then subjected to follow. In other words, perceptual intake and imaginative rendering of the "riprap of things" precedes conceptualization. Actually, the poems do not only precede it but do not even attempt to reach it. Like the real objects in the world (Snyder prefers to call them "people": "Standing Tree People," "Flying Bird People," "Swimming Sea People"), the poems have no predetermined "meaning" or "idea"; they are "only" themselves in their own reality. They are like a road of riprapped stones upon which the "body of the mind" may begin its own journey.

As with all ideogrammic poets, and particularly the projectivists, Snyder does not set himself up as lord and master over the creative act. He does not "force" the song but follows what is "given" in a spirit of obedience. Not that he denigrates closed form, what he calls the "contrived" poem. But there the subjective mind of the maker is seen to be in control, arranging and ordering the particulars of experience and memory as *it* sees fit, taking its cue from a corresponding human metaphysic, an almost visible anthropomorphic cosmology. A poem thus contrived may be a source of pride and accomplishment, but for Snyder the "art" of poetry has an entirely different significance and one opposed to that of the closed poem:

> the pure imagination flow leaves one with a sense of gratitude and wonder, and no sense of "I did it"—only the Muse. *That* level of mind—the cool water—not intellect and not—(as romantics and after confusingly thought) fantasy-dream world or unconscious. This is just

the clear spring—it reflects all things but is of itself transparent. Hitting on it, one could try to trace it to the source; but that writes no poems and is in a sense ingratitude.[24]

Snyder's "Muse," "the clear spring" which lies underneath or behind things, is the same mysterious presence which Duncan named *It*. *It* is utterly real and alive, yet cannot be known, and it is in fact presumptuous of us to try and pursue it; for *It* is present and essentially embedded in all existent things. The poet can, and should, do no more than show forth the things themselves as they are perceived. Their unseen relations and interdependence allude to *It* without overt human meddling and interference. Snyder's poems are, of course, *human* works, but in and through them the poet does not want to either copy or outdo nature. He only sees that the "riprap" of the universe is in harmony. It is that harmony which he wants to re-create with the aid of natural yet specifically human resources in the "riprap" of his poems.

Snyder said, "The poems speak of place, and the energy-pathways that sustain life. Each living being is a swirl in the flow."[25] His humility and unassuming naturalness—his "snake-stance"—do not allow him to even interpret his perceptions. As a result, metaphors of any kind are seldom present in the poems, with the exception of the "language beyond metaphor," the compressed, suggestive verbs and the elliptical juxtapositions of adjectives and nouns like those employed by Ginsberg. The use of connectives is reduced to a minimum. In its unadorned, unpretentious simplicity and quick juxtapositions of natural data, the Snyder poem comes closest perhaps to the Fenollosian definition of the Chinese ideogram: "a vivid shorthand picture of the operations of nature." The emphasis is on *operations*, not on mere outward appearance, and on the poet's own indelible presence in the "swirl" of the living universe. And when Snyder stresses the merging of the human with the nonhuman flow of nature, even the frequently used strong and active verbs are dispensed with and are replaced by the more pliant gerund, suggesting a transcendence of human control. Strong transitive verbs Snyder usually reserves for the depiction of natural things in action. Many of Snyder's juxtapositions have at their basis the more fundamental opposition of, on the one hand, civilization, society, and the state, often symbolized by the city, and, on the other hand, forests, mountains, rocks, and animals, subsumed under the concept of wilderness, as in "Mid-August at Sourdough Mountain Lookout" in *Riprap*. At times this persistent dichotomy is presented objectively, but more often than not it is colored by Snyder's vigorous and committed partisanship.

After *Riprap* Snyder's poems assume an increasingly projectivist shape, with perception and breath setting the pattern of line length and position on the page. In the books *Myths & Texts*, *Regarding Wave*, *The Back Country*, and *Turtle Island*, the form is coextensive with the material. As Snyder comments,

"Each poem grows from an energy-mind-field-dance, and has its own inner grain."[26] The locus of "creation," as indicated by Snyder's paratactic compression of four words linked by hyphens, is a process: energy invades the mind, expands out into a field from which the poem, the dance of words, comes into being. At the same time, the poem itself contains within it all four elements, capable of releasing its dance of energies in the mind of the attentive reader. Though not on the scale of Duncan's almost limitless variety of form, Snyder has used different devices, changing and adapting them to suit his particulars to be expressed. Even strict oriental forms such as the haiku became in his hands singularly Snyderian, for the haiku, the basic ideogrammic form, conforms in structure to the "riprap" of things in nature, and is essentially an open, projective poem. Some of Snyder's best haiku are in a series written in that form, a record of travels playfully titled "Hitch Haiku."[27] All the poems are pieces of two, three, four, or five lines (Snyder naturally abandons the traditional number of lines and syllables of the Japanese haiku), and they capture concrete detail in the simplest language without commentary. As in haiku in general, what remains unsaid in these poems is just as important as the "luminous detail" the poet presents. As Snyder writes in *Earth House Hold*, "Form—leaving things out at the right spot / ellipse, is emptiness."

Elliptic juxtapositions patently dispense with logic. In Snyder's case, his studies in Zen Buddhism have strengthened his instinctive distrust of logic and abstract thinking. As exemplified by the Zen *koan*, or philosophical riddle, the mind is powerless to deal with the world through logic alone. Each *koan* (such as "What is the sound of one hand clapping?" "What was your face like before you were born?" or "When I hear I see, and when I see I hear") is a lesson on the limits of human reason. Snyder's statement that form is emptiness, is just such a *koan*. As a practicing Buddhist he has stepped beyond the pitfalls of assertion and negation, for he knows that in nature there is no negation. The essence and existence of the world is one and inseparable—a fundamental insight transported to the West by Fenollosa and shared by all ideogrammic poets. The paradoxes and nonsensical postulations of the *koan* are meditative devices to prod consciousness to recognize the true oneness of the universe. "The impasse in which 'Koans' place us," writes Robert Linssen in his seminal work *Living Zen*, "cannot be solved by the mind. Before the simultaneity of two contradictory affirmations—opposite but complementary facets of a more vast Reality—logic is forced to suspend its usual process."[28] Logic is detrimental to a true seeing and hearing, to a true knowledge of the world *as it is*—to *gnosis* or, in Buddhist terms, *satori*, enlightenment; that is, to a sensing of the unknowable, what Snyder termed "the clear spring" which is the hidden flow manifested in the interacting and coinhering "riprap" of the material world.

Snyder, with his own independent oriental "archeology," has further enriched the method of ideogrammic composition in its use of nonlogical, "unreasonable" juxtapositions of particulars, as a not-too-distant relation of even such seemingly alien practices as the *koan*. The aim of juxtapositions is not to point to a reality *beyond* the external appearance of things but to direct attention *inward* into the living thing as an entity. The entity is at once real and transcendental, transcendental not in a humanistic-metaphysical sense but as a thing embodying unceasing motion. It is never still but at all times involved in a transformation of force—a meeting point of metamorphosing energies. The poems in *Myths & Texts* move steadily toward this vision, realized in the final section entitled "Burning." In part 7, for example, the theme of permanence-in-impermanence is delicately presented through a series of juxtapositions from a variety of sources, a device based on the idea of "riprap," the haiku, and the *koan*, but also showing Poundian and projectivist influences. The first section is a complex of heterogeneous elements:

> Face in the crook of her neck
>   felt throb of vein
> Smooth skin, her cool breasts
> All naked in the dawn
>   "byrdes
> sing forth from every bough"
>   where are they now
> And dreamt I saw the Duke of Chow.

In sensuous brush strokes of visual and tactile imagery, Snyder delineates a sleeping woman, probably the beloved. The scene is reminiscent of the medieval alba—hence perhaps the echo of a line of archaic poetry in the mind of the speaker as he gazes at the woman's body in the dawn light. The words "where are they now" seem like the half-conscious thoughts of the speaker as he drifts back to sleep. "They" may refer to the birds in the old poem or, like Villon's "*mais où sont les neiges d'antan*," may allude to the impermanence of earthly beauty and human existence. The Duke of Chow, whom the speaker sees in the dream, is no less real.

In the second section Snyder presents an image of eternal reality:

> The Mother whose body is the Universe
> Whose breasts are Sun and Moon,
>   the statue of Prajna
> From Java: the quiet smile,
>   the naked breasts.

The following brief section shifts back to human reality and to the transience of human relationships as Snyder quotes the question of a little girl, "Will you still love me when my breasts get big?"—to which the poet answers with a paraphrase of a doctrine from Hindu scriptures, thus ending part 7:

> "Earthly Mothers and those who suck
> the breasts of earthly mothers are mortal—
> but deathless are those who have fed
> at the breast of the Mother of the Universe."

The word "deathless" does not imply the promise of a "heaven"; it does quite definitely signify a *stepping beyond* the dualistic concepts of life and death, real and unreal, finite and eternal, for they are constructs of the mind. An escape from such conflicts can come about if none of the constituent parts of the total reality is disregarded or made to exist separately from each other. In this heightened vision of cosmic relations the earthly woman and the Mother of the Universe are not irreconcilable, mutually exclusive realities, but the one is the other and the other is the one. This is of course my very inadequate rationalization, for the reverse is also true: neither is the one the other, nor the other the one. Snyder's point may perhaps be better illustrated by a Zen *koan* which runs as follows:

> At the beginning, the mountains are mountains.
> In the middle, the mountains are no longer mountains.
> At the end, the mountains are once again mountains.

The *koan* describes the steps leading to *satori*. At first, as in the first line of Snyder's poem, the mountains are what we observe through our sense organs: actual rocks, boulders, ravines; stones as stones, earth as earth. But after meditating on this reality, we may suddenly see *into* another reality of the mountain, not as thing, but as motion, something that has come into being through immense forces of energy. These forces are still at play in the mountain, working changes in it from moment to moment, and there will be a time when the mountain will no longer be the thing we now see but transformed into something else. The "thing-ness" of the mountain in this second phase of seeing disappears; its materiality and its actual contours which before were all too real are perceived now as illusory, a mirage. Only those essential forces which are immaterial are now "real." In the third stage, we begin to see that thing and motion are not really different; matter and essence are one: "things in motion, motion in things." The mountains are once again mountains, neither purely material nor exclusively essential and illusory. At this level of true vision we also realize, as Linssen writes, that "the creator of illusions has been finally unmasked: it is none other than our own mind."[29] The attainment of *satori* is seeing things and events in their true relation, acting out their destiny in the vast field of the living universe and seeing our own place in this field as another force among many.

Snyder's poems are steps toward this vision of cosmic unity. They are a testament of nonlogical, posthumanist ways of thinking, feeling, and living. They unify, as Ginsberg's later poems do, the objective and visionary modes of composition. The poetics and ecological writings point to the emergence of a new type of human community, as distinct from "society," a combination of resuscitated archaic values and contemporary exigencies. In this community the poet can once again function as Pound had prophesied: as a teller of the tale of the tribe—not as a kind of "unacknowledged legislator," but as one human being functioning to the fullest potential among equals. Snyder has no trust in the world as he finds it. Rather, his activities and writings seem to be preparations for a saner, more human future, signs of which he already recognizes all around him. As he says,

> Industrial society indeed appears to be finished. Many of us are, again, hunters and gatherers. Poets, musicians, nomadic engineers and scholars; fact-diggers, searchers and researchers scoring in rich foundation territory.[30]

With this new posthumanist, postindustrial consciousness the poet assumes an age-old role in the community, that of shaman and healer. This poetry is, as Snyder writes, "the kind of healing that makes whole, heals by making whole. . . ."[31] He further clarifies his ideas of the poet's work as healing:

> I'm obviously not a doctor. I'm not doing magic on anybody's head, either. I'm simply striving to get our heads clear to certain wholenesses that are there anyway; like our oneness with nature, the oneness of mind and body, the oneness of conscious and unconscious, our oneness in society with each other. These are basic and ancient conditions from which we flourish.[32]

Snyder's poetry, then, is a poetry of true transition, the work of a poet who has consciously absorbed and synthesized the most useful elements of Eastern and Western art and philosophy—and by "Western" I do not simply mean European, but Hopi and Navajo in equal proportion. In fact, Snyder's *oeuvre* proves that method is process, and process is consciousness. It is a "new beginning," and thus it does not end the line of ideogrammic composition but makes the method ready and available for use by poets to come.

Concluding Note

Absolute originality in the arts, a total break with the past, is neither possible nor desirable. If it were, such "absolutely original" work, as Eliot noted, would be absolutely incomprehensible, for it could not then have any relation to the world as it is. Most of the artists involved in the modernist revolution have not sought such a break. It is true, they did sever most drastically their ties with a *certain* tradition, but only to reaffirm another, nearly extinct, heritage: the archaic and the primitive. In all the arts modernism has meant both a rejection and a renewal of values and correlated compositional techniques. The change did not occur in a vacuum. The emergence of non-representational/archaic forms in painting and sculpture, together with the collage; the casting-off of conventional harmonics and melody in music; the appearance of nontransitional, paratactic modes in poetry, particularly in Pound's, have come about concurrently with a profound change in our view of ourselves and the universe as a result of the empirical sciences. The new science, revolutionary though it has been in dealing a final blow to the anthropocentric world picture, has itself, like the arts, reached back to its own archaic antecedents. In a much more sophisticated way, supplanting naive observation with controlled experiments, it has picked up and expanded the work of the early Greek thinkers (Heraclitus, Anaximander, the atomists), who were all but buried under Platonic idealism and scholastic logic. "Poetry agrees with science and not with logic," proclaimed Fenollosa, and modernist poetry can be seen as a confirmation of that agreement.

This study was not intended to monopolize the terms "modernism" and "modernist" for those poets whose method has been, and is, predominantly juxtapositional or ideogrammic. What I did intend was to demonstrate that the ideogrammic method, as taken up and "made new" by successive poets after Pound, has been a consistent and reliable instrument to approximate the method of scientific observation and thus give poetic voice to the new *Weltanschauung*. The method is not an end-all in itself, and none of the poets in my survey has used it as such. It is the tip of an iceberg, the visible form of a multileveled content, an extension of that content or context which the poets in the ideogrammic stream share to varying extent.

The first common element and perhaps the most obvious in that shared context is the ideogrammic poets' vision of the universe as alive and inseparable, a constantly changing field of energy transference. There are of course subtle divergences within this context from poet to poet in the ideogrammic stream. In fact, one of the reasons that we can talk about a "progress" or "evolution" of the method is that the poets kept up to date with the newest advances of science: Pound hearkened to the new biology, psychology, and anthropology; Williams studied Einstein; Oppen derived ideas from higher mathematics; Olson lectured on Whitehead and read Heisenberg; Duncan read and incorporated in his poetics all of the above, plus Schrödinger, Köhler and the Gestalt, Dirac and microphysics; and Gary Snyder supplemented his oriental and ecological studies with the findings of Lévi-Strauss and a host of "fact-diggers" such as H. C. Conklin and Stanley Diamond. For these poets the unit of the world is not a metaphysical but a nuclear-physical and astronomical proposition, one in which quantitative changes in the arrangement of atomic or subatomic particles produce qualitative change. The universe is an infinite field of force consisting of things in motion, motion in things; matter is not scalar but vector; relations are not static but dynamic. The world is *both* discrete/separate *and* continuous.

From Pound on, the ideogrammic poets have sought to redefine and revaluate the human being's position in accordance with this view, so that humans would no longer be seen as different in kind from the other objects in nature—as held by an arrogant and presumptuous humanism—but different in degree of complexity, a force in a field of force. But the weight of the past, the anthropocentrism of two and a half millennia, could not so easily be shaken off. As Olson said, speaking of all "archeologists of morning," "We are still in the business of finding out how all action, and thought, have to be refounded."[1]

This refounding means of course the deflation of our self-constructed supranatural *telos*, a puncturing of our metaphysical dimension. Yet the ideogrammic poets do not see this as a cause for despair—on the contrary, we thereby may regain our physicality and a chance to reestablish our true relation with "space" and with the natural world. This recognition of the cosmic process as ultimately functional and not somehow moral (or immoral) and the desire to be an integral part of this living process, not a lost creature wandering in an alien universe waiting for "redemption"; this acceptance, without trauma or hysteria, of the "death" of the Judeo-Christian God and, with it, the demise of metaphysical-humanist "man" is one of the salient features of the ideogrammic poets' conception of the world, one that sets them apart from most European modernists. K.'s last words at the end of Kafka's *The Trial*, "Like a dog!" are filled with shame, grief, and a rage against cosmic "injustice." By contrast, Williams's "just another dog / among a lot of dogs" in *Paterson* signified a calm acceptance of the human place in, and proper relation to, the totality of nature. To deprive us of our false metaphysical image does not diminish our true stature; for with the revelation that we are a functional force in an infinite field, nature ceases to be a mere backdrop to our self-appointed quest for immortality. Instead of succumbing to silence, resignation, rage, or defiance, we may simply acknowledge that what we misinterpreted and misused is our home, therein to dwell in harmony. Our human attributes, science, art, language are not the products of our ego and intellect; even the very shape, the basic structure of speech, as Fenollosa had shown, follows the movement of the process; or, as Pound wrote in Canto LXXXI, "it is not man / Made courage, or made order, or made grace," but rather these are gifts of nature.

For an accurate artistic expression of this posthumanist reality the ideogrammic method has been found the most suitable by three generations of American poets. The world is not "man-made," and in this sense neither is the ideogrammic method. Like the sentence, it was "forced upon" the poet by nature itself. Ideogrammic construction consequently abandons logic and ratiocination, remnants of human-centered "positive capability," which directed the will to impose a human order on the world as well as on the poetic representations of the world. What has become imposed form in the humanist era fulfilled in archaic times natural functions. "Rhythm" was "measured motion," and the metric foot referred both to the beat of the song and to the "beat" of the physical foot in the dance. As human beings became further and further alienated from nature and caught up in the dream of their own magnificence, the forms remained but became devoid of true meaning. They became vehicles of the grandiose image of "man" as Ruler through Reason, as witnessed by "his" inventions—rigid metre and stanza pattern, the tyranny of "poetical" stock images, artificial conventions in diction, and the spread of arbitrary, noninterpretative metaphor, or, in other endeavors, St. Peter's Basilica and the gardens of Versailles. As Duncan commented,

> Fact and reason are creations of man's genius to secure a point of view protected against a vision of life where information and intelligence invade us, where what we know shapes us and we become creatures, not rulers, of what is. Where, more, we are part of the creative process, not its goal. . . . The rationalist gardener's art is his control over nature, and beauty is conceived as the imposed order visible in the pruned hedge-row and the ultimate tree compelled into geometric globe or pyramid that gives certainty of effect.[2]

This kind of imposition of rules and regulations on life stems from "rational man's" fear that the universe is alien, chaotic, even monstrous, and that it is our cosmic destiny to give it order. It is diametrically opposed to a different kind of ordering—that of "primitive" peoples, whose cosmogony, art, and life-style have at all times aimed at a harmonious coexistence with the fundamental natural laws. The ideogrammic poets without exception, but Olson and Snyder in particular, became spokesmen for this more sane and truly *humane* planetary consciousness, and they have shied away from the need or validity of human-centered imposition of control. "Control-addiction" in its various manifestations, and this includes closed, nonprojective poetic form, became for them not only boring and repetitious but, on a more basic level, unnatural. As Duncan remarked further, in connection with Robert Frost's well-known adage, "I would as soon write free verse as play tennis with the net down":

> But, for those who see life as something other than a tennis game, without bounds, and who seek in their sciences and arts to come into that life, into an imagination of that life, the thought comes that the counterpart of free verse may be free thought and free movement. The explorer displays the meaning of physical excellence in a way different from that displayed by the tennis player.[3]

The ideogram, then, is ultimately the method of explorers, of "diggers," of spiritual voyagers who are at the same time rooted in the reality of their physical space. With objectivity and imagination they grasp and gather up in luminous "heaps" particular pieces of their reality, as did in the *periplus* the cartographers of old. The method is a tool, supple and flexible. And, like all real tools, it partakes of the personality and objective reality of the person who puts it to use.

To place the ideogrammic method in the larger contemporary aesthetic context is a fairly straightforward task. As mentioned above, the method does not imply that absolutely anything and everything can be "heaped" together in a poem. Ideogrammic writing, although different from closed composition in essence, structure, and form, is rarely a passive "ego-trip," a dream talk, a complete letting-go of the conscious mind. Although the method was greatly enriched by surrealism, particularly in its latest metamorphoses, it is not "pure psychic automatism," to use Breton's definition of his own great poetic method. It should be recognized that although different measures apply in cumulative and contrastive juxtapositions, in fugal, overlapping, collagistic, or elliptical groupings of particulars, all ideogrammic poets insist on certain determining factors in the inclusion or exclusion of material. In all instances it is always a *field*, a definite imaginative-perceptual-factual space, a "field of reference," a "context," a "geography of requiredness" which is *given* to the poet; and the poems come about, as Williams wrote, "by our having heard their structural elements new-spoken as hints immediately about us."[4] The ideogrammic poet does not stand outside but moves inside the "field," moving from one perception immediately to another. The poet is involved in an organizing activity without actually doing the organizing. In other words, the poet presents one facet or one aspect of a series of object-events until their unseen relations become apparent and can "register" in the mind of the reader as insight or revelation. The ideogrammic method, therefore, is not based on an association by contiguity. That is, it does not postulate that just because two or more things are grouped together, an ideogram will inevitably result. In an ideogram the particulars are *functionally interrelated*, not simply by their proximity or the possibility of an association. It is true, as Gestalt psychology has demonstrated, that the human mind is capable of forming associations between the most heterogeneous elements if placed side by side. As an example, Köhler gives a series of noun pairs: lake—sugar, boot—plate, girl—kangaroo, pencil—gasoline. How can the mind combine these units into meaningful entities? By the imagination, says Köhler:

> When I read those words I can imagine, as a series of strange pictures, how a lump of sugar dissolves in a lake, how a boot rests on a plate, how a girl feeds a kangaroo, and so forth. If this happens during the reading of the series, I experience in imagination a number of well-organized, though quite unusual wholes.[5]

Apart from the rather meager results of the great psychologist's imagination, one of the interesting aspects of the experiment is that organization comes about *through particularization*. The more important fact, however, is that the organized wholes are purely subjective. Different readers would imagine any number of "strange pictures" according to their own immediately preceding sense impressions, memory, whim, or associational ability, as they do with inkblots in a Rorschach test.

Juxtapositions such as "Seven Lakes and Geryon" or "hydrogen jukebox" are of a different category. Indeed, the ideogrammic method relies on no such "stretch of the imagination" as mentioned by Köhler. First and foremost, ideogrammic composition *begins with particulars*—with, in Zukofsky's words, "historic and contemporary particulars." Thus, in interpreting a juxtaposition the result will likely be some measure of objective predication, whereas if we were to ask Köhler why the boot is on the plate, or, similarly, if we were to ask the surrealist why the particular association, they could only say, "That's the way my consciousness operates, that's the power of *my* mind." Second, in ideograms natural pictures and/or images are juxtaposed paratactically. The poet interferes little or not at all to make overt connections: the juxtaposed units establish relations among themselves. Third, the method demands that the reader, like the writer, become an explorer, not simply expecting entertainment or spoon-feeding, but bringing an openness and a willingness to communicate and to commune to the text.

Readers must naturally ease the mind into the contours of the work as they would the physical self into new surroundings.

The ideogrammic method, therefore, in comparison to closed composition on the one hand, and associational or surrealistic writing on the other, appears to be situated somewhere between the two. It is somewhat closer, of course, to the latter than to the former. More important than this placing, the method's virtue is its readiness to depict the world in accordance with the processes of nature. The presence in poetic ideograms of incongruous units put side by side without transition is not gratuitous. The universe, in its multifarious and varied reality, itself appears incongruous; but ideograms attempt to reveal its essential oneness, the "clear spring" flowing through all. Ideograms point to a reality and an order which is not human; at the same time they seek to affirm that human beings, neither the rulers nor the freaks of nature, are an integral part of the cosmic process.

This is the sense in which I take ideogrammic form, in its progression from Pound to Snyder and beyond a constructive, fully contemporary, syncretic form. Although issuing from the great crucible of modernism, it has become more acclimatized in America than elsewhere. And the values and energies underlying it, from Fenollosa on, have come more and more to be identified with the ancient and still potent world view of native Americans. The aim is not, as some critics have mistakenly said, "to go backwards," but, like the Indians, to be conscious of a larger spatial-temporal context and not to take technological, producing/consuming, nuclear society as the norm. When Snyder was asked, "You're going against the grain of things all the time, aren't you?" he replied, "It's only a temporary turbulence I'm setting myself against. I'm in line with the big flow."[6] Ideogrammic form is coextensive with this pre-logical and posthumanist outlook, which does not want to control and mar the reality of the living universe, but accepts and respects it in all its creatures, seeks to live in harmony with its processes, and wants to love it and to enact its mysteries in art.

In ideograms containing "a sufficient phalanx of particulars" we find that the mythic, religious, historical, factual, and personal "textual particles" are sharply defined, retaining their affective power in their juxtapositions. In Snyder's ideogram of the sleeping girl and the Mother of the Universe the respective identities are not blurred. Only through one common aspect—the breast—is their essential oneness and their latent unity suggested. The particulars explain one another, as Oppen said, not themselves. In Canto LXXXIII Pound presents a new-born wasp, "an infant, green as new grass," sticking its tiny head out of the bottle-like nest its parent has built on the poet's tent. The birth of this insect is part of nature's vernal renewal, which the poet sees all around him: "mint springs up again," and "the clover leaf smells and tastes as its flower." And then he sees:

> The infant has descended,
> from mud on the tent roof to Tellus,
> like to like colour he goes amid grass-blades
> greeting them that dwell under XTHONOS ΧΘΟΝΟΣ
> ΟΙ ΧΘΟΝΙΟΙ; to carry our news
> εἰς χθονίους to them that dwell under the earth,
> begotten of air, that shall sing in the bower,
> of Kore   Περσεφόνεια
> and have speech with Tiresias, Thebae.

The juxtaposition of the wasp's descent with Persephone and then with Odysseus' *katabasis* reveals the identical direction of natural and human processes. Human beings go through their life descending and returning, as the wasp and the mint go through theirs. And, as part of the ideogram, there is Pound himself, in the tent of the Pisa Disciplinary Training Center, having descended into his own purgatory. But there is no implied "meaning" that "The wasp is Koré" or "The wasp is Odysseus" or "Odysseus is Pound." The particulars of the ideogram remain distinct, and from their dynamic interaction arises the universal concept of nature's "latent" unity. "The plan is in nature rooted," wrote Pound in Canto XCIX. This is the belief, the *gnosis*, that underlies the poetics of all ideogrammic poets and is the basis of the ideogrammic method itself. This form is nothing more than an extension of that content.

For those poets of the fourth and subsequent generations of modernism who share or will come to share this belief, those who will enter into the poetic activity as explorers rather than tennis players, the ideogrammic method will hold continued possibilities from which to evolve their individual theories of composition. Like the ideogrammic poets, they will not likely think of themselves as "creators"; they will be creatures of the world, not its rulers. Consequently, they will dispense with the humanist notion that poems are supposed to manifest some sort of "creative" ordering. Instead, they may begin their journey with the ideogrammic assumption that order is latently present in the material universe; that nature is not disordered and chaotic, in need of human "rectifying"; and that reason and logic may be consigned to more fitting realms than myth and art.

On occasion even ideogrammic poets have given voice to fears and doubts about the unity of their work and of the world, too. As Oppen wrote in *Of Being Numerous*:

> war in incoherent
> sunlight it will not
> COHERE it will NOT
> that other

Pound also remarked near the end of *The Cantos*, in Canto CXVI:

> And I am not a demigod,
> I cannot make it cohere.

But a few lines later, in the same canto, as if suddenly sensing that he need not be, or pretend to be, a demigod to impose order on his epic—for it is *as it is*, a confirmation and revelation of the Process—he added:

> to "see again,"
> the verb is "see," not "walk on"
> i.e. it coheres all right
>   even if my notes do not cohere.

For indeed it coheres, as *It* and the entire universe cohere.

Notes

Introduction

1. Herbert Schneidau, "Wisdom Past Metaphor: Another View of Pound, Fenollosa, and Objective Verse," *Paideuma* 5 (1976): 15.

2. Ezra Pound, *Literary Essays*, p. 205.

3. Edward Thomas in *English Review* (1909), quoted by Charles Norman, *Ezra Pound*, p. 37.

4. Pound, "D'Artagnan Twenty Years After," in *Selected Prose, 1909–1965*, p. 453.

5. Hugh Kenner to Louis Zukofsky, Zukofsky Collection, Humanities Research Center, University of Texas, Austin. Subsequent references to material at this location will be abbreviated as HRC, Texas.

6. Harold Bloom, *The Anxiety of Influence* (New York: Oxford University Press, 1973), p. 7.

7. The corrective note of Bloom's eminent colleague, Geoffrey H. Hartman, may be cited here: "Bloom's theory of the relation of literary sons and fathers, while a significant contribution, is a strangely literal transfer to art of one strain of Freud's thinking." See Geoffrey Hartman, *The Fate of Reading and Other Essays* (Chicago: University of Chicago Press, 1975), p. 53.

8. Louis Zukofsky, *Prepositions*, p. 127.

9. Guy Davenport, "The Symbol of the Archaic," *Georgia Review* 28 (1974): 647.

10. Ludwig Wittgenstein, *Tractatus Logico-Philosophicus*, trans. D. F. Pears and B. F. McGuinness (London: Routledge & Kegan Paul, 1961) 2:18.

11. Hugh Kenner, *The Poetry of Ezra Pound*, p. 84.

12. Wai-lim Yip, *Ezra Pound's Cathay*, p. 32.

1. From Metaphor to Vortex

1. Edward Thomas, *English Review* (1909), reprinted in J. P. Sullivan, ed., *Ezra Pound: A Critical Anthology*, p. 35.

2. William Carlos Williams, *Selected Letters*, p. 225.

3. T. S. Eliot, in the introduction to Ezra Pound, *Selected Poems*, p. 11.

4. Charles Reznikoff, for example, called himself "a kind of archeologist," and Charles Olson similarly referred to himself as an "archeologist of morning."

5. Pound, "Credo," *Literary Essays*, p. 11.

6. Ronald Bush, *The Genesis of Ezra Pound's Cantos*, p. 11.

7. Pound, "A Retrospect," *Literary Essays*, p. 3.

8. Hugh Witemeyer, *The Poetry of Ezra Pound*, p. 39.

9. Pound, "A Retrospect," *Literary Essays*, p. 9.

10. See Dante Alighieri, *De Vulgari Eloquentia* (Padova: Editrice Antenore, 1968), Bk. II, Sec. I. Dante writes that "optima loquela non convenit nisi illis in quibus ingenium et scientia est" (p. 33).

11. Walt Whitman, *Leaves of Grass*, Comprehensive Reader's Edition, ed. Harold W. Blodgett and Sculley Bradley (New York: New York University Press, 1965), p. 714. The quote appears in the 1855 preface to *Leaves of Grass*.

12. Ralph Waldo Emerson, *Essays*, 2d Ser. (Boston: Houghton Mifflin, 1968), pp. 9-10.

13. Pound, "I Gather the Limbs of Osiris," *Selected Prose*, p. 27.

14. Ibid., p. 27.

15. Herbert Schneidau, *The Image and the Real*, p. 97.

16. Pound, *The Spirit of Romance*, p. 14.

17. Pound, "The Serious Artist," *Literary Essays*, p. 42.

18. Pound, *ABC of Reading*, p. 22.

19. Pound, *The Spirit of Romance*, p. 30.

20. Ibid., p. 33.

21. Ibid., p. 158.

22. Helen Gardner, in the introduction to *The Metaphysical Poets* (Harmondsworth: Penguin, 1957), p. 19.

23. Pound, *The Spirit of Romance*, p. 159. Pound refers to "epithets of primary apparition" in a footnote concerning Fenollosa's statements that poetry "must appeal to emotions with the charm of direct impression, flashing through regions where the intellect can only grope" (Fenollosa, *The Chinese Written Character*, p. 21).

24. Pound, "I Gather the Limbs of Osiris," *Selected Prose*, p. 22. Cf. *The Spirit of Romance*, p. 87: "The interpretive function is the highest honour of the arts, and because it is so we find that a sort of hyper-scientific precision is the touchstone and assay of the artist's power, of his honour, his authenticity."

25. Pound, "I Gather the Limbs of Osiris," *Selected Prose*, p. 33.

26. Stuart Y. McDougal, *Ezra Pound and the Troubadour Tradition*, p. 147.

27. Pound, "A Visiting Card," *Selected Prose*, p. 319. See also Pound, *Polite Essays*, p. 50.

28. Pound, "Vorticism," reprinted in Pound, *Gaudier-Brzeska: A Memoir*, p. 92.

29. Pound, "Serious Artist," *Literary Essays*, p. 49.

30. Pound, "I Gather the Limbs of Osiris," *Selected Prose*, p. 36.

31. Pound, "Vorticism," *Gaudier-Brzeska*, p. 86.

32. Pound, "Affirmations—As for Imagisme," *Selected Prose*, p. 374. William C. Wees writes in *Vorticism and the English Avant-Garde* that vorticist paintings "were totally abstract designs composed of sharply defined geometrical elements—arcs, circles, ovoids, triangles, irregular rectangles, etc.—which overlapped, intersected, and generated larger geometrical patterns that unified the work as a whole without obscuring the separate parts that made it up" (p. 179).

33. Pound, "Vorticism," *Gaudier-Brzeska*, p. 94.

34. Ibid., p. 89.

35. Excerpts from Kandinsky's *Über das Geistige in der Kunst* were cited in a prepublication review of the work by Edward Wadsworth in *Blast* 1 (20 June 1914): 120.

36. Schneidau, *The Image and the Real*, p. 188.

37. Pound, *The Spirit of Romance*, p. 91.

38. Wyndham Lewis, "Manifesto," *Blast* I (20 June 1914): 33.

2. The Impact of Fenollosa

1. Wyndham Lewis, "Ezra Pound," *Blast* II (July 1915): 82.

2. Pound, *Cathay*, title page; reprinted in Pound, *Selected Poems*.

3. Pound, *Selected Letters*, p. 61.

4. Ibid., p. 82.

5. Ibid., p. 90.

6. Ibid., p. 101.

7. Hugh Kenner, *The Pound Era*, p. 231; Donald Davie, *Articulate Energy*, p. 33.

8. Noel Stock, *Poet in Exile: Ezra Pound* (Manchester: Manchester University Press, 1964), p. 142.

9. First manuscript draft of *The Chinese Written Character*, Fenollosa Papers, Pound Collection, Beinecke Rare Book and Manuscript Library, Yale University. Subsequent references to unpublished manuscripts by Fenollosa will be abbreviated as Fenollosa, Yale.

10. Fenollosa, *The Chinese Written Character*, p. 7.

11. Ibid., p. 8. The phrase "but unforgettable once you have seen it" is Pound's addition.

12. Ibid., p. 10.

13. Ibid., pp. 21-22.

14. Fenollosa, Yale.

15. Fenollosa, *The Chinese Written Character*, p. 22.

16. Ibid., p. 11.

17. Ibid., p. 10.

18. Ibid., p. 15.

19. Ibid., p. 19.

20. Ibid., p. 10.

21. Ibid., p. 23.

22. Ibid., p. 23.

23. Ibid., p. 28.

24. Ibid., p. 32.

25. Fenollosa, Yale.

26. Fenollosa, *The Chinese Written Character*, p. 33.

27. Ibid., p. 25.

28. The sinologue who first pointed out Fenollosa's misconceptions, calling the essay "a small mass of confusion," was George Kennedy in "Fenollosa, Pound, and the Chinese Character," *Yale Literary Magazine* 126, no. 5 (December 1958): 24-36.

29. See Bernhard Karlgren, *Sound and Symbol in Chinese* (London: Oxford University Press, 1923), pp. 32-54.

30. These errors were corrected with meticulous care by Achilles Fang in "Fenollosa and Pound," *Harvard Journal of Asiatic Studies* 20 (1957): 213–233.

31. Kenner, *The Pound Era*, pp. 225 and 231.

32. Hugh Gordon Porteus, "Ezra Pound and His Chinese Character: A Radical Examination," in Peter Russell, ed., *An Examination of Ezra Pound*, pp. 212 and 216.

33. Ibid., pp. 216–217.

34. Wai-lim Yip, *Chinese Poetry: Major Modes and Genres* (Berkeley: University of California Press, 1976), p. 11.

35. Ibid., p. 18.

36. Fenollosa, *The Chinese Written Character*, p. 32.

3. The Poundian Ideogram

1. Pound, "Date Line," *Literary Essays*, p. 77.

2. Pound, "Immediate Need of Confucius," *Selected Prose*, p. 78.

3. Fenollosa, *The Chinese Written Character*, pp. 25–26.

4. Ibid., p. 26.

5. Pound, *ABC of Reading*, p. 19.

6. Ibid., p. 22.

7. Hugh Kenner, "Ezra Pound and Chinese," *Agenda* 5 (October–November 1965): 38.

8. Pound, "T. S. Eliot," *Literary Essays*, p. 420.

9. James Wilhelm, *The Later Cantos of Ezra Pound*, p. xvi.

10. Pound, "Abject and Utter Farce," *Polite Essays*, p. 106.

11. Pound, *ABC of Reading*, pp. 17–18.

12. Werner Heisenberg, *Physics and Beyond: Encounters and Observations* (New York: Harper & Row, 1972), p. 63. I have used this work of Heisenberg's because it presents both sides of the arguments succinctly.

13. Ibid., p. 63.

14. Ibid., p. 69.

15. Pound, "The Teacher's Mission," *Literary Essays*, p. 61.

16. Pound, "How to Read," *Literary Essays*, p. 39.

17. Pound, *ABC of Reading*, p. 87. See Leslie H. Palmer, "Matthew Arnold and Ezra Pound," *Paideuma* 2 (1973): 193–198.

18. Pound, *ABC of Reading*, p. 24.

19. Wolfgang Köhler, *Gestalt Psychology* (New York: Liveright, 1947), p. 84.

20. Pound, *Guide to Kulchur*, p. 152.

21. Kenner, *The Poetry of Ezra Pound*, p. 76.

22. M.-L. von Franz in Carl G. Jung, *Man and His Symbols* (New York: Doubleday, 1964), p. 164.

23. J. P. Sullivan, *Ezra Pound and Sextus Propertius*, p. 89.

24. Fenollosa, "The Logic of Art," *Golden Age* (May 1906), quoted in Lawrence W. Chisolm, *Fenollosa: The Far East and American Culture* (New Haven: Yale University Press, 1963), p. 203.

25. Pound, *Guide to Kulchur*, p. 82.

26. M. L. Rosenthal, *A Primer of Ezra Pound*, pp. 44–45.

27. James E. Miller, Jr., *The American Quest for a Supreme Fiction: Whitman's Legacy in the Personal Epic* (Chicago: University of Chicago Press, 1979), p. ix.

28. Eric A. Havelock, *Preface to Plato* (Oxford: Blackwell, 1963), p. 180. Cf. Max Nänny, "Oral Dimensions in Ezra Pound," *Paideuma* 6 (1977): 13–26.

29. George Seferis, "The Cantos," in Russell, ed., *An Examination of Ezra Pound*, p. 79.

30. Walter L. Fischer, "Ezra Pounds chinesische Denkstrukturen," in Eva Hesse, ed., *Ezra Pound: 22 Versuche über einen Dichter*, p. 170.

31. Daniel Pearlman, "Pound and the Postromantics," *Contemporary Literature* 21 (1980): 309. Pearlman's *The Barb of Time* is an important study of *The Cantos*.

32. Leon Surette, *A Light from Eleusis: A Study of Ezra Pound's Cantos* (Oxford: Clarendon Press, 1979), p. 23.

33. Achilles Fang to Noel Stock, 20 July 1955, Pound Collection, HRC, Texas.

4. Sincerity and Objectification

1. Pound, *Selected Letters*, p. 266.

2. Robert Creeley, *Contexts of Poetry*, p. 17

3. Louis Zukofsky, *Prepositions*, p. 76.

4. Zukofsky, "Ezra Pound: His Cantos," *The Observer* 2, no. 2 (January-February 1934): 4. The revised version included in *Prepositions* has a slightly different wording.

5. Zukofsky, *Prepositions*, p. 134.

6. Zukofsky to Carl Rakosi, Zukofsky Collection, HRC, Texas.

7. Pound, *Selected Letters*, p. 228.

8. Ibid., p. 231.

9. Zukofsky, "The 'Objectivist' Poet: Four Interviews," introduced and conducted by L. S. Dembo, *Contemporary Literature* 10 (1969): 203.

10. Ibid., p. 204.

11. Zukofsky, "Sincerity and Objectification," *Poetry* 37 (1931): 274.

12. Ibid., p. 284n.

13. Zukofsky, *An "Objectivists" Anthology*, p. 10.

14. Zukofsky, *"A" 1–12*, p. 29.

15. Ibid. p. 66.

16. Ibid., p. 134.

17. Ibid., pp. 66–67.

18. René Taupin, *Poetry* 37 (1931): 290–291.

19. Zukofsky, "Sincerity and Objectification," *Poetry* 37 (1931): 278.

20. L. S. Dembo, "Louis Zukofsky: Objectivist Poetics and the Quest for Form," *American Literature* 44 (1972): 79.

21. Zukofsky, *Prepositions*, pp. 12 and 15. See also Zukofsky, *Bottom: On Shakespeare*, regarding science and poetry.

22. Zukofsky, *An "Objectivists" Anthology*, pp. 22 and 25.

23. Guy Davenport, "Zukofsky's 'A'-24," *Parnassus: Poetry in Review* 2, no. 2 (Spring/Summer 1974): 18–19.

24. Zukofsky to Felicity Andrew, 29 August 1966, Zukofsky Collection, HRC, Texas.

25. Ibid.

26. Zukofsky to Margaret Caetani, 15 November 1951, Zukofsky Collection, HRC, Texas.

27. G. S. Fraser, "A Pride of Poets," *Partisan Review* 35 (1968): 471.

28. Zukofsky, "A Statement for Poetry (1950)," *Kulchur 3*, no. 10 (Summer 1963): 49.

29. Quoted in Dembo, "The 'Objectivist' Poet: Four Interviews," p. 193.

30. Ibid., p. 194.

31. Ibid., p. 198.

32. Ibid., pp. 194–195.

33. Ibid., p. 202.

34. Ibid., p. 202.

35. Ibid., p. 172.

36. Ibid., p. 161.

37. Ibid., p. 163.

38. Oppen, *Collected Poems*, p. 134.

39. Quoted in Dembo, "The 'Objectivist' Poet: Four Interviews," p. 161.

40. Hugh Kenner, *New York Times Book Review*, Oct. 19, 1975, p. 5.

41. Oppen, *Collected Poems*, p. 147.

42. Ibid., p. 143.

43. See Martin Heidegger, "Bauen Wohnen Denken," *Vorträge und Aufsätze* (Pfullingen: Neske, 1954; 3d ed., 1967), 2: 19–36. Heidegger notes that etymologically both *wohnen* and *bauen* derive from the root verb *buan* which contains both meanings (dwelling and building) as one concept.

44. L. S. Dembo, "Individuality and Numerosity," *The Nation*, November 24, 1969, p. 574.

45. Oppen, *Collected Poems*, p. 155.

5. Dr. Williams: Ideas in Things

1. William Carlos Williams, *I Wanted to Write a Poem*, p. 17.

2. Williams, *Autobiography*, p. 148.

3. Ibid., pp. 138 and 146.

4. Williams to Cid Corman, 11 August 1950, Williams Collection, HRC, Texas.

5. Williams, *Selected Letters*, p. 225.

6. Williams, *Autobiography*, p. 241.

7. Williams, "Spring and All," *Imaginations*, pp. 149–150.

8. Williams, *Autobiography*, p. 357.

9. Ibid., p. 391.

10. Williams, *Selected Letters*, p. 130.

11. Williams to Marcia Nardi, 27 September 1949, Williams Collection, HRC, Texas.

12. Williams, "Kora in Hell," *Imaginations*, p. 14.

13. Creeley, *Contexts of Poetry*, p. 17.

14. Williams, *Interviews: Speaking Straight Ahead*, p. 53.

15. Williams, "Spring and All," *Imaginations*, pp. 110–111.

16. Williams, "Kora in Hell," *Imaginations*, p. 19.

17. Williams, "Spring and All," *Imaginations*, p. 101.

18. Ibid., p. 101.

19. Williams, *Autobiography*, p. 359.

20. Williams to Frances Steloff, 15 March 1939, Williams Collection, HRC, Texas.

21. Williams, *Selected Letters*, p. 187.

22. Williams, *I Wanted to Write a Poem*, pp. 82–83.

23. Williams, *Interviews*, p. xi.

24. Williams, *I Wanted to Write a Poem*, p. 83.

25. James E. Breslin, *William Carlos Williams: An American Artist*, p. 173.

26. Williams, *Selected Essays*, p. 256.

6. Projective Verse I: The Hieroglyphs of Olson

1. Williams, "Kora in Hell," *Imaginations*, pp. 16–17.

2. Richard Kostelanetz, *Possibilities of Poetry* (New York: Dell, 1970), p. 5. Hugh Kenner's assessment of prevailing conditions at the time is similar in *A Homemade World: The American Modernist Writers*, pp. 173–174.

3. Charles Olson, *Charles Olson and Ezra Pound: An Encounter at St. Elizabeths*, p. 102.

4. Quoted by Robert Creeley in his introduction to Olson, *Selected Writings*, p. 6.

5. Olson, *Letters for Origin, 1950–1956*, p. 129.

6. Olson, *Call Me Ishmael*, p. 100.

7. Ibid., pp. 14–15.

8. Olson in a 1956 lecture, reprinted in Ann Charters, *Olson/Melville: A Study in Affinity*, p. 85.

9. Olson, *The Special View of History*, p. 42.

10. Olson, "Human Universe," *Selected Writings*, p. 55.

11. Ibid., p. 55.

12. Ibid., p. 56. Also: "If you leave the particular as the occurrence of force—as the vector—you lose the force" (Charters, *Olson/Melville*, p. 90).

13. Olson, "Projective Verse," *Selected Writings*, p. 16. All subsequent quotations from the essay refer to this edition.

14. Ibid.

15. Ibid.

16. Ibid., p. 17.

17. Olson, "Projective Verse," *Selected Writings*, p. 21. Robert von Hallberg, "Olson's Relation to Pound and Williams," *Contemporary Literature* 15 (1974): 15–48, completely disregards Olson's enthusiastic affirmation of Fenollosa's ideas, among them the theory of the sentence as power transference; he also misinterprets Olson's poem "La Torre" (pp. 17–18). These and other inaccuracies have not been corrected in Robert von Hallberg, *Charles Olson: The Scholar's Art* (Cambridge: Harvard University Press, 1978).

18. Olson, "Projective Verse," *Selected Writings*, p. 24.

19. Stephen Stepanchev, *American Poetry since 1945* (New York: Harper & Row, 1965), p. 145.

20. Olson, "Human Universe," *Selected Writings*, pp. 53–54.

21. Ibid., p. 58.

22. Olson, "Mayan Letters," *Selected Writings*, p. 112.

23. Ibid., p. 113.

24. Creeley, in the introduction to Olson, *Selected Writings*, p. 4.

25. Olson, "Letter 27," *Maximus Poems IV, V, VI*, p. [15].

26. Ibid., p. [15].

27. Olson, *Additional Prose*, p. 40.

7. Projective Verse II: Duncan's Collages, Creeley's Pieces

1. Olson, *Causal Mythology*, p. 11.

2. Robert Duncan, *Notes on Grossinger's "Solar Journal: Oecological Sections,"* p. [3].

3. Duncan, *An Interview with Robert Duncan*, with George Bowering and Robert Hogg, p. [7]. Cf. "My sense of the total poem is that it is a community where every word is a worker" (Duncan, "Interview with Robert Duncan," with Ekbert Faas, *Boundary 2* 8, no. 2 [Winter 1980]: 4). Also, "It is our experience of the universe really which makes open form seem appropriate" (ibid., p. 3).

4. Duncan, "From the Day Book," *Origin*, Second Series 10 (July 1963): 7.

5. *An Interview with Robert Duncan*, with Bowering and Hogg, p. [16].

6. Ibid., pp. [26-27].

7. Mersmann, "Robert Duncan: Irregular Fire—Eros against Ahriman," *Out of the Vietnam Vortex*, p. 168.

8. Duncan, *The Opening of the Field*, p. 83.

9. Duncan, *Bending the Bow*, p. vii.

10. Duncan, "Toward an Open Universe," *Poets on Poetry*, ed. Howard Nemerov (New York and London: Basic Books, 1966), p. 139.

11. Duncan, "From the Day Book," *Origin*, 2d ser. 10 (July 1963): 10, and Duncan, "Some Letters to Charles Olson," *MAPS*, no. 6 (1974), p. 59.

12. Duncan, "The Lasting Contribution of Ezra Pound," *Agenda* 5, no. 4 (October-November 1965): 23.

13. Jess, *Translation* (Los Angeles: Black Sparrow Press, 1971).

14. Duncan, "Toward an Open Universe," *Poets on Poetry*, ed. Nemerov, p. 139.

15. Duncan, *The Opening of the Field*, p. 12.

16. A. K. Weatherhead, "Robert Duncan and the Lyric," *Contemporary Literature* 16 (1975): 174.

17. Duncan, *Bending the Bow*, p. ix.

18. Ibid., pp. ix-x.

19. Duncan, *Tribunals*, appended pamphlet.

20. Creeley, *Contexts of Poetry*, p. 77.

21. Ibid., p. 40.

22. Ibid., pp. 34-35.

23. Creeley, *A Sense of Measure*, p. 48.

24. Ibid., p. 50.

25. Warren Tallman, *Three Essays on Creeley*, pp. [1] and [14].

26. Joyce Carol Oates, *The New Republic*, Dec. 18, 1976, p. 27.

27. Creeley, *A Sense of Measure*, p. 33.

28. Creeley, *Contexts of Poetry*, p. 16.

29. Ibid., p. 14.

30. Ibid., p. 162.

31. Creeley, in the introduction to Olson, *Selected Writings*, p. 4.

32. Creeley, *Contexts of Poetry*, p. 100.

33. Williams, unpublished fragment, William Carlos Williams Collection, Lockwood Memorial Library, State University of New York, Buffalo.

34. Quoted in Creeley, *Contexts of Poetry*, p. 27.

35. Ibid., p. 192.

36. Fred Moramarco, "A Gathering of Poets," *Western Humanities Review* 24 (1970): 204.

37. Creeley, *Contexts of Poetry*, p. 185.

38. Creeley, *A Sense of Measure*, p. 41.

39. Creeley, *Pieces*, pp. 6–7.

8. Ellipsis and Riprap: The Ideograms of Ginsberg and Snyder

1. Allen Ginsberg, *Allen Verbatim: Lectures on Poetry, Politics, Consciousness*, p. 139.

2. Ibid., p. 141.

3. Ginsberg, "A Talk with Allen Ginsberg," with Alison Colbert, *Partisan Review* 38 (1971): 295–296.

4. Ginsberg, *Allen Verbatim*, pp. 144–145.

5. Jack Kerouac, "Interview," with Ted Berrigan, *Paris Review*, no. 43 (Summer 1968), p. 83.

6. Ginsberg, "Notes for *Howl and Other Poems*," album cover, Fantasy Records 7013.

7. Ibid.

8. Ginsberg, *Journals, Early Fifties Early Sixties*, p. 95.

9. Ginsberg, "Interview," *Paris Review*, no. 37 (Spring 1966), pp. 28–29.

10. Quoted by Stepanchev, *American Poetry since 1945*, p. 133. Ginsberg distinguishes sharply between closed form and spontaneous composition: "The difference is between someone sitting down to write a poem *in* a definite preconceived metrical pattern and filling in that pattern, and someone working with his physiological movements and *arriving* at a pattern, . . . arriving at it organically rather than synthetically" ("Interview," *Paris Review*, no. 37 [Spring 1966], pp. 15–16).

11. Walt Whitman, "Backward Glance O'er Travel'd Roads," *Leaves of Grass*, pp. 573–574.

12. See Olson, *Charles Olson and Ezra Pound*, p. 97.

13. André Breton, *Arcane 17* (1947; reprinted Paris: Collection 10/18, 1975), p. 37.

14. Ginsberg, *Indian Journals*, p. 41.

15. Ibid., pp. 93–94.

16. Quoted in Michael Reck, "A Conversation between Ezra Pound and Allen Ginsberg," *Evergreen Review*, no. 55 (June 1968), p. 29.

17. Ginsberg, "Interview," *Paris Review*, no. 37 (Spring 1966), p. 30.

18. Gary Snyder, *Earth House Hold*, p. 117.

19. Quoted in David Kherdian, *Six Poets of the San Francisco Renaissance: Portraits and Checklists*, p. 52.

20. Thomas Parkinson, "The Poetry of Gary Snyder," *Southern Review*, New Series 4 (1968): 617.

21. Alan Williamson, "Language against Itself: The Middle Generation of Contemporary Poets," in Robert B. Shaw, ed., *American Poetry since 1960*, p. 62.

22. Donald M. Allen, ed., *The New American Poetry*, pp. 420–421.

23. Robert Kern, "Recipes, Catalogues, Open Form Poetics: Gary Snyder's Archetypal Voice," *Contemporary Literature* 18 (1977): 179.

24. Snyder, *Earth House Hold*, pp. 56–57.

25. Snyder, introduction to *Turtle Island*, n.p.

26. Snyder, "Some Yips & Barks in the Dark," in Stephen Berg and Robert Mezey, eds., *Naked Poetry*, p. 357.

27. Snyder, *The Back Country*, pp. 28–31.

28. Robert Linssen, *Living Zen*, trans. Diana Abrahams-Curiel (New York: Grove Press, 1960), p. 320.

29. Ibid., p. 95. For the interpretation of this *koan* I am indebted to Linssen, although the linking of its principles with Fenollosa's ideas is my own.

30. Snyder, *Earth House Hold*, p. 111.

31. Snyder, *The Real Work: Interviews and Talks, 1964–1979*, p. 171.

32. Ibid., p. 157.

Concluding Note

1. Olson, *Selected Writings*, p. 48.

2. Duncan, "Ideas of the Meaning of Form," in Donald M. Allen and Warren Tallman, eds., *The Poetics of the New American Poetry*, p. 207.

3. Ibid., p. 209.

4. Williams to Marianne Moore, 21 May 1948, Williams Collection, HRC, Texas.

5. Köhler, *Gestalt Psychology*, p. 157.

6. Snyder, *The Real Work*, p. 112.

Select Bibliography

Primary Works

Creeley, Robert. *Contexts of Poetry: Interviews 1961–1971*. Bolinas, Calif.: Four Seasons Foundation, 1973.

———. *Pieces*. New York: Scribner's, 1969.

———. *A Sense of Measure*. London: Calder & Boyars, 1972.

Duncan, Robert. *Bending the Bow*. New York: New Directions, 1968.

———. "From the Day Book." *Origin*, Second Series 10 (July 1963): 1–47.

———. "Iconographical Extensions." In Jess, *Translation*. Los Angeles: Black Sparrow Press, 1971.

———. *An Interview with Robert Duncan*. With George Bowering and Robert Hogg. Toronto: Beaver Kosmos, 1971.

———. "Interview with Robert Duncan." With Ekbert Faas. *Boundary 2* 8 (1980): 1–20.

———. "The Lasting Contribution of Ezra Pound." *Agenda* 5, no. 4 (1965): 23–26.

———. "Note to Olson," *Origin*, no. 12 (1954), pp. 210–211.

———. *Notes on Grossinger's Solar Journal: Oecological Sections*. Folder. Los Angeles: Black Sparrow Press, 1970.

———. *The Opening of the Field*. New York: New Directions, 1973.

———. "Some Letters to Charles Olson." *MAPS*, no. 6 (1974).

———. *Tribunals, Passages 31–35*. Los Angeles: Black Sparrow Press, 1970.

Fenollosa, Ernest. *The Chinese Written Character as a Medium for Poetry*. Edited by Ezra Pound. San Francisco: City Lights Books, 1969.

———. Pound Collection. Beinecke Rare Book and Manuscript Library. Yale University, New Haven.

Ginsberg, Allen. *Allen Verbatim: Lectures on Poetry, Politics, Consciousness*. Edited by Gordon Ball. New York: McGraw Hill, 1974.

———. *"Howl" and Other Poems*. San Francisco: City Lights Books, 1956.

———. *Indian Journals*. San Francisco: David Hazelwood/City Lights Books, 1970.

———. "Interview." *Paris Review*, no. 37 (Spring 1966), pp. 12–55.

———. *Journals, Early Fifties Early Sixties*. Edited by Gordon Ball. New York: Grove Press, 1977.

———. *The Fall of America: Poems of These States, 1965–1971*. San Francisco: City Lights Books, 1972.

————. *Wichita Vortex Sutra*. San Francisco: Coyote, 1966.

Olson, Charles. *Additional Prose: A Bibliography on America, Proprioception and Other Notes and Essays*. Edited by George F. Butterick. Bolinas, Calif.: Four Seasons, 1974.

————. *Call Me Ishmael*. San Francisco: City Lights Books, 1947.

————. *Causal Mythology*. San Francisco: Four Seasons, 1969.

————. *Charles Olson and Ezra Pound: An Encounter at St. Elizabeths*. Edited by Catherine Seelye. New York: Grossman Viking, 1975.

————. *Letters for Origin, 1950-1956*. Edited by Albert Glover. London: Cape Goliard, 1969.

————. *The Maximus Poems*. New York: Corinth Books, 1960.

————. *Maximus Poems IV, V, VI*. London: Cape Goliard, 1968.

————. *Selected Writings*. Edited by Robert Creeley. New York: New Directions, 1966.

————. *The Special View of History*. Edited by Ann Charters. Berkeley: Oyez, 1970.

Oppen, George. *Collected Poems*. New York: New Directions, 1975.

Pound, Ezra. *ABC of Reading*. London, 1934. Reprinted New York: New Directions, 1960.

————. *The Cantos, 1-117 and 120*. New York: New Directions, 1972.

————. *Gaudier-Brzeska: A Memoir*. London, 1916. Reprinted New York: New Directions, 1961.

————. *Guide to Kulchur*. London, 1938. Reprinted New York: New Directions, 1952.

————. *Literary Essays*. Edited by T. S. Eliot. London: Faber & Faber, 1954.

————. *Pavannes and Divagations*. New York: New Directions, 1958. Reprinted 1974.

————. *Polite Essays*. London: Faber & Faber, 1937.

————. Pound Collection. Beinecke Rare Book and Manuscript Library. Yale University, New Haven.

————. *Selected Letters*. Edited by D. D. Paige. New York: Harcourt Brace Jovanovitch, 1950. New edition New York: New Directions, 1971.

————. *Selected Poems*. Edited by T. S. Eliot. London: Faber & Faber, 1928. Reprinted 1961.

————. *Selected Prose, 1909-1965*. Edited by William Cookson. New York: New Directions, 1975.

————. *The Spirit of Romance*. London, 1910. Reprinted New York: New Directions, 1968.

Reznikoff, Charles. *Collected Poems*. Edited by Seamus Cooney. 2 vols. Los Angeles: Black Sparrow Press, 1976-1977.

————. *Holocaust*. Los Angeles: Black Sparrow Press, 1975.

————. *Testimony: The United States, 1885-1890*. New York: New Directions/San Francisco Review, 1965.

Snyder, Gary. *Earth House Hold*. New York: New Directions, 1969.

————. *Myths and Texts*. New York: Totem Press, 1960.

————. *The Real Work: Interviews and Talks, 1964-1979*. Edited by William Scott McLean. New York: New Directions, 1980.

————. *Riprap*. San Francisco: Origin Press, 1959.

————. *Six Selections from Mountains and Rivers without End Plus One*. San Francisco: Four Seasons, 1978.

———. *Turtle Island*. New York: New Directions, 1974.

Williams, William Carlos. *Autobiography*. New York: Random House, 1951.

———. *Imaginations*. Edited by Webster Schott. New York: New Directions 1970.

———. *Interviews: Speaking Straight Ahead*. Edited by Linda Welshimer Wagner, New York: New Directions, 1976.

———. *I Wanted to Write a Poem: The Autobiography of the Works of a Poet*. Edited by Edith Head. London: Jonathan Cape, 1967.

———. *Paterson: I–V, Fragments of VI*. New York: New Directions, 1963.

———. *Selected Essays*. New York: New Directions, 1954.

———. *Selected Letters*. Edited by John C. Thirlwall. New York: McDowell, 1957.

———. Williams Collection. Humanities Research Center. University of Texas, Austin.

Zukofsky, Louis. *Bottom: On Shakespeare*. Austin: Ark Press for The University of Texas, 1963.

———. *"A" 1–12*. London: Jonathan Cape, 1966.

———, ed. *An "Objectivists" Anthology*. Var, France, and New York: Le Beausset, 1932.

———. *Prepositions: The Collected Critical Essays*. London: Rapp & Carroll, 1967.

———. Zukofsky Collection. Humanities Research Center. University of Texas, Austin.

Secondary Works

Allen, Donald M., ed. *The New American Poetry*. New York: Grove Press, 1960.

——— and Warren Tallman, eds. *The Poetics of the New American Poetry*. New York: Grove Press, 1973.

Berg, Stephen and Robert Mezey, eds. *Naked Poetry*. Indianapolis and New York: Bobbs-Merrill, 1969.

Breslin, James E. *William Carlos Williams: An American Artist*. New York: Oxford University Press, 1970.

Bush, Ronald. *The Genesis of Ezra Pound's Cantos*. Princeton: Princeton University Press, 1976.

Charters, Ann. *Olson/Melville: A Study in Affinity*. Berkeley: Oyez, 1968.

Chisolm, Lawrence W. *Fenollosa: The Far East and American Culture*. New Haven: Yale University Press, 1963.

Davenport, Guy. "The Symbol of the Archaic." *Georgia Review* 28 (1974): 642–657.

Davie, Donald. *Articulate Energy*. London: Routledge & Kegan Paul, 1955.

Dembo, L. S. "The 'Objectivist' Poet: Four Interviews." *Contemporary Literature* 10 (1969): 155–219.

Hesse, Eva, ed. *Ezra Pound: 22 Versuche über einen Dichter*. Frankfurt: Athenäum, 1967.

Kenner, Hugh. *A Homemade World: The American Modernist Writers*. New York: Alfred A. Knopf, 1975.

———. *The Poetry of Ezra Pound*. London: Faber & Faber, 1951.

———. *The Pound Era*. Berkeley: Univ. of California Press, 1971.

Kern, Robert. "Recipes, Catalogues, Open Form Poetics: Gary Snyder's Archetypal Voice." *Contemporary Literature* 18 (1977): 173–197.

Kherdian, David. *Six Poets of the San Francisco Renaissance: Portraits and Checklists.* Fresno: Giligia Press, 1967.

McDougal, Stuart Y. *Ezra Pound and the Troubadour Tradition.* Princeton: Princeton University Press, 1972.

Mersmann, James F. *Out of the Vietnam Vortex.* Lawrence: University Press of Kansas, 1974.

Nänny, Max. *Ezra Pound: Poetics for an Electric Age.* Bern: Francke, 1973.

————. "Oral Dimensions in Ezra Pound." *Paideuma* 6 (1977): 13–26.

Norman, Charles. *Ezra Pound.* New York: Minerva, 1969.

Pearlman, Daniel. *The Barb of Time.* New York: Oxford University Press, 1969.

Reck, Michael. "A Conversation between Ezra Pound and Allen Ginsberg." *Evergreen Review* 55 (June 1968): 24–29, 84.

Rosenthal, M. L. *A Primer of Ezra Pound.* New York: Macmillan, 1960.

Russell, Peter, ed. *An Examination of Ezra Pound.* New York: Gordian Press, 1950. Revised edition 1973.

Schneidau, Herbert N. *Ezra Pound: The Image and the Real.* Baton Rouge: Louisiana State University Press, 1969.

Shaw, Robert B. *American Poetry since 1960.* Chester Springs: Dufour, 1974.

Stock, Noel. *The Life of Ezra Pound.* London, 1970. Reprinted Harmondsworth: Penguin, 1974.

Sullivan, J. P., ed. *Ezra Pound: A Critical Anthology.* Harmondsworth: Penguin, 1970.

————. *Ezra Pound and Sextus Propertius: A Study in Creative Translation.* Austin: University of Texas Press, 1964.

Wees, William C. *Vorticism and the English Avant-Garde.* Toronto and Buffalo: University of Toronto Press, 1972.

Wilhelm, James. *The Later Cantos of Ezra Pound.* New York: Walker, 1977.

Witemeyer, Hugh. *The Poetry of Ezra Pound: Forms and Renewal 1908-1920.* Berkeley: University of California Press, 1969.

Yip, Wai-lim. *Chinese Poetry: Major Modes and Genres.* Berkeley: University of California Press, 1976.

————. *Ezra Pound's Cathay.* Princeton: Princeton University Press, 1969.

Index

Printed and bound by CPI Group (UK) Ltd, Croydon, CR0 4YY

13/04/2025

14656492-0005